COMPETITION FOR CALiFORNIA WATER
Alternative Resolutions

SPONSORING ORGANIZATIONS
The University of California
Cooperative Extension
Division of Agricultural Sciences
Giannini Foundation of Agricultural Economics
Institute of Governmental Studies
Public Service Research and Dissemination Program
Water Resources Center
with partial funding by the Western Water Education Foundation

ORGANIZING COMMITTEE
Robert M. Hagan, Chairman
Professor of Water Science and Extension Water Specialist
University of California, Davis

Raymond H. Coppock
Communications Specialist, Cooperative Extension
University of California, Davis

John Cummins
Director, California Policy Seminar, Institute of Governmental Studies
University of California, Berkeley

Noreen Dowling
Director, Public Research and Dissemination Program
University of California, Davis

Ernest A. Engelbert
Professor of Public Administration
University of California, Los Angeles

J. Herbert Snyder
Director, Water Resources Center and Professor of Agricultural Economics
University of California, Davis

L. T. Wallace
Economist, Cooperative Extension
University of California, Berkeley

William W. Wood, Jr.
Economist, Cooperative Extension
University of California, Riverside

Marcia Kreith
Conference Coordinator
University of California, Davis

This publication is a part of the information exchange program in water resources research. The CALIFORNIA WATER RESOURCES CENTER sponsors projects in water resources and related research on the several campuses of the University of California with funds provided by the Office of Water Research and Technology (USDI) and from the State of California. Copies of Center publications may be examined at either the location of the Water Resources Center Archives Collection: 410 O'Brian Hall, Berkeley Campus (415) 642-2666 or 2801 Engineering I, Los Angeles, Campus (213) 825-7734, or at the

WATER RESOURCES CENTER
University of California
2102 Wickson Hall
Davis, CA 95616
(916) 752-1544

Competition for

CALIFORNIA WATER

Alternative Resolutions

Edited by
Ernest A. Engelbert
with
Ann Foley Scheuring

University of California Press
Berkeley Los Angeles London

University of California Press
Berkeley and Los Angeles, California
University of California Press, Ltd.
London, England
© 1982 by
The Regents of the University of California

Printed in the United States of America

Library of Congress Cataloging in Publication Data
Main entry under title:

Competition for California water.

    1. Water-supply—California.   I. Engelbert, Ernest A.
II. Scheuring, Ann Foley.
TD224.C3C65   333.91 '17 '09794   81-40109
(hardbound) ISBN 0-520-04822-9   AACR2
(paperback) ISBN 0-520-04823-7

1 2 3 4 5 6 7 8 9

CONTENTS

PREFACE

This publication grew out of a University of California conference on "Competition for California Water: Alternative Resolutions," which was held September 30 to October 2, 1981, at Asilomar. The goals of the conference and of this volume have been to identify competing needs and demands for water in California, to seek out realistic water policy options, and to point out areas where cooperation and compromise can help in developing state water policies.

Planning for the conference began in 1980. By the end of that year the Organizing Committee had invited thirty researchers and other professionals from twenty-five departments and research units on seven campuses of the University to work in teams to prepare drafts of analytical papers. The papers were discussed at a meeting of all of the teams in July 1981. Revised versions then were reviewed, primarily by informed persons outside the University. After further changes, the papers became the basis of a draft volume discussed by the conferees at Asilomar.

The conference was attended by 141 persons representing diverse viewpoints and interests, including water experts, decision makers, planners, administrators, and others from concerned agencies and organizations. Principal groups represented were agriculture, environmental organizations, water districts and associations, state, federal and local agencies, universities and public interest organizations. Also represented were consulting firms, business interests, utilities, labor unions, educational agencies and research institutes.

The conference was structured to encourage discussion both in plenary sessions and in small groups. To assure diversity of opinion, participants were assigned to mixed groups, and to encourage individual expression, persons were not identified by organizational affiliations. Reports from discussion groups and individual responses during plenary sessions were made available to the authors of this volume for their consideration in the revision of their manuscripts.

The first chapter of this volume provides an introduction to California's water resources and problems. It also sets forth the assumptions and future scenarios on which the volume is based. Following the introduction are five chapters that analyze competition over California's water resources from the perspectives of the major water-using sectors: agriculture, municipal and domestic, industry, energy, and the environment including recreation. This analysis is followed by four chapters which examine the major water-using sectors in the context of the social forces and trends which will shape the course of California's development, including lifestyles, economics, institutions and political dynamics. A concluding integrative chapter highlights some of the underlying themes of the volume and reports on reactions of the conference participants to some of the controversial issues.

Each chapter reflects the approach and expertise of its particular team of authors. The policy analyses, findings and conclusions are those arrived at by the author teams after nearly a year of team dialogue and discussion. It should be emphasized that the authors are solely responsible for the contents of their chapters. The contents of the volume do not represent a University position, nor University advocacy of particular viewpoints. Nor, it should be added, does the volume reflect the views of conference participants or those experts who reviewed the manuscripts during the course of their preparation.

The primary purpose of the University in sponsoring the water policy conference and in publishing this volume has been to encourage small teams of faculty members to analyze and participate in public discussion of important aspects of California water needs and water policy implications. This is part of the University effort to encourage faculty to bring research findings to bear upon long-range public policy issues. We recognize that this approach does not necessarily produce a complete and balanced analysis of the entire scope of immensely complex water issues. It may well be that other options and other conclusions should also be considered. The Organizing Committee, however, hopes that the information and views contained in this volume will represent a useful effort by the University to work with others toward resolution of California's difficult water problems.

Robert M. Hagan
Chairman, Organizing Committee

ACKNOWLEDGMENTS

Many individuals gave generously of their time and services to make possible the University of California conference and volume on "Competition for California Water: Alternative Resolutions." Grateful appreciation for their significant contributions is extended to the following persons and groups:

Members of the Organizing Committee who planned, guided and contributed to this activity through many meetings and discussions over a two-year period. The committee developed the format for the conference and the volume, selected the participants, and supervised and participated in all of the events.

Marcia Kreith who served as Conference Coordinator and who so capably handled all of the organizational arrangements. Without her dedication and energy this undertaking would not have succeeded.

The authors and contributors to this volume who undertook the substantial task of preparing a set of analytical papers on the major facets of California water policy. They devoted many hours to this collective enterprise and carried out their assignments in addition to their regular teaching and research activities without any additional compensation.

University faculty members Margaret FitzSimmons, John Harte, Laura Lake, Walter B. Lawrence and Robert Williams for assistance in developing the outlines of the early versions of some of the manuscripts.

Reviewers who made constructive criticisms of the manuscripts in their initial stages.

The conference participants who took time from busy schedules to review the manuscripts and participate in three days of meetings. Many of their valuable comments and suggestions have been incorporated into this volume.

Leaders and recorders of conference discussion groups who were responsible for guiding the dialogue into constructive channels and providing group reactions to water policy issues for the plenary sessions. Without their efforts the goal of intellectual interchange at the conference would not have been attained.

Members of the University staff who provided invaluable administrative assistance at various stages of this undertaking, notably Betty Esky and Ruth Laidlaw of the Department of Land, Air and Water Resources, Marian Cain and Kelly Carner of the Public Service Research and Dissemination Program, and Otto Helweg and Patricia Farid of the Water Resources Center.

Ernest A. Engelbert
Editor

CHAPTER I

INTRODUCTION:
THE PROBLEM, THE RESOURCE, THE COMPETITION

by

Raymond H. Coppock, Robert M. Hagan, and William W. Wood, Jr.

ABSTRACT

Water development, water distribution and water use inevitably are central concerns of public policy in California. This University of California study looks at the competition for California's increasingly costly water resources in the light of (1) the requirements for different water uses in the state, and (2) the socioeconomic trends and constraints which condition the allocation of water supplies. All of these involve basic public policy considerations.

This chapter provides an introduction to the water problems and water resources of California. Water is both a physical and economic resource and a natural ecosystem. It also is a prime determinant of land use in this state. The need to use the resource efficiently and at the same time to protect the ecosystem creates extremely difficult policy problems. It is important to keep in mind, however, that only the broadest policy considerations apply uniformly to the entire state. Water problems, like water supplies, often are local or regional in nature. Therefore, generalizations—of which this volume necessarily has its share—may or may not apply to specific local or regional situations.

Some of the important policy issues discussed in the following chapters are highlighted here. This introductory chapter also describes a set of common assumptions and scenarios for future water development in California which have been employed by other chapter authors in their respective analyses.

PERCEPTIONS OF THE PROBLEM

The debate over water policy in California is complex and confusing. In no state in the nation are there so many geographical variations in water supply and availability, or such a diversity of water-oriented interest groups as in California. Consequently many views prevail about which water problems are most real and/or urgent. There are at least three categories of perceived water problems in this state:

- *The risk of future crisis.* Demands for water are expected to increase as the population and the economy grow, while new supplies will be increasingly costly and difficult to develop. Under these circumstances the possibility and impact of another drought as severe as that which occurred in 1976-77 is a serious concern. (Population estimates for this volume are based on California Department of Finance projections of 25 million Californians sometime between 1985 and 1990, 30 million between 2000 and 2005, and 34 million between 2015 and 2020.)

• *Regional water supply and quality problems that presently exist even in years of normal precipitation.* Groundwater overdraft, most severe in the San Joaquin Valley, is the most significant of these. Other regional problems include low streamflow and deteriorating water quality in the Trinity, San Joaquin and other rivers; adverse environmental impacts of water diversions, as for example at Mono Lake; and worsening soil and water salinity in the lower San Joaquin Valley.

• *Problems of inefficient water distribution and use.* Physical management of water distribution and irrigation systems is one perceived problem. Other concerns are economic and political in nature, involving the feasibility and efficiency of water allocation through institutional or market systems.

THE RESOURCE

Surface and Groundwater Supplies

At the center of the statewide debate is the resource itself—the annual flow of surface water within California, the groundwater stored in the state's immense aquifers, and some inflow and outflow across the borders. Figure 1 shows recent estimates by the California Department of Water Resources (DWR) of surface water supplies and disbursements. The actual amount of streamflow within the state naturally varies from year to year, but the average supply is about 70.8 million acre-feet (MAF) annually. About two-thirds of this supply originates in North Coast and Sacramento basin rivers. The remainder includes streamflow farther south in the Central Valley and elsewhere in the state. In addition, about 4.7 MAF are imported from the Colorado River and about 1.4 MAF flow in from Oregon. As Figure 1 also shows, recent changes in land use (conversions of native vegetation to irrigated agriculture, and also urban expansion) are estimated to have increased total runoff by 1.5 MAF.

What happens to this surface flow? Figure 1 shows DWR's estimates for 1980, a normal year, and how much remains in-stream. These figures reflect long-term average flows. It should be kept in mind that both intensity and duration of seasonal precipitation in California vary greatly from year to year.

A crucial component of this surface supply is the amount that is diverted for use. California's more than 50 major reservoirs—those with capacity larger than 100,000 AF—have a combined capacity of about 77 MAF. The yields from these reservoirs, together with direct diversions, permit delivery of about 20.4 MAF of surface water in an average year. Some of this water is delivered to more than one user, for successive use.

The state's other immense water resource is the underground supply, which provides about 40 percent of the water used in California. Usable storage capacity of the state's groundwater basins has been estimated at about 143 MAF—about twice the gross storage capacity of surface reservoirs. Approximately 16.5 MAF are pumped out in an average year. Of this, only about 5.3 MAF are naturally recharged, thus providing sustained yield. (This includes 4.2 MAF from streambed percolation and 1.1 MAF from deep percolation of precipitation). Artificial recharge is estimated to add 1.8 MAF. An additional 6.9 MAF of

Figure 1

Surface Water Supplies in California
Long-term average—1980 development level
(Millions of acre-feet)

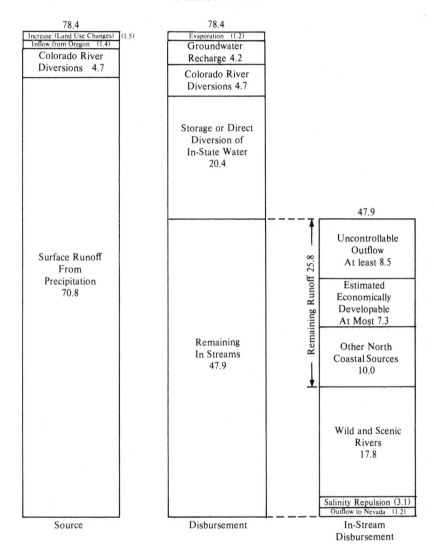

Adapted from *Policies and Goals for California Water Management: The Next 20 Years,* State Water Resources Control Board and the California Department of Water Resources, State of California, Bulletin No. 4, June 1981.

pumped water are supplied by irrigation return flows to underground basins, and by conveyance and other losses. The remainder, about 2.3 MAF, is overdraft. (Overdraft during the 1976-77 drought was variously estimated at 5 to 8 MAF per year.)

The principal area of overdraft is the San Joaquin Valley, where the net loss is about 1.5 MAF yearly, but DWR studies have identified "critical" overdraft situations in 16 groundwater basins. In many of these, the groundwater has not yet dropped to the level at which a steady state would be economically optimum. In others, however, it apparently is at or below that level—and pumping is still continuing because of the "common pool" problem.

Another water source being given increasing attention is reclaimed wastewater. By the year 2000, DWR estimates about 0.6 MAF from planned reuse projects will become available.

Based on 1980 estimates by DWR, about 40.6 MAF are delivered for use yearly in California—85 percent for agriculture and 15 percent for municipal/industrial use. This developed supply includes 2.5 MAF from the State Water Project, 7.9 from the Central Valley Project, 1.1 from other federal works, and 9.2 from local development; 4.7 MAF from the Colorado River; 16.5 MAF from groundwater; and about 0.8 MAF from reclaimed wastewater, of which 0.2 is planned and 0.6 is incidental. Of this total delivered water, DWR estimates the net use at approximately 34 MAF, with the remainder flowing back into the state's water system.

Storage and Distribution

A network of reservoirs and canals, mostly constructed by quasi-public or public agencies, permits storage and transfer of water throughout much of California. The earliest large-scale projects were built by cities. Later came the federal Central Valley Project (CVP), largely for agricultural use; and in the 1960s the State Water Project (SWP) began delivering water to both agricultural areas and cities.

Urban supply systems. The city of Los Angeles gets much of its water from the two Owens Valley aqueducts. In addition, the Metropolitan Water District of Southern California (MWD) has tapped 1.2 MAF annually from the Colorado River. About half of that will be lost later in the 1980s, as a result of a Supreme Court decision which reduced California's total rights. The MWD also has contracts for 1.5 MAF yearly of SWP water to be delivered currently, and another 500,000 acre-feet later. The MWD covers six counties—Los Angeles, Orange, Riverside, San Bernardino, San Diego, and Ventura—and serves nearly 11 million people. The Bay Area has two major municipal systems: San Francisco's Hetch Hetchy project on the Tuolumne River, which also serves other cities on the Peninsula and the South Bay; and East Bay Municipal Utility District's project on the Mokelumne, which serves much of Alameda and Contra Costa counties.

Central Valley Project. Operated by the federal Bureau of Reclamation, the CVP stores waters of the Sacramento, American, Trinity, and San Joaquin rivers and conveys them to largely agricultural areas in the Sacramento and San Joaquin valleys. Major reservoirs are Shasta, Trinity, Folsom, and Millerton (Friant Dam). Water from the first three reservoirs flows down the Sacramento River and through the Delta, is pumped into the Delta-Mendota Canal, and is transferred halfway down the San Joaquin Valley. Water from Millerton serves the east side of the lower San Joaquin Valley through the Friant-Kern and Madera canals. The San Luis Reservoir, a joint federal-state project, provides offstream storage just south of the Delta. Farther north, the western Sacramento Valley is served through the Tehama-Colusa Canal. In a normal year, CVP deliveries total almost 8 MAF. More than 80 percent of this goes to irrigate nearly 2 million acres of farmland. The U.S. government pays costs of the CVP, but is partially reimbursed by agricultural, municipal and industrial consumers of water and power. Two important policy issues involving CVP water are the 160-acre limitation and water price subsidies to agriculture.

State Water Project. The key storage facility of the SWP is Oroville Dam on the Feather River. SWP water, like that of the CVP, flows down the Sacramento River and through the Delta. There it is pumped into the 444-mile California Aqueduct and flows to the west side of the lower San Joaquin Valley and across the Tehachapi Mountains to Southern California. The SWP was financed by state bonds. Water users will repay about 74 percent of the total costs of building the system, plus transport charges which vary with distance. Power users will pay about 11 percent. In a normal year, the SWP yields about 2.3 MAF; however, it is presently committed to delivering more than 4 MAF by the end of the century. This fact creates a many-sided policy problem—for the DWR, which has the contractual commitment; for water users in the southern half of the state, who say they are counting on future expanded deliveries; and for all others who are concerned about the issues of water development, or lack of development. One proposed means of acquiring more water for the SWP is the Peripheral Canal. By allowing more efficient flushing of salty water from the Delta, the canal would permit between 0.5 and 1 MAF of additional water to be transferred south in a normal year. (The actual amount would depend on operational management of the canal, and whether it is used as a joint federal-state facility.)

Nonurban, local water projects. A number of irrigation districts have separate water supplies. For example, the Modesto, Turlock and Merced districts own their own dams on rivers flowing out of the Sierra Nevada, and various other districts have long-established rights to streamflow. Many districts also supplement their surface supplies with groundwater. In total, nonurban local water agencies with independent supplies provide about 5 MAF to their users in a typical year.

Development Costs

Of California's approximately 48 MAF of undeveloped runoff, the DWR estimates that only slightly over 7 MAF, mostly in the Central Valley, can be developed economically. This figure is based on the assumptions that:

- There are commitments of over 22 MAF to North Coast "wild and scenic rivers," to salinity repulsion in the Delta, and to Nevada outflow.

- About 10 MAF of additional North Coast water is unavailable because of engineering and economic constraints.

- About 8.5 MAF consists of very large flood flows beyond the capacity of storage reservoirs, or of small streams that would be uneconomic to dam.

Others see more potential for development. They point out that more than half of the state's total surface supply still flows into the ocean in an average year.

This viewpoint, of course, suggests that the "wild and scenic rivers" should not be permanently excluded from development.

What would be the cost of "new" water from the surface sources considered developable by the DWR? What about the costs of other additions to the state's usable water supply—from wastewater reclamation, for example?

Any figures are necessarily estimates. Involved in the computations are questions of increasing costs, financing methods, pricing and subsidies, environmental impacts and other cost/benefit considerations. Nevertheless, the relative costs of different potential water sources can be roughly compared.

Table 1 gives estimates for water yields and costs of a number of proposed federal and state water projects in California. Some of these cost figures come from the DWR, the Corps of Engineers, or the Bureau of Reclamation. Others were calculated from capital cost and water yield figures provided by those agencies. In any case, it is important to keep in mind that many years would be required to complete most of these proposed projects. Except for New Melones, there is little possibility of any significant new additions to the water supply within the next decade.

To these cost figures must be added transportation costs. According to the DWR, these range from $10 to $40 per acre-foot in the North Bay area, about $40 in the South Bay, $15 to $35 in the San Joaquin Valley, and from $100 to $125 in Southern California.

There are other possibilities for increasing California's developed water supply or "stretching" the present supply. These include:

- *Wastewater reclamation.* Costs for water usable by agriculture are estimated at between $240 and $350 per acre-foot in the area of the treatment plant. Additional transportation costs would vary. At present, about 200,000 acre-feet yearly of reclaimed water are being put to planned use in the state for agriculture, landscape irrigation, and groundwater recharge. Dependable further yield is estimated at between 200,000 and 400,000 acre-feet. At least part of the cost of reclaimed water may be borne by the city doing the discharging, which gets the value of disposal; hence, the actual cost to users may be less than the figures given above.

- *Desalinization of brackish water.* Drain water from the San Joaquin Valley could be desalted for about $300 to $330 per acre-foot (preliminary estimate). The yield potential is estimated at up to 300,000 acre-feet yearly. A drainage disposal problem would remain for the effluent, which would be extremely salty.

- *More lining of canals.* For example, lining the All-American Canal in the Imperial Valley area would eliminate an estimated 132,000 acre-feet of water loss. Cost estimates are unavailable.

- *Watershed management.* Runoff from brush-covered watersheds can be increased by replacing the chaparral with a less water-demanding cover such as grass. In regions with greater than 15 or 20 inches of rainfall, substantial extra runoff—from one-fourth to almost one-half acre-foot per acre of watershed—has been consistently recorded over long periods of time. Although environmental impacts have been studied, the economic potential for significantly increasing regional or statewide water supplies is still unknown. One substantial benefit is reduced hazard from wildfire.

Table 1

Water Yields and Costs of Proposed
Water Projects in California

	Yearly Dependable Yield in Acre-Feet*	Cost per A/F (At Delta, or Delta Equivalent
Peripheral Canal (Sacramento-San Joaquin Delta area)	700,000	$100
Groundwater storage south of the Delta	400,000	55
Thomes-Newville (small version of Glenn Reservoir in Tehama and Glenn counties)	220,000	245
Los Vaqueros (off-canal storage in Contra Costa County)	265,000	325
Cottonwood (west side of Sacramento (Valley)	200,000	238
⅄Auburn (American River east of Sacramento)	318,000	250
New Melones (already constructed on Stanislaus River)	213,000	125
High Shasta (northern end of Sacra- mento Valley)	1,400,000	85

*This is additional water that otherwise would not be available. In the case of dams, it represents captured flood flows that otherwise would go to the sea. In the case of the Peripheral Canal, it is water that would not be "lost" during transfer across the Delta. In the case of groundwater storage, it is flood flows that would be stored in underground basins instead of surface reservoirs for conjunctive use.

THE COMPETITION FOR WATER

California's water resources, summarized in the previous section, are at the center of an intense economic and political struggle. Some balance must be reached between the supply and demand for water, but it is far from certain that all Californians will get as much water as they want at a price they feel is right. The two central policy issues in the debate over water are:

• How much of California's potentially available water supply should be developed, and how much left undeveloped?

• Who should get how much of the developed supply, and by what process of allocation?

The chapters that follow provide background for discussion of more specific issues of policy and fact, including:

• *The issue of costs.* What would be the water yields and what would be the costs, in dollars and in less tangible values, of developing new surface sources of water by building new reservoirs, or by other means such as watershed management, lining of canals, desalinization, or wastewater reclamation?

• *The issue of environmental protection.* To what extent should environmental values, such as fish and wildlife resources and whitewater rivers, be protected amid changes in the state's water system?

• *The issue of cost-sharing.* How much of the cost of water development and distribution should be borne by the general public, by the water users, and by other beneficiaries? This raises questions of financing methods, pricing, subsidies, and environmental impacts.

• *The issue of institutional reform.* Can changes in California's laws and institutions produce a more efficient statewide system of water supply and management? Would these changes substantially reduce the need for more water development?

• *The issue of conservation.* To what extent can the need for new water development be offset by conservation and/or more efficient water use by the various types of users?

• *The issue of agriculture's role.* How much increased cost and/or loss of water could California agriculture bear and still remain competitive with other production areas? What kinds of impacts on cropping patterns would occur, and how would they affect different regions within the state? What would be the effects on the state and national economies and on consumers?

Assumptions and Scenarios

The teams of authors responsible for the following chapters approached the policy issues primarily from the viewpoints of their individual disciplines. However, to provide relationships among the chapters, the authors proceeded from a common set of assumptions and scenarios. The common assumptions for the volume are:

(1) No real disasters, or technical or social breakthroughs for California, e.g.:

   a. No world war.
   b. No dramatic change in climate.
   c. No unforeseen environmental threat or epidemic.

     d. No collapse in political, economic, or social system.

(2) No dramatic developments significantly easing California's socioeconomic problems and pressures, e.g.:

     a. No limit on immigration from other states.
     b. Continued immigration from Mexico.
     c. No cheap new energy source. Rising energy prices.
     d. No dramatic discovery of a new means of water supply or pollution treatment.

(3) Demographic projections based upon California Department of Finance Report 77-P-3, Series E-150, December 1977.

(4) Continuing pressure from the danger of disruptions in international commerce, energy supply and food supply. This includes the possibility of famine.

Three scenarios projecting alternative futures for state water supply and demand were chosen. These scenarios do not necessarily represent the authors' preferences but were selected to provide a uniform set of alternatives for discussion. Although these scenarios are based upon specific assumptions and project distinct courses of action, California's policy choices undoubtedly will reflect combinations of these scenarios and possibly other directions for change.

The three scenarios are:

Current status. This alternative assumes that there will be no major institutional or legal changes; that there will be only small, incremental adjustments in water supply (no big new projects); that crises will be managed on an ad hoc basis; and that there will be a gradual shift of water from agriculture to urban-industrial uses.

Substantial reallocation. This alternative assumes that there will be no major increase in water supply, but that there will be two significant institutional changes: (1) major revisions of federal and/or state law, providing well-defined and separable property rights to water so as to permit exchanges among willing parties, and (2) development of a marketlike system under state or other sponsorship fostering the buying and selling of water.

New development. This alternative assumes no major institutional changes, but development of a significant amount of "new" surface water. The sources that might be considered are those listed in Table 1. (The various proposed water development projects in California are not discussed in detail in this volume. Those projects have been extensively studied by federal, state and local water agencies, and there seems to be no need to repeat the information here.)

Figure 2 provides a visual framework for placing the three scenarios in the context of real-world multiple policy choices. Note that the diagram shows two indicated directions of change from the current status: one toward institutional and/or regulatory shifts, and the other in the direction of more water supply. Located somewhere along these lines are the second and third scenarios described above. The first scenario, of course, is the "current status" box.

It is important to note that these two possible directions of change are not mutually exclusive. California's actual policy choices may well include some of both; on the diagram, such a solution could be located in the area between the two lines.

Figure 2

A Framework for Defining the Scenarios

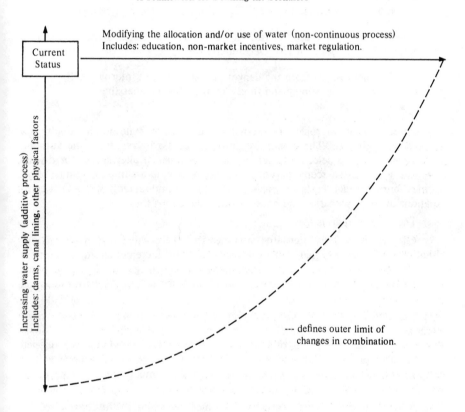

CHAPTER II

AGRICULTURE

by

B. Delworth Gardner, Raymond H. Coppock, Curtis D. Lynn,

D. William Rains, Robert S. Loomis, and J. Herbert Snyder

ABSTRACT

Climate, soil and water all determine cropping patterns in California. Limits of the developed supply of water are being approached; in fact, the serious overdraft of groundwater, particularly in the San Joaquin Valley, shows that the replenishable supply is being exceeded. Some undeveloped runoff flows to the ocean—almost 48 million acre-feet in an average year. Much of that, however, is in the protected rivers of the North Coast. Of the developed water supply, agriculture consumptively uses about 85 percent.

Under these circumstances, the question of agricultural water use efficiency in California is crucial. Two sets of forces, physical/biological and economic, determine the amount of irrigation water used by the state's farmers.

The basic water requirement for crop growth is for the process of evapotranspiration (ET), which has two components—evaporation from soil and water, and transpiration through the leaves of plants. Most ET losses take place through transpiration, which is directly related to crop production through photosynthesis. Production and water use efficiency may drop substantially if the crop is not well cared for; pest, weed and disease control are important, as is adequate nutrition. Overall efficiency of water use in agriculture is closely related to units of crop produced per unit of water applied.

Some crops use more water than others, largely because of differences in growing season and in length of growing period. Also, some irrigation methods use more water than others, with sprinkler and drip systems often—though not always—more efficient.

Another factor that determines agricultural water use is its cost, particularly the marginal cost of applying additional water. Many irrigation districts use fixed (per-acre) charges or a combination of fixed and variable charges which may be related to average consumptive use, but do not reflect the incremental cost of water. One possibility for reducing on-farm water use would be to charge all or most of the cost of surface water at a variable (per-acre-foot) price. Groundwater pumpers, of course, already pay according to the amount they use.

How much water could California agriculture save? Most of the unused water associated with less efficient irrigation is recovered—it returns to the basin water system and is used again. As "recoverable losses," these are not really losses at all in a physical sense, although their recovery is not costless in an economic sense. There also are very large "nonrecoverable losses," mostly through ET, most of which could not be reduced without a concomitant reduction in crop biomass.

In response to higher water costs and/or decreased supplies, farmers may: (1) change cropping patterns, (2) cease irrigating some cropland, (3) in some cases, cut water applications to a point below the crop's maximum need, or (4) adopt new irrigation technology. The first two alternatives would save water for use elsewhere, but of course would affect crop production; the third would reduce nonrecoverable losses, but might be risky, and the fourth would reduce mostly recoverable losses, hence might not significantly increase basinwide water supplies.

Factors that will influence future water use by California agriculture are: the worsening overdraft problem; expected future water price increases; environmental constraints; future demand for agricultural products; the trend toward more efficient, and expensive, irrigation technology; the issue of varying values of water (implying that economic efficiency gains could be made by transferring water from one area to another); and the issue of water subsidies, particularly the question of whether a proposed project would create more, or less, total wealth than it costs.

Three alternative futures for California agriculture are:

(1) Status quo. This would mean higher real water costs for agriculture without necessarily making more water available for other uses. The potential loss of some Colorado River water and continued overdrafts would add to the pressure on agriculture. Direct economic impacts would be regional, concentrated primarily in the San Joaquin Valley where we would expect some decline in agriculture.

(2) Marketlike systems for water transfer. Some water might move out of agriculture, but probably not very much. Most water exchanges would take place within agriculture, from areas of lower crop value with higher water use (particularly the Sacramento Valley) to areas of water scarcity and/or high water prices—particularly the San Joaquin Valley.

(3) Development of new supplies. This scenario is strongly preferred by agriculture. However, prospective costs for "new" irrigation water are so high that either "blend pricing" or water subsidies must be involved. Nevertheless, agriculture argues that developing new surface water supplies is necessary to relieve the most critical constraint on California's farm output, which is a mainstay of the state's economy and of the nation's food supply.

AN OVERVIEW OF CALIFORNIA AGRICULTURE

In the debate over California water policy, productivity of the state's agriculture is a central issue. In California, as in few other places in the world, it is apparent that irrigation is one of the most effective means of increasing farm production.

The state has a total land area of about 100 million acres, most of which is mountains, desert, or rangeland. About 11 million acres now produce crops; about 8 million are under irrigation. From this relatively small fraction of California's land comes the abundance of food and fiber which is so important in the economy of the state and which contributes significantly to the food supply of the nation and the world.

California agriculture has developed a complex system—production, processing, transportation, distribution and input supply—that is well suited to its unique combination of natural resources.[1] As one result, the state's gross cash receipts from farm sales have consistently approached 10 percent of the U.S. total every year since 1960. Year after year, California ranks first among the states in cash receipts from crops, and second or third in livestock and livestock products.

The Economic Contribution

What is agriculture's role in the state's overall economy? One recent study[2] indicates that production-level agriculture creates 3 percent of private sector sales and about 3 percent of the state's personal income. Processing-level activities add 6 percent in sales and another 3 percent in personal income. These are direct contributions; when the "multiplier effect" is considered, the two sectors together create about 20 percent of the private sector sales in California and about 15 percent of personal income. This does not include value added after processing, such as transportation, or wholesale and retail sales.

The same source indicates that about 5 percent of private sector jobs are directly connected with farm production and another 2 percent with processing—representing, with a multiplier effect, about 14 percent of the jobs in the state. California paid over 20 percent of the nation's hired farm labor bill in 1978.[3] On an annual average basis, there are more than 200,000 hired workers on California farms—nearly three times as many as in the second state, Texas.[4] In the peak months of September and October over 300,000 farm workers are hired.[5]

California ranks first in the nation in production of more than 20 farm commodities, including such important crops as sugarbeets, processing tomatoes, strawberries, lettuce, peaches, grapes, and navel oranges. It is second in dairy products and cotton. California also produces sizable amounts of red meat, feedgrains, oil crops, and hay—even though it is a net importer of those commodities.

California agricultural exports contribute substantially to the U.S. balance of trade. Major crops exported include cotton, rice, dry beans, wheat, almonds, grapes, fresh deciduous fruits, raisins, strawberries, and vegetables. The value of exported farm products in 1980 was $4 billion.[6] About one-third of the state's cropland currently is used for producing commodities for export sales.

The Resource Base

This agricultural output is made possible by California's unique combination of climate, land and water—all particularly favorable for highly diverse crop production. Dry summers and a long growing season permit a wide range of irrigated crops that are largely free from the plant diseases and weather risks that plague more humid regions.

Climate is crucial in the state's crop production. Warm winters in the desert valleys and cool summers in the central coast make it possible to produce a number of cool-season vegetable crops the year around. Climatic differences lengthen the marketing season of important vegetable and fruit crops. Varying coastal valley climates produce some of California's world-famed specialty crops—lettuce, strawberries, wine grapes. Perhaps most significant, the San Joaquin and Sacramento valleys, with their long, hot, and dry summers, are suited for high yields of quality deciduous fruits and nuts, as well as the field and row crops that provide a substantial share of California farm income.

California has some of the finest agricultural soils in the world. The deep alluvial fans found over much of the San Joaquin and Sacramento valleys are productive and, in general, relatively easy to farm. Most soils in the cool coastal and hot southern desert valleys also are well fitted for crop production. Much of the land in California's valleys is relatively level, requiring minimal grading for surface irrigation. Modern farming tools, such as leveling equipment and deep rippers, have made it possible to modify and irrigate some of the less desirable soils. More recently, sprinkler and drip systems have permitted irrigated agriculture to move on to rolling and hilly land.

Along with climate and soils, the third crucial resource that makes possible California's agricultural output is irrigation water. Abundant water, a traditional goal of California's farmers as well as its industries and cities, exists in certain parts of the state—particularly in the northern one-third and along the western slope of the Sierra Nevada. Unfortunately, limits of the developed supply are being approached and there is fierce competition for what available water is left.

Since most precipitation in California occurs in the winter, storage is essential for providing water in late spring and summer when irrigation demands are highest. Significant natural storage occurs as winter snowpack at the higher elevations in the central and northern mountains. Reservoirs on practically all the major interior streams in the state provide much more of the needed storage.

In addition to surface supplies, California farmers pump large quantities of water from underground. Some growers rely entirely on surface water, others get their total supply from groundwater, and many others use a mix of surface and groundwater. As described in Chapter 1, groundwater overdraft is a crucial problem.

Much of the remaining undeveloped surface water is protected from development under the wild and scenic rivers program, which includes the major North Coast streams. Furthermore, any additional water development would be costly, both because construction costs are escalating and because the more easily developed water already has been captured.

Agricultural growth and productivity in many parts of California are constrained today by scarcity and/or cost of one resource—water. This is evidenced by the extent of summer fallow and minimum-water crops that can be seen even in prime agricultural districts. If irrigation water becomes less available, physically or economically, the acreage of dryland grain and pasture will increase.

Another growing threat to the state's agriculture is deterioration of soil quality from waterlogging and increased salinity, mostly as a result of irrigation.[7] (Much irrigation water in California and the West carries significant amounts of salts. These accumulate in the soil as the water is removed by evapotranspiration.) This is no problem on lands where there is adequate drainage, but in many lowland areas—including possibly one-fourth of the San Joaquin Valley—irrigated agriculture cannot exist indefinitely without drainage.

DETERMINANTS OF WATER DEMAND
IN CALIFORNIA AGRICULTURE

Two interlocking sets of forces determine the amount of irrigation water used by California farmers. The first set is physical and biological, and is based on the water requirements of crop plants and the losses inherent in conveying and applying irrigation water. The second is economic, and is based on the relationships between the cost of irrigation water, the costs of other inputs such as land and labor, and the prices received by farmers for what they sell.

Water Needs for Crop Production

The amount of water used to grow a crop depends upon a number of physical and biological factors, the most important of which is evapotranspiration, or ET. (Another important requirement may be for leaching salts from the root zone.)

Table 1 shows average daily and seasonal rates of "potential" ET for various regions in California. ET has two components: (1) direct evaporation of water from soil and water surfaces and (2) transpiration of water through the plant. The potential ET rates in Table 1 are the maximum amounts of water that plants will use if adequate soil moisture is available, and if the foliage covers all or nearly all of the ground. ET rates of full-cover crops are controlled by solar radiation, moisture in the air, temperature, wind speed, the reflectiveness of the surface, and water supply.

These rates vary from .02 inches per day during winter in far northern California to almost .40 inches per day during summer in the desert. However, actual crop water use under field conditions usually is below the potential ET because of less than full cover and because crops are often stressed by lack of soil moisture.

In considering irrigation efficiency and potential water savings, both components of ET—evaporation and transpiration—are important. However, for full-cover crops with adequate soil moisture, 90 percent or more of water loss is by transpiration. Since transpiration is the chief water need, it will be discussed first.

Transpiration Factors: The Basic Plant Requirement. There is a direct physical relationship between the transpiration of water from plant leaves and photosynthetic production. Transpiration and photosynthesis both depend on energy (sunlight), and both involve the exchange of gases—water and CO_2 —through the stomatal pores of the leaves. Those pores must open for CO_2 intake to occur, but water is lost whenever they are open. It turns out that there is a more or less constant ratio between the production of biomass and this loss of water. That ratio is *plant water use efficiency* (WUE):

$$WUE = \frac{dry\ matter\ production}{transpirational\ water\ loss}$$

In our climate, WUEs of healthy crops vary between 3 and 5 pounds of production per 1000 pounds (125 gallons) of water. Since only 30 to 50 percent of plant production flows to economically useful portions like grain, efficiencies per pound of food or feed go as low as 1/1000.

Not much can be done to change basic WUE. There are, however, adaptive strategies for maximizing production with limited supplies of water, and most of them are already employed to varying degrees in California's agriculture. WUE is greater during the cool season, with crops such as wheat and broccoli, than during the summer. Also, some summer crops such as corn and grain sorghum have intrinsically higher efficiency than others such as sugarbeets and tomatoes.

In the real world, plant water use efficiency may drop well below its potential. That happens when yields decline because the crop is not kept free of pests, diseases and weeds or not provided with adequate nutrition. This is a critical point; it means that overall efficiency of water use in irrigated agriculture reflects not just the amount of water put on the land, but units of crop produced per unit

Table 1

Daily and Seasonal Potential Evapotranspiration
Rates in California*

	Northeastern Mountain Valleys	North Coast-Coastal Valleys and Plains	North Coast-Interior Valleys	Sacramento Valley	San Joaquin Valley	Central Coast-Coastal Valleys and Plains	Central Coast-Interior Valleys	Sierra (Tahoe Basin)	South Coast-Coastal Valleys and Plains	South Coast-Interior Valleys	Southern California Desert
					Inches Per Day						
January	0.02	0.02	0.03	0.04	0.03	0.06	0.05	--	0.06	0.06	0.09
February	0.04	0.04	0.04	0.06	0.06	0.08	0.08	--	0.09	0.09	0.13
March	0.07	0.06	0.08	0.1	0.1	0.1	0.11	--	0.1	0.11	0.19
April	0.12	0.08	0.11	0.15	0.15	0.13	0.14	0.10	0.13	0.14	0.25
May	0.16	0.11	0.16	0.19	0.21	0.15	0.18	0.13	0.14	0.16	0.33
June	0.19	0.12	0.20	0.24	0.25	0.16	0.21	0.16	0.17	0.20	0.38
July	0.26	0.11	0.23	0.26	0.25	0.17	0.22	0.20	0.18	0.22	0.37
August	0.23	0.11	0.20	0.22	0.21	0.16	0.19	0.17	0.18	0.22	0.31
September	0.16	0.09	0.15	0.17	0.16	0.13	0.16	0.13	0.15	0.17	0.28
October	0.09	0.06	0.09	0.11	0.11	0.1	0.12	0.09	0.11	0.12	0.2
November	0.03	0.04	0.04	0.05	0.05	0.07	0.08	--	0.09	0.08	0.12
December	0.02	0.02	0.02	0.03	0.02	0.05	0.05	--	0.07	0.06	0.06
					Seasonal Total Inches						
November-March	5.1	5.3	6.3	8.5	7.9	10.7	10.8	--	12.1	11.5	17.7
April-October (growing season)	37.1	20.8	34.9	40.7	40.7	30.6	37.5	30.0	32.3	37.9	65.1
Annual	42.2	26.1	41.2	49.2	49.0	41.3	48.3	--	44.4	49.4	82.2

*These are the rates of water loss one would observe from a well-watered lawn. They vary seasonally in response to solar radiation and atmospheric humidity. The maximum rate, 0.38 inches/day, corresponds to 0.032 feet/day, so that 1 acre-foot of water would be needed every 31 days to maintain an acre of vegetation.

Source: California Department of Water Resources, *Vegetative Water Use in California, 1974,* Bulletin No. 113-3, except for figures for Sierra (Tahoe Basin) which are University of California observations for the growing season.

of water applied. Under some circumstances, in fact, application of more water per acre results in increased water use efficiency because of higher productivity.

Table 2 lists seasonal ET requirements of major crops in the San Joaquin Valley. These numbers relate more or less directly with those in Table 1— cropping season and crop duration are dominant factors.

Table 2

Table 2

Seasonal Evapotranspiration of Major Field Crops
in the San Joaquin Valley

Crop	Season	Days	Total Seasonal ET (in.)
Annual Crops			
Small grains	11/1 - 5/15	200	13
(wheat and barley)	12/1 - 5/31	180	16
	1/1 - 6/30	180	21
Beans (pinto)	4/1 - 7/31	120	21
	5/1 - 8/15	110	20
	6/15 - 9/30	110	18
Grain sorghum	5/1 - 9/30	150	24
	6/15 - 10/31	140	18
Corn	3/15 - 8/15	150	27
	4/15 - 9/15	150	28
	5/15 - 9/30	140	24
	6/1 - 10/15	140	23
Cotton	4/1 - 9/30	180	31
	4/15 - 10/15	180	31
	5/1 - 10/31	180	32
Sugarbeets	2/1 - 8/31	210	36
	3/15 - 9/15	180	35
	5/1 - 1/31	280	36
	6/15 - 3/15	300	29
Rice	4/1 - 8/31	150	39
	5/1 - 9/30	150	39
Perennial Crops			
Alfalfa	All year, with winter dormant period		48
Pasture	All year, slower growth in winter		49
Grapes	March through mid-November		
Wine, raisin			30
Table			40
Deciduous orchards	February/March—November		
Clean cultivated			36
With cover crop			up to 48

Source: David C. Davenport and Robert M. Hagan, Proc. Agric. Water Conservation Workshop, Fresno, Nov. 6, 1980. (Figures are based on
Interagency Agricultural Information Task Force "Drought Tips").

As the table shows, it is possible to change total water use by varying the acreage and growth duration of crops. In most of inland California during the summer growing season, ET removes 0.2 to 0.3 inches of water per day from a well-irrigated crop that is past the developmental stage. At a rate of 0.3 inches per day for 150 days, a crop would consume about 45 inches of water. Replacing it with a crop that matured in 100 days would reduce water use to about 30 inches. Replacement by a winter cereal averaging only 0.1 inches per day for 180 days would give a further reduction to 18 inches. Although seasonal water use may be reduced by such changes in cropping patterns, production is generally reduced in proportion. Unless some other input is limiting, the amount of crop growth depends on the amount of solar energy—in effect, days of sunshine—that the plants receive. Hence, annual crops of long growth duration generally produce more than short-season ones.

The question is sometimes asked whether acreage of certain low-value and/or high-water-requirement crops might not be reduced in order to save water for other uses. This issue is discussed later, under "Shifts in Cropping Patterns."

Evaporation Factors: Delivery and Application. Since the evaporation of water is strongly determined by solar radiation, temperature, humidity, and wind velocity, evaporation rates are much greater during the hot, dry summers of the Central Valley compared to more temperate climates. These losses occur during storage and delivery, as water evaporates from reservoirs and canals, and there also are seepage losses during delivery. Open earth ditches, for example, may lose 20 to 40 percent of their water (evaporation plus seepage), while concrete-lined ditches lose only about 10 percent during delivery.

Other evaporative losses, as well as deep percolation and runoff, occur during application of water in the field. The method of irrigation is an important factor here. Table 3 lists types of irrigation systems used in California, and the acreage they cover. One important factor in the choice of application methods is soil type. On very light, sandy soils, infiltration is so rapid that sprinklers and drip systems are necessary. However, the fact that border and furrow methods are more commonly used with surface water, and sprinkler and drip systems with groundwater, reflects primarily economic considerations. Surface water is often relatively cheaper, so lower cost—and less efficient—delivery and application systems are more likely to be used. Poorly managed flood, furrow or border methods can result in irrigation efficiency as low as 55 or 60 percent, although it is usually higher. (In fact, well-designed and well-managed surface systems can be very efficient, particularly on heavy soils.)

With groundwater, which often is more expensive, sprinkler and drip systems are more common because they generally have smaller losses. Sprinkler efficiencies range from 75 to 85 percent, and drip efficiencies may be slightly higher. This approaches the maximum that is possible under most conditions.

On-Farm Use of Irrigation Water

In addition to the physiological needs of various crops, water use in agriculture is inextricably linked to the economic environment of crop production. Important factors are: (1) the availability and cost of the water itself, (2) the per-unit costs of other inputs such as land, labor, energy and machinery, and (3) prices received by farmers for what they sell.

Table 3

Irrigation Methods and Acreage in California
and Water Sources

Method	Surface Water Acreage	Ground Water Acreage
Flood	197,000	296,000
Border	2,031,000	897,202
Furrow	1,810,215	956,181
Sprinkler	694,362	880,290
Drip	5,218	34,183
Total	4,737,795	3,063,856

Source: Allan Highstreet, Carole Frank Nuckton, and
Gerald L. Horner, *Agricultural Water Use and
Costs in California,* Giannini Foundation Infor-
mation Series No. 80-2, Division of Agricultural
Sciences Bulletin No. 1896 (University of Cali-
fornia: Giannini Foundation, July 1980).

Water Prices. In California, irrigation water is distributed to farmers by several hundred nonprofit irrigation companies, irrigation districts and water districts of various types. (Chapter IX describes these institutions and their operating procedures.) Usually the cost of water to a farmer is his pro-rata share of the costs of operating and maintaining the district system. Districts close to their source of supply, especially those that own their own storage facilities, tend to have relatively low costs and low water charges; those farther from the source must charge more. Hence, the extreme range of irrigation water prices in the state—from possibly $1 per acre-foot in certain districts along the western slope of the Sierra Nevada to as much as $150 in districts at the southern end of the state.[8]

The federal Central Valley Project (CVP) and California's State Water Project (SWP) supply water to many districts, and greatly influence irrigation water prices. The CVP requires districts to reimburse it for a predetermined portion of the project costs, and sets water prices by an "ability-to-pay" rule. (This involves public subsidies of irrigation water and the so-called "160-acre limit." Water prices and subsidies will be discussed later in this chapter.)

SWP water is priced closer to its full supply cost. All SWP water users receiving entitlements of water pay a proportionate share of the project's fixed capital cost, as well as a transportation charge that varies with distance from the water source and the amount of pumping required. Thus, SWP water prices in Southern California are much higher than those farther north in the Central Valley.

Water Prices vs. Water Use. Water planners and managers sometimes tend to think of irrigation water solely in terms of a per-acre "need" or "requirement." However, water prices greatly influence the amount of water that irrigators use.

The quantity of water a farmer desires depends both on its cost to him and its value in terms of potential income. Only if an additional unit of water is worth more to him than its cost will a rational farmer wish to use it.

Suppose the extra cost (the marginal cost) of an additional acre-foot is very low—say, $2 to $5—and the farmer can use all he wants. How might he react? He might choose a longer season crop that uses more water, if it is otherwise profitable. He would choose an irrigation method that is quite efficient in conserving other valuable inputs such as labor, land and capital even though it is less efficient in using water. He might choose a "safe" irrigation schedule that would use more water but would reduce the risk of reduced yields. Obviously, some of these choices might be different if the price were $50 to $100 per acre-foot.

"Elasticity of demand" reflects the percentage change in water use associated with a 1 percent change in the water price. For example, an elasticity of -0.5 indicates that water use could be expected to decline by 0.5 percent if the water price were to increase by 1 percent (5 percent for a 10 percent increase).

What do we know about elasticity of demand for irrigation water? Not as much as we would like. Unfortunately, very few free water markets exist where prices can be observed directly. A number of economic studies do exist, however, and they show that elasticities vary a good deal among geographic areas and among crops. Water used to produce field crops such as cereals, feedgrains, cotton and sugarbeets would be expected to have a more elastic demand than that for high-valued vegetable crops and orchards.[9] Why the difference? Water costs are likely to be a smaller part of total costs for truck and orchard crops which have high per-acre costs (and revenues)—this tends to decrease elasticity.

Another critical factor is the degree of flexibility the farmer has in changing crops or acreage in response to the changing water price; the more the flexibility, the higher will be the elasticity of demand. For example, a farmer cannot move in and out of orchard production as he might with a field crop, since the orchard takes years to establish and entry and exit costs are high. In California, soils and climate patterns are also strong factors in restricting flexibility.

A Test Case: Kern County.[10] To test the hypothesis that farmers use water more efficiently when marginal water costs to them are high, water prices paid in various Kern County water districts were correlated with district irrigation efficiency. The data are shown in Table 4. (Irrigation efficiency was estimated by comparing the amount of water delivered to a district with crop acreage times an expected consumptive factor. Acreage must be estimated and actual consumptive use may vary considerably with field management, so the figures are subject to error.)

Total surface water costs as shown in Table 4 were plotted against the estimated district irrigation efficiencies. The results indicated little relationship between estimated efficiency and cost up to $30 per-acre foot. Beyond that price, there are several examples of high efficiency (e.g., Cawelo District). For the entire table, about 50 to 56 percent of the variation in efficiency can be associated with price. (This amount of explained variance is statistically significant at the 5 percent probability level.) The correlation for groundwater is slightly higher than for surface water—which is not surprising, since it is entirely under the grower's control, and a direct expense. More detailed analyses are needed before we can draw clear conclusions about efforts made by growers to improve irrigation efficiency in response to higher water costs. Irrigation practices have been improved through

Table 4

**Variable and Total Water Costs* and Estimated District
Irrigation Efficiency in Kern County, 1975**

	Surface Water		Groundwater		Estimated District Irrigation Efficiency
	A	B	C	D	Y
	Variable cost	Total cost	Variable cost	Total cost	
	per acre-foot				percent
Arvin-Edison	14.93	20.83	22.88	30.51	69
Belridge	25.18	25.18	--	--	71
Berrenda Mesa	12.53	33.51	--	--	75
Buena Vista	5.67	8.68	10.60	16.05	65
Buttonwillow	19.62	20.75	15.73	21.23	65
Cawelo	46.00	51.07	22.80	30.60	83
Delano-Earlimart	3.47	6.68	19.54	25.47	65
Henry Miller	15.83	28.20	9.93	16.60	61
Kern Delta	8.22	11.67	12.03	17.32	64
Kern-Tulare	--	--	31.31	40.03	77
Lost Hills	11.87	20.04	16.80	24.55	67
North Kern	10.27	11.94	16.25	22.44	65
Pond Poso	--	--	14.46	20.32	65
Rag Gulch	35.60	35.60	20.64	26.75	67
Rosedale-Rio Bravo	--	--	13.94	19.12	64
Semitropic	--	--	14.19	19.77	65
Shafter-Wasco	4.01	8.15	19.08	26.79	65
Southern San Joaquin	6.00	7.43	21.87	28.27	66
West Kern County	--	--	18.24	24.48	65
Wheeler Ridge-Maricopa	44.92	46.96	23.35	31.70	71

*Actual irrigation costs considered by the farmer include the labor and equipment costs associated with water application and drainage.

Source: William D. Watson, Carole Frank Nuckton, and Richard E. Howitt, *Crop Production and Water Supply Characteristics of Kern County,* Giannini Foundation Information Series No. 80-1, Division of Agricultural Sciences Bulletin No. 1895 (University of California: Giannini Foundation, April 1980).

time, and much land is being laser-levelled, but the estimated efficiencies in Table 4 do not seem to change with variation in certain other practices which should affect efficiency—for example, the proportion of acreage under sprinklers.

The high cost districts generally have unique structural, soil, and/or climatic conditions that affect irrigation efficiency and cropping patterns. Typically, lower valued crops (grains and alfalfa) are not produced with high cost water. The correlation coefficient for the Kern County districts between water costs and the percent of district acreage in high valued crops (orchards, vineyards and vegetables) was 0.51—not large, but statistically significant.

It would be a mistake, however, to assume that a grower of grain or alfalfa would automatically switch to higher value crops as water prices increase. To the extent feasible, those crops have already spread to lands with cheap water. Field crops simply occupy the remaining niches of land. Where water is very costly, revenues from lower value crops won't cover variable costs, so land is taken out of production.[11]

Pricing Practices of Water Districts. The way an input is priced at the margin is critically important to the amount that is demanded, and to the efficiency of the allocation process. Many agricultural inputs, such as fertilizer, gasoline, tractors and even hired labor, have well-defined market prices. This is not so in the case of water. Marginal water costs to farmers in California vary widely, not only because of actual differences in district costs (high or low capital costs, as with new and old dams), but also because of pricing practices.

The most common components of total irrigation water price have been identified as:[12]

• A water toll or "user charge" based on the number of acre-feet used.

• A general service charge, usually on a per-acre basis. (This is a fixed cost not related to the amount of water delivered.)

• Land taxes levied on behalf of the district by the local tax assessor.

These components of water price vary tremendously among districts. For example, in Kern County (Table 4) the Rag Gulch District, which depends relatively more on declining groundwater tables, charged $35.60 per acre-foot as a variable water toll, with no fixed per-acre charge. Berrenda Mesa, using "surplus" state water, collected $12.53 as a variable toll and the equivalent of $20.98 per acre-foot as a fixed charge. Therefore, although farmers in Berrenda Mesa paid a total price for water that was the equivalent of $33.51 per acre-foot, they were able to obtain an additional acre-foot for only $12.53. It seems likely that over a time period long enough for adjustment the quantity of water demanded in Berrenda Mesa would be substantially different if the marginal cost were the higher figure.

Fixed per-acre water charges may vary by crop. As an example, the Glenn-Colusa Irrigation District's regular water rates (effective February 7, 1980) were $17.25 per acre for rice; $12.10 per acre for sugarbeets and tomatoes; $10.35 per acre for pasture, clover, corn, alfalfa, and orchards; and $6.90 per acre for barley, vine crops, wheat, grain sorghum, other cereal grains, and silage corn.[13]

Why do so many water districts use a large proportion of fixed per-acre charges, rather than a variable per-acre-foot toll? There are two important reasons:

(1) The need to capture enough revenue to meet district indebtedness and other overhead costs. For example, assured income from fixed charges makes the district's financial status appear more secure; hence, bonds are easier to sell.

(2) The desire by districts to distribute all the surface water to which they have rights. If their surface supply is relatively plentiful, low per-acre-foot water tolls (marginal costs) to the farmer are used to increase surface water use. If sur-

face water is in short supply and the district must pump expensive groundwater, then high water tolls can be used to decrease total water demand.

Another reason that water may be priced on a per-acre rather than per-volume basis is the difficulty and cost of measuring how much is delivered. This is especially true of surface water diversions and for riparian users. But there are reliable methods, such as meters and weirs, for measuring water deliveries. For example, districts receiving federal water from the Tehama-Colusa Canal deliver it to their users through meters. Whether more efficient allocation would result from wider use of such devices needs to be determined.

These reasons for using fixed water charges may be perfectly sensible from the viewpoint of the district's management. From the broader viewpoint of water policy, however, a central question is the impact of fixed per-acre charges on agricultural water use. In the case of the Glenn-Colusa District, for example, a sugar-beet grower would pay the same flat water rate to apply 45 inches of water as for 35 inches; and a rice grower could get 6 acre-feet for the same price as 4. We do not mean to imply that putting more water on crops is costless—additional labor may be required and sometimes there are even deleterious effects on the crop. There will always be factors constraining water use, but the fact remains that, under circumstances of fixed per-acre water charges, the water cost per se invokes no incentive to use less water.

An even more tenuous relationship exists between water price and water use when land taxes are used to raise district revenues to pay water supply costs. Again, the marginal water cost to the grower is zero, so there is no incentive to use water more efficiently.

Basin Efficiencies and Water Savings

Our discussion of elasticity of demand for water and the impacts of pricing practices might be taken to suggest that irrigated agriculture wastes large amounts of water and that a significant quantity could be acquired for other uses by improving irrigation methods. This viewpoint is commonly expressed. Those holding it point out that on-farm or district irrigation efficiencies are seldom higher than 90 percent, and in some situations are as low as 50 or 60 percent. Why, they ask, should not irrigated agriculture in California be able to reduce its water use by, say, one-tenth? This would at least double supplies available for municipal, industrial and other nonagricultural uses and might avoid, or at least delay, the need for major new water projects.

Recoverable and Nonrecoverable Losses. At best, this viewpoint is only partially correct. The reason is that where irrigation is less efficient much of the unused water is recovered—it returns to the basin water system, where it is used again by others. Hence, water that runs off farmland or percolates below the plant root zone is not wasted when it replenishes either the surface or the groundwater supply.[14]

Return flows of this kind are known as *recoverable losses.* They include: (1) water that leaks or spills from storage and delivery systems, (2) surface water that runs off the lower end of an irrigated field, and (3) subsurface water that percolates below the reach of plant roots.

There are important costs linked with such inefficient use of water by individual farmers, even though much of the loss is recoverable. Drainage problems may be created. Water quality may be lowered by additional salts in water that escapes below the root zone, and possibly by pesticide or fertilizer residues in surface runoff. There may be additional power costs for pumping the extra water to the field. It may cost more to collect and reuse the water than if it had not been used in the first place.

But, despite these costs, water is not really lost unless it (1) moves into the atmosphere through evapotranspiration, (2) flows to some salt-sink such as the Salton Sea or the ocean, or (3) percolates into subsurface formations from which it cannot be feasibly recovered. These are *nonrecoverable losses*. Mostly in the form of evapotranspiration, they are very large—over 22 million acre-feet yearly in the state (see Figure 1, Introduction).

In determining how much of the water lost during irrigation could be saved for other uses, it is important to take into account a crucial difference between recoverable and nonrecoverable losses—which is that recoverable losses affect downstream flow. In the lower San Joaquin Valley, for example, irrigation water use is so efficient that very little streamflow leaves the basin. (This is a serious problem for downstream water users, primarily because of high salt concentrations in the water. But there is no other way for the lower Valley to export salts and maintain salt balance in the soil.) As a contrasting example, streamflows leaving the Sacramento Valley—composed in part of recoverable losses from irrigation—contribute to headgate supplies for the CVP and SWP, and to salt water repulsion in the Delta.

To summarize, preventing recoverable on-farm losses might save water and energy and/or improve water quality, but it is also likely to reduce downstream flow. On the other hand, preventing nonrecoverable losses, if possible, would result in a net gain in the total water supply.

Potential for Water Savings. To reduce both recoverable and nonrecoverable on-farm losses of irrigation water, four kinds of action are possible. Farmers may:

- Increase irrigation efficiency by improving existing systems or adopting more efficient new technologies. Sprinkler or drip systems, or advanced surface systems, if properly adapted and managed, may be more efficient than present systems.
- Reduce water applications below the crop's maximum need.
- Change cropping patterns.
- Cease irrigation of some cropland.

Water-saving possibilities within these categories must be evaluated in light of their potential for reducing losses (particularly nonrecoverable losses) and also their economic impacts on the farmer and on California's farm production.

How much potential is there in California for improving on-farm irrigation efficiency by more use of sprinkler and drip systems and/or better designed surface systems? As shown in Table 3, the more traditional surface irrigation methods presently account for almost 80 percent of total irrigated acreage. Flood (mostly rice) accounts for 6 percent; basin (forages, small grains, irrigated pastures), 38 percent; and furrow methods (most field and vegetable crops), 35 percent.

During the past decade there has been a significant increase in more efficient irrigation technology, with emphasis on sprinkler and drip systems. These methods are most likely to be used where water is expensive or limited in supply or where surface irrigation is less effective and/or efficient because of slope, soil texture or other reasons.

In any case, it is likely that increases in water and energy costs, plus improved technology such as level-basin or nearly level border irrigation and low-pressure traveling sprinkler systems, will continue the trend toward more efficient—although often far more expensive—irrigation systems. The chief water-saving benefit of these systems is less excess percolation and surface runoff and, in case of drip, less evaporation from the soil. They also cut labor costs. One disadvantage is high capital costs for sprinkler and drip systems and the use of increasingly expensive energy for pressurizing the water. Another is the possibility that increased efficiency will reduce the leaching of salts, resulting in salt build-up in the soil profile. Drip systems, particularly, may cause localized salt accumulations.

It is also possible to reduce recoverable losses by such means as:

• Improved irrigation scheduling, which helps in applying water in the right amounts at the right time.

• Better drainage and salinity management, which will reduce water needs for these practices.

• Automation of systems to increase application efficiency.

• Shorter irrigation runs (at the expense of more labor).

• Use of lined ditches or pipelines.

• Use of tailwater recovery systems.

In addition, nonrecoverable water losses can be reduced within existing cropping patterns by controlling weeds and aquatic plants, and by limiting or eliminating cover crops. All these techniques must be evaluated for cost effectiveness.

Shifts in Cropping Patterns. Other potential water-saving management practices involve the crop itself, and are primarily concerned with reducing seasonal evapotranspiration. As Table 2 shows, crops vary widely in length of growing season, time of growing season, and amount of foliage cover—all of which directly affect seasonal ET losses. To take advantage of these factors, farmers could change their present cropping patterns (choosing a short-season variety of an annual crop, for example); reduce multiple cropping; or shift to a different crop.

However, the question of overall potential savings from reduced ET is still open. Although over 22 million acre-feet of water are consumed each year through crop ET in California, the consequences of significant reductions would be very complex—and are still largely unknown.

It has been suggested, for example, that acreages of rice, alfalfa or irrigated pasture could be reduced to save water for other uses. Rice has a relatively high seasonal ET loss of almost 40 inches and has been planted on more than 500,000 acres in recent years, mostly in the Sacramento Valley. Rice is grown on very heavy soils which are poorly suited for most other crops, but it has been estimated that possibly half of the acreage could be shifted to, for example, corn and beans. This would save an estimated 300,000 to 375,000 acre-feet of water yearly that is now lost to ET.

Whether such a shift could be economically justified is quite another question. Arguments will be made that California's rice crop fills a unique role in world food supplies. With average yields near 7,000 pounds per acre—the highest in the world—the state's rice fields provide nearly one-half of the world's trade in that commodity. California rice also is a critical source of human food for Latin America, Asia and Europe. And, despite its high consumptive use of water, rice is exceeded in California only by wheat and sugarbeets in the amount of digestible human food produced per unit of water.

Alfalfa and pasture are crops with even larger ET requirements—about 48 inches yearly, depending on the area, climate and growing season. Alfalfa is grown on approximately one million acres in the state, many of them on the better soils. Shifts from alfalfa to certain other field crops could save one or more acre-feet of water per acre yearly. Irrigated pasture is grown on about 1.12 million acres, many with shallow soils, and tends to be located where water is cheap. Its seasonal ET is about the same as that of alfalfa, and shifts to other crops, where feasible, would further reduce ET losses. Both of these crops, however, are critical elements in the livestock complex. They are the main sources of protein and energy feeds for dairy animals, and are decisive factors in carrying range animals through the dry season. An estimated 20 percent of the state's alfalfa crop goes to maintain its horse population, and additional large fractions are used for poultry and for pet foods. In addition, alfalfa, a legume, serves an important role in the cropping system by producing its own nitrogen biologically. Besides contributing vital protein to the food system without need of fertilizer, it leaves large residues of nitrogen in the soil for subsequent crops. It also plays important roles in weed control and physical conditioning of the soil.

It appears that possibly a million acre-feet of water could be saved yearly by substantial shifts away from California's heaviest water-using crops—rice, alfalfa and pasture. However, immense and highly complex impacts on the food system—economic and otherwise—could be expected to follow.

Stressing the Plants. It may be possible to reduce evapotranspiration by applying less water than is actually needed for maximum crop yield. The critical relationship is the effect on yield of decreasing applications of water. University research on water-deficient agriculture has indicated that a 10 percent water deficit would, at the least, reduce alfalfa yield by 10 percent; cotton, 12.5 percent; corn, 12.5 percent; grain sorghum, 10 percent; pinto beans, 23.5 percent; and pink beans, 21 percent.[15] These reductions would be even higher if the water deficit occurred at critical periods, such as during pollenation. These figures indicate that, in most cases at least, cutting irrigation below ET requirements results in lower yields. Income may subsequently be lower or higher, depending on costs and returns.

However, preliminary results of continuing research indicate that "deficit irrigation" might be adapted to some permanent crops such as raisin and wine grapes, and almonds—but only in areas where there is sufficient rain or available winter irrigation water to satisfy salt-leaching requirements. Research on deficit irrigation in cotton also is continuing, with some promising results.

Stressing the plant by deficit irrigation may increase the risk of sharp yield reductions. Because weather conditions are unpredictable, because water-holding capacity of the soil varies within many fields, and for other reasons, the timing and quantity of irrigation often cannot be managed with extreme precision. Risks to the farmer of applying too little water and stressing the plant may well be higher than the costs of applying too much.

FUTURE WATER USE BY AGRICULTURE

Besides those factors discussed thus far—crop requirements for water, price influence on water utilized, and possibilities for using water more efficiently—certain other trends and constraints will shape future water use by California agriculture. These include the continuing overdraft, water price trends, and unanswered policy questions such as the possibility of new water development and the potential role of subsidies. All of these topics will be discussed briefly, with particular emphasis on what might be expected in the near future.

Trend to More Efficiency

In recent years, agriculture has made large investments in laser leveling, pipelines, and in sprinkler and drip systems to improve irrigation efficiency. This will result in some water saved at the basinwide level, but not as much as is commonly believed because most of the on-farm savings simply reduce recoverable losses.

For example, the only major agricultural areas in the state where percolation losses are not recoverable are in the Imperial and Coachella valleys and on the west side of the San Joaquin Valley, where these losses end as saline drainage water. However, irrigation efficiency is relatively high on the west side because water is costly and in short supply.

The principal reason that farmers are investing in improved irrigation efficiency is not to save water on a regional basis, but to improve crop production, stretch their on-farm water supplies, and reduce water costs.

The Overdraft Problem

Groundwater overdrafting is high on the list of public concerns about water policy in California. Overdrafting implies an imbalance of demand and supply. It also means that pumpers are taking water from greater and greater depths, thus incurring higher pumping costs. If overdrafting continues, eventually it will simply be uneconomic to pump.

Continued and serious overdrafting occurs primarily because of a "common pool" problem. Groundwater is common property and each farmer knows that if he doesn't use it, even to the point of no economic return, somebody else will. Since individual farmers have no exclusive rights to water left in the ground, they tend to disregard the future value of that stored water. Therefore, instead of remaining at a somewhat higher level where most growers can make at least some profit, the entire groundwater basin will be drawn down to a no-profit level.[16]

If the current overdraft in the San Joaquin Valley of 1.5 million acre-feet yearly continues and the farmers respond by discontinuing irrigation, how much acreage would be eventually lost to irrigated production? Assuming a seasonal crop water use of 36 inches (see Table 2), the answer would be 500,000 acres.

To correct the "common pool" problem, it has been suggested that management entities be created to manage at least some aquifers in the best interests of the joint pumpers. Legislation has been introduced that would limit groundwater use to the average annual aquifer recharge. Farmers, however, have almost universally condemned these proposals and have resisted even local or regional groundwater control. Why is this, when at first glance it appears that farmers would be the primary beneficiaries? There are several reasons:

(1) Farmers in many areas realize that their aquifers are not being over-utilized, either from the individual or basin viewpoint. This means groundwater use plans should be flexible enough to adjust to local conditions; and this implies local rather than state-level controls.

(2) Other cost and price trends may be disguising the impact of increasing pumping costs on a farmer's total costs.

(3) Farmers fear that regulation of groundwater use, especially at the state level, could shift control of the resource to nonfarmers.

(4) Farmers fear the immediate costs of reduced pumping, including the possibility of having to watch some acreage go dry. This would affect not only crop profits but land values.

(5) Farmers still hope that new surface water will be made available to offset the overdraft.

Future Water Prices

Since water costs influence irrigation technology and cropping patterns, and thus the amount of water demanded, a crucial question is what lies ahead for water prices. The answer is, it depends on the water supply source—but the trend is generally upward.

In the case of federal water supplied by the Bureau of Reclamation, water repayment schedules have been set by ability-to-pay rules established in 40-year contracts. Most of these contracts in California will not be renegotiated formally until the mid-1990s. Some pressure is being brought by the Bureau to update water rates every five years. Changes in the ability to pay and in agency supply costs will be monitored, and the plan is to increase rates to the level of whichever of the two is lower. However, water users can be expected to resist renegotiations that would increase prices. Meanwhile, the Bureau plans to make available some water from New Melones Reservoir—that which does not incur additional pumping or transportation costs—at $3.50 per acre foot.[17]

The situation regarding the State Water Project is more clearcut. Water clients are required by law to pay the full supply costs, although there is disagreement about exactly what these costs are. The costs are updated every 10 years, and new rates will be set in 1984. A large fraction of the supply costs is for pumping, mostly for electric power. Moore[18] has shown that the growth in the cost of energy from 1973 to 1980 was an estimated 24 percent per year, compared to 11 percent annually for the Consumer Price Index. Since power costs will have risen relatively sharply during the previous 10 years, almost everyone agrees that State Water Project prices will increase substantially in 1984.

The same will be true for agricultural users of groundwater. Pumping costs are increasing rapidly for two reasons: (1) in many areas, especially the southern end of the San Joaquin Valley, water is being pumped from great depths, and the overdraft is continuing; and (2) power rates are increasing. Watson, Nuckton, and Howitt[19] have shown that pumping costs in Kern County in 1975 ranged between $16.05 and $40.03 per acre-foot (Table 4). These costs are likely to be much higher today, and will almost certainly be higher still in the future. A rule of thumb is that the energy costs alone are about 10 cents per acre-foot per foot of lift.

As pointed out in Chapter I, the full supply costs of most "new" water in California will be $100 per acre-foot or higher, and even more when the conveyance costs are included. Meanwhile, studies show that, in general, irrigation water used in California has a value to the grower of somewhat less than $100 per acre-foot. This means that much of the new irrigation water would either have to be subsidized (see the next section) or that the higher costs would have to be averaged in with lower ones for existing supplies to yield a blend price that would be "affordable." This blending of high and low prices is a practice strongly advocated by those favoring new development and is now widely used by some water districts. It is a threat to efficient allocation of resources, however, because it hides the true costs of new water development—which may exceed the benefits.

No discussion of water pricing would be complete without reference to California's specialty crops, those for which the state has a high proportion of total national production. Because of limited competition, the market price of these crops will be largely determined by how much is grown in California. Cost increases for crops that are grown mostly or totally in California will be more easily passed on to consumers because they cannot turn to other production areas. This point is significant in determining the competitive advantage of California agriculture; in general, it means the specialty crops such as fruits and nuts will be more competitive than field crops such as cotton and wheat in the face of rising water prices.

Benefits/Losses From Subsidies

One of the most controversial aspects of water policy in the western U.S. and California is the water "subsidy" given to farmers. Nearly everyone agrees that some farmers get water at prices below its full supply cost, especially water from federal projects, but there is sharp disagreement about how much the subsidy is—as well as whether or not it is justified.

Per-acre subsidies were recently estimated for certain federal water projects in California and are shown in Table 5. Column 1 shows the per-acre subsidy, which is the difference between what the water costs to develop and what the farmers pay for it. This subsidy, which represents a loss to the taxpayers, varies among projects so much because the full irrigation supply costs of the more recent projects listed in the table are much higher than those of earlier ones. Column 2 shows the percentage of total irrigation supply costs that the subsidy in the first column represents. Column 3 lists the estimated per-acre increases in land value that occurred because project water was worth more to the farmers than its cost to them, and the difference became capitalized into land values. (Estimating land values is a hazardous undertaking under the best of circumstances. However, it is often assumed that increases in land value reflect fairly accurately the net benefits of the water captured by landowners.)

There are important implications here as to the economic feasibility of the projects. Where enhanced land values captured by land owners exceeded the subsidy's cost to the taxpayers—as in the cases of Goleta and Glenn-Colusa—it could be argued that more net wealth has been created in the economy as a whole. The equity of this wealth transfer from taxpayers to farmers may be questioned, but it is economically efficient. On the other hand, if the taxpayer loss is greater

Table 5

Per-Acre Subsidies and Land Values for
California Federal Water Districts

District	Subsidy	Percent of Irrigation Supply Costs Subsidized	Estimated Increase Per Acre in Land Value
	dollars (1)	percent (2)	dollars (3)
Goleta	1,378	81.4	2,000
Glenn-Colusa	101	90.7	500
Westlands	1,422	84.7	950
Coachella	1,000	69.5	550
Imperial	149	73.5	100

Source: United States Department of the Interior, *Acreage Limitation,* Interim Report, Water and Power Resources Service,
March 1980.

than the landowner benefits, then there is a net loss of wealth to the economy.
This was the outcome in the Westlands, Coachella and Imperial districts.

Varying Marginal Values

Ordinarily, a grower will continue to apply irrigation water, even though its
return to him diminishes, as long as the water's marginal value exceeds its cost.
Therefore, where costs are low, water may be used for relatively low-value purposes even though it may be worth much more to other water users.

A crucial question, then, is: Within a region or basin, how much variation is
there in the value of the last acre-foot of irrigation water applied (marginal
value)?

This question has been addressed by a study of water use in Yolo County.[20]
An economic-hydrologic model was used to estimate the marginal values of irrigation water, both pumped and surface-delivered, being used in six areas of the
county. The values ranged from $2.44 per acre-foot near the Sacramento River
where costs are low (water is plentiful and the pumping lift is less than 20 feet) to
$61.13 in another area 25 miles away where costs are higher because water is
pumped more than 100 feet.

This disparity in values suggests that large economic gains could be captured
by transferring water from areas of low value to areas of high value. (The case
for water transfers is discussed in Chapter VIII.)

Environmental Constraints

Directly competitive with irrigation are in-stream uses of water such as
fishing, boating, dilution of pollutants, and repulsion of saline water (see Chapter

VI). Water law provides rights for water diversions for beneficial uses, but does not adequately take account of such in-stream uses.[21] If the law is changed to give rights to in-stream uses or if administrative rules provide generous quantities of water for these uses via minimum-flow standards, the impact on irrigated agriculture could be substantial.

Another potential environmental constraint is water quality problems created by agricultural return flows. Irrigated farms may be "nonpoint sources" of water pollutants—salts, nitrates and pesticide residues. The emphasis in nonpoint source control, however, appears to be directed toward erosion and sedimentation; and, in California, these problems are more severe in nonirrigated lands such as ranges and forests. Furthermore, the trend toward more efficient on-farm water use will help to solve the return-flow pollution problem. Less surface runoff and percolation proportionately reduce salts, nitrates and pesticide residues leaving the land.

Future Demand for Agricultural Products

Forces outside agriculture but impinging on it always have been critical to a healthy farming industry. Historically, a growing economy with near full employment has produced jobs for excess labor in agriculture and has provided a strong demand for agricultural products. As discussed in the first section of this chapter, California agriculture is not only a mainstay of the state's economy, but is inextricably linked to the national and world economies and will rise or fall as conditions change in those markets.

Because of world population dynamics and the real costs of growing food, the United States Department of Agriculture expects a rise in the relative price of food over the next half century, reversing a long-time trend toward cheaper prices for raw food compared to other goods. The outlook is for rising relative prices particularly in food grains and crops used to produce cooking oil. Marginal shifts of acreage to wheat, beans, rice, and the oil crops such as sunflower and safflower might be expected. California acreage in wheat and rice in 1981 will be more than a million acres, and there is still room for further expansion, especially in wheat. The implications for water demand are not clear, however, as rice is a relatively heavy water user whereas wheat and the oil crops are not.

On the other hand, rising energy prices have increased the cost of moving California produce to eastern markets. If they continue to escalate, some loss of markets could occur in those products which are expensive to ship. This would include fresh fruits and vegetables, which are fairly heavy water users. Chapter V, however, presents indications that energy prices may not increase substantially in real terms in the near future, and thus there may not be much further impact on California agriculture.

ALTERNATIVE FUTURES: THREE SCENARIOS

Status Quo

This scenario assumes that no significant amounts of new water will become available to California agriculture, and that no change in water-allocation institutions will make it easier to transfer water. Even though this alternative future is described as "status quo," it would bring significant change to the state's agriculture—at least to those production regions where existing trends in water costs and availability have most impact.

One force for change, not entirely predictable, will be the shifting national and international demands for California agricultural products. Of course, increasing demand for a particular crop would add to its competitive advantage in an era of generally rising costs.

A second major force producing change under the "status quo" scenario is virtually certain: increasing real water costs. Higher prices charged for surface water, at least by the SWP, and higher pumping costs for groundwater will significantly boost water costs in many regions. This, in turn, can be expected to increase pressure for on-farm irrigation efficiency in the affected areas, and the trend to advanced irrigation technology. In addition, there might well be shifts to crops with lower seasonal ET requirements and/or to crops giving higher returns to water. Unless drought conditions reappear, however, these changes probably would be relatively slow and orderly.

It cannot be assumed that higher on-farm irrigation efficiencies would make much more water available for redistribution, either within agriculture or outside. For one thing, as noted before, reducing the recoverable losses does not necessarily increase the total supply. Also, water prices would be expected to increase most in the San Joaquin Valley and Southern California, where transport costs are highest and where pumping lifts are greatest. These are the precise areas that already have done the most to improve irrigation efficiency; whether substantial further improvements are feasible there is an open question.

On the other hand, the variability in per-acre-foot tolls charged by water districts in Kern County and elsewhere in the Valley indicates that at least some districts have not, so far, made use of pricing practices as an incentive to reduce water demand. Furthermore, the lower prices charged for federal water—even for new federal water coming on line—implies the possibility of shifting cropping patterns as a result of potential changes in federal pricing policy. But changing to higher-valued crops does not necessarily mean a reduction in total water use. A shift from single-cropped corn to orchards, for example, would mean higher water use, although from alfalfa to grain sorghum would not.

The Supreme Court ruling in favor of Arizona will reduce California's share of Colorado River water by some 650,000 acre-feet annually beginning sometime in the mid-1980s. Most of this water has been used by the Metropolitan Water District (MWD) in Southern California and, unless the contracting agencies for this water raise their prices to reduce demand, they obviously will be looking elsewhere for replacement supplies. In the past, during years of normal or higher rainfall, MWD has had surplus water which was sold to farmers in Kern County at low prices. The annual quantities have varied tremendously, but in 1979 the Kern County Water Agency received over half a million acre-feet of this surplus water.

Particularly if the MWD were to use all of its contracted state water to replace the lost Colorado River supply, the imbalance of water demand and supply in the San Joaquin Valley would worsen. If this happens (under the "status quo" scenario), either the overdrafting of groundwater will accelerate, higher variable water tolls will induce increased irrigation efficiencies, or some land will cease to be irrigated—or, more likely, some combination of these outcomes will take place. There do not seem to be other feasible choices.

Decreased water availability and increased water prices, unless offset by very favorable agricultural output prices, would almost certainly reduce net income to farmers and result in lower land values. There could be associated impacts on consumers in the form of higher food prices or less availability of certain crops, or both.

It appears, however, that under the "status quo" scenario these impacts of water supplies and prices on farmers will be regional, and will be felt mostly in the San Joaquin Valley and in certain parts of Southern California (not including the Coachella and Imperial valleys). Because output of many crops south of the Tehachapis already has been reduced by urbanization, the bulk of the economic impact would be in the San Joaquin Valley.

Marketlike System for Water Transfer

If legal and political institutions were modified to permit transfers or market exchanges of water, no doubt the effects would be far-reaching and dramatic. The details of a market system are discussed more fully in Chapter VIII. Our interest here is the expected impacts on agriculture.

It has been shown that the value of water to a farmer versus what he pays for it affects his decisions on irrigation methods and on cropping patterns—and thus his water demand. It also has been shown that marginal values of water among uses and users are highly disparate. This means the potential gains to the traders from voluntary transfers would likely be large. In addition, the impact of a water market on total water use is likely to be significant. This is because a farmer using water for low-valued uses has little incentive to conserve; but if he could market water at higher prices than its value on his farm, his approach to water use would change. He would be motivated to save water, to shift to crops that use less water, or perhaps to move out of farming altogether. However, the exchange would be voluntary and he would not sell his water, or any part of it, unless he believed he would be better off.

Under such voluntary market exchanges, the price of water would be established at market-clearing levels and would serve as signals to direct water movement and development. The question is, how much water would move and where?

Under this scenario, some water might move out of agriculture, but probably not very much. The demand for water in domestic, commercial, and industrial uses is quite price-inelastic, and there are no apparent unsatisfied demands waiting to be filled, except for the Colorado River loss mentioned before. Some nonagricultural users might buy up water anticipating future growth, but might well lease it back to agriculture until the growth actually occurred.

Rather, most of the water exchanges would be expected within agriculture. High water-using crops with relatively low value such as pasture and rice would become, in effect, more costly to grow if the opportunity existed to sell some or all of the water used on them. (Rice acreage in the state has varied in recent years between 310,000 acres in 1977 to an estimated 555,000 acres in 1981, showing that its acreage response to other economic and physical forces is great.)

Despite the high conveyance costs of moving water to the San Joaquin Valley, water values are high enough there to suggest some movements in that direction. Much depends on market conditions for the crops grown (vegetables, fruits, nuts, cotton) and whether or not increases in production would depress market prices. It follows that if northern water could be purchased and moved south more cheaply than groundwater can be pumped there, the market process also could mitigate the groundwater overdraft.

Notwithstanding these claimed advantages to water markets, many in the agricultural community are resisting. Growers fear there would be losses of water during transfer that would have to be accounted for. They are concerned about impacts on third parties such as irrigation districts, adjacent landowners, allied businesses, and local communities. They point to possible legal tangles. (Could a farmer sell his surface water and then continue to farm by pumping? Could long-term contracts create other "Owens Valley" situations?)

Some of these concerns could be mitigated by allowing a water owner to sell only that water which otherwise would be consumptively used by his crops. But the question of whether whole areas would cease irrigation altogether, or simply save water by using it more efficiently, needs to be carefully researched before a market system is widely adopted. It should not be overlooked that marketlike transfers of water are already occurring every year and were particularly significant during the drought years when normal patterns of distribution were disrupted.

Development of New Supplies

This is the scenario widely preferred by the agricultural community for solving its water-shortage problems. While they realize that new development is highly controversial and presents difficult political and economic problems, many California farmers—particularly those in water-short areas—believe that other proposed solutions (groundwater regulation, water markets or increased water prices) are either impractical, insufficient, or present even greater problems.

As pointed out in Chapter I, of the 25 or 26 million acre-feet of "remaining surface runoff" in California (1980 conditions), possibly 7 million are considered by the Department of Water Resources to have potential for capture and diversion to new uses. This is only about one-sixth of the 42 million acre-feet of presently developed supply, but the argument is that it is crucially important that this water be available for use.

The problem is the development and conveyance costs of "new" water. As shown in the introductory chapter, cost estimates for irrigation supplies from proposed new projects in California start at or near $100 per acre-foot and range up to $200 or $300. Additional conveyance costs would range from $10 to $40 in the North Bay area to $100 to $125 in Southern California.

There are some, but very few, situations in California agriculture where water is worth in excess of $100 per acre-foot at today's prices for crops. Of course, if inflation continues as in recent years, $100 per acre-foot for irrigation water may not be out of reach some time in the future; but $200 to $300 is another question.

These cost figures suggest that if there is to be demand within agriculture for available new water, then either blend pricing or water subsidies must be involved. Both have been previously discussed in this paper. Both are commonly practiced and justified by farmers and others in society. Many types of development projects are subsidized: e.g., airports, highways, postal service, railroads, public housing, education, urban renewal, wastewater treatment, and health services. Farmers ask, why not water projects and especially irrigation, since all eat and benefit from lower priced food?

There is an additional question as to whether use of new subsidized water should be restricted to areas of groundwater overdraft. Groundwater replenishment may not take place automatically, especially if prices for the new surface supply are relatively high. Since wells already are in place, pumping will continue as long as variable pumping costs are lower than the new water prices. In the absence of controls, therefore, the newly developed water might move to new lands where it would be less expensive than the total costs of putting in new wells and pumping.

Under this scenario, the pricing of new water can be used as a public policy device to influence the amount of land in agricultural production, as well as the distribution of water and the profitability of irrigated agriculture.

Courses of Action

An argument for further development of water for agriculture in California goes like this:

California agriculture's historic economic advantage is both crucial and endangered. The lower the per-unit costs of the state's farmers relative to their competitors, the larger will be the producing, processing, transportation, and marketing sectors—and the more California's economy and consumers, as well as its farmers, will gain.

Water, not land, is the most critical constraint on farm output in the state. The more water that is available to agriculture, therefore, the more land will be in intensive irrigated production—and the larger the volume, if not the value, of farm output. Availability of more irrigation water, however, depends directly on more development of surface streamflow in the state; there is no other feasible source on a sustainable basis. Saving irrigation water in situations where efficiency is not already high would help stretch the supply—but it is highly questionable whether that alone could even make up the existing deficit, much less allow new growth.

There are, however, additional losses and gains to be weighed in considering the above rationale for new development of water. These include:

- The significant taxpayer losses that occur when new projects are subsidized and total costs exceed total benefits.

- The gains to the overall economy that come with more efficient allocation and use of existing supplies of water that are induced by higher prices, even though there are some losers.

- The environmental benefits associated with in-stream uses that would be foregone if more water is diverted.

Nevertheless, from the specific viewpoint of agriculture in California, the logical recommendation is for development of some additional surface water, priced at a level that farmers could afford. Such a solution would clearly benefit agriculture in the state, and losses to California taxpayers would be at least partly offset by indirect benefits to the state's economy and in lower food prices.

In any case, it is important not to underestimate the resiliency of irrigated agriculture in California. On a per-acre basis, costs of farm production in the state—for land, water, labor, energy and capital—are as high as anywhere in the nation and higher than in many competing areas. But the state also has an offsetting advantage: lower costs per unit of output for most of its crops, resulting largely from the unique combination of climate, soil, water, and technology, and especially a highly skilled and innovative group of farm managers.

REFERENCES AND NOTES

1. Chester O. McCorkle and Carole Frank Nuckton, "The Dimensions of California Agriculture," in *A Guidebook to California Agriculture* (Berkeley, California: University of California Press, forthcoming).
2. Calculations by George Goldman based on data in *Measuring Economic Impacts: The Application of Input-Output Analysis to California Water Resource Problems*, Bulletin No. 210, Department of Water Resources (Sacramento, California: The Resources Agency, 1980).
3. U.S. Department of Commerce, Bureau of the Census, *1978 Census of Agriculture*, Preliminary Report, California, July 1980.
4. U.S. Department of Agriculture, *Agricultural Statistics, 1980* (Washington, D.C.: United States Printing Office, 1980), p. 430.
5. California Employment Development Department, *Report 881-M*, January 1978.
6. California Crop and Livestock Reporting Service, *Exports of Agricultural Commodities Produced In California, Calendar Year 1980*, August 1981.
7. William L. Kahrl, ed., *The California Water Atlas*, prepared by the Governor's Office of Planning and Research in cooperation with the California Department of Water Resources, 1979, p. 103.
8. Adrian Griffen, California Department of Water Resources, personal communication, July 1981.
9. Richard E. Howitt, William D. Watson, and Richard M. Adams, "A Reevaluation of Price Elasticities for Irrigation Water," *Water Resources Research*, 4(1980):4,623-629.
10. The information in this section is from William D. Watson, Carole Frank Nuckton, and Richard E. Howitt, *Crop Production and Water Supply Characteristics of Kern County*, Giannini Foundation Information Series No. 80-1, Division of Agricultural Sciences Bulletin No. 1895 (University of California: Giannini Foundation, April 1980).
11. The authors are indebted to George Ferry, County Director of Cooperative Extension in Kings County, for some of these ideas.
12. Watson, Nuckton, and Howitt, op. cit.
13. Glenn-Colusa Irrigation District, Water Rates and Due Dates Adopted by the Board of Directors, Feb. 7, 1980.
14. David C. Davenport and Robert M. Hagan, "Assessing Potentials for Agricultural Water Conservation," *Western Water*, November-December 1979, pp. 6-11.
15. J. Ian Stewart, "Conservation Irrigation of Field Crops: A Drought-Year Strategy," *California Agriculture*, 31(1977):4, 6-9.
16. B. Delworth Gardner, Richard E. Howitt, and Carole Frank Nuckton, "The Case for Regional Groundwater Management," *California Agriculture*, 35(1981):1 and 2, 9-10.
17. Bee Capital Bureau, Capital Report, "New Group to Push Initiative to Restrict Filling of Melones," *The Sacramento Bee*, July 23, 1981, p. A19.
18. Charles V. Moore, "Impact of Increasing Energy Costs on Pump-Irrigated Agriculture," *California Agriculture*, 35(1981):1 and 2, 23-24.
19. Watson, Nuckton, and Howitt, op. cit.
20. Jay E. Noel, B. Delworth Gardner, and Charles V. Moore, "Optimal Regional Conjunctive Water Management," *American Journal of Agricultural Economics*, 62(1980): 3, 489-498.
21. For 1977, California Crop and Livestock Reporting Service, *Field Crop Statistics*, 1977-78; for the 1981 estimate, United States Department of Agriculture, Crop Reporting Board, *Prospective Planting*, March 1981.

CHAPTER III

MUNICIPAL AND DOMESTIC USE

by

William H. Bruvold, Frank G. Mittelbach, and Christian Werner

ABSTRACT

The paper begins by considering population projections for California for the five decade years beginning with 1980. The 1980 population estimate is 23 million and the 2020 population projection is 35 million. Daily per capita use of water is then considered with a figure of 200 gallons per person estimated for urban use. The combined population and water use estimates yield a projected urban use of 2.555 x 10^{12} gallons for the year 2020. Based on the evidence cited and assumptions developed by this paper it is projected that, if urban use remains constant at 200 gallons per person per day, the safe operating capacity of urban water supply systems for California taken as a whole will be exceeded by the year 2000.

The population of California will not grow at the same rate in the various regions of the state. Over one-half of California's population growth during the next 40 years is projected for Southern California, the region most reliant on water imported over long distances. Obviously, regions with rapid population growth will face urban water shortages sooner than less rapidly growing regions if current pricing and allocation practices continue. Control of urban development and urban water conservation are identified as major factors intimately related to future urban water supply management.

Future urban water use in California may decrease or increase from the current estimated use of 200 gallons per person per day. The paper considers decreased uses of 100 and 150 gallons per person per day and increased usages of 250, 300 and 350 gallons per person per day. Very interesting is the dramatic finding that average uses of 100 or 150 gallons per person per day would not, for the state as a whole, exceed estimated safe operating capacity before the year 2020—whereas average uses of 250, 300 and 350 gallons per person per day would currently exceed it. This general result is then considered more specifically, first for regions and then for selected cities.

Three major policy options are identified which respond to the urban water supply situation in California. One policy option involves increasing the supply to the urban sector. The second involves control over urban development in the regions of California experiencing the most rapid population growth. The third policy option involves urban conservation and reuse. The relative merits of the three policy options are considered and the paper concludes with a recommended policy for urban water use in California for the next half-century.

MUNICIPAL NEEDS AND SUPPLIES

Population and Use Estimates

The population of California in 1980 was estimated to be 22,798,900 by the California Department of Finance[1] and 23,669,000 by the United States Bureau of the Census.[2] For the purposes of this chapter a population estimate of 23 million in 1980 is appropriate. Further, following projections of the California Department of Finance,[3] California's population is estimated to be 26 million in 1990, 29 million in 2000, 32 million in 2010 and 35 million in 2020.

This chapter will use population figures and gallons per person per day estimates to develop its analyses and positions. The residential component of municipal use is estimated to be 100 gallons per person per day. The commercial and public agency component of municipal use is estimated to be 50 gallons per person per day.[4] For our purposes, municipal use will include the residential, commercial, and public agency components. Industrial use may be estimated at 50 gallons per person per day. Urban use will include municipal and industrial use.

Daily residential use for California as a whole is estimated to be 2.30×10^9 gallons; yearly residential use is estimated to be 0.839×10^{12} gallons. Daily municipal use for California as a whole is estimated to be 3.45×10^9 gallons; yearly municipal use, 1.259×10^{12} gallons. Daily urban use for California as a whole is estimated to be 4.60×10^9 gallons; yearly urban use, 1.679×10^{12} gallons. The accuracy of these estimates may be checked against 1972 figures provided by the Department of Water Resources[5] which indicates that urban use in California then totaled 4.50×10^9 gallons per day and 1.642×10^{12} gallons, or 5.1 million acre-feet, per year. Thus the current estimate of 200 gallons per person per day for urban use is reasonable. Further, recent estimates of daily per capita use developed by the City of Los Angeles, Department of Water and Power, shown in Table 1, also support the present estimate of 200 gallons per capita per day.

2020 Population and Use

If it is assumed that the 200 gallons per capita per day urban usage rate remains constant to the year 2020, and if California's population is 35 million in that year, then daily urban use would be 7.00×10^9 gallons per day and 2.555×10^{12} gallons, or 7.8 million acre-feet, per year. Daily and yearly urban use estimates derived in this way using 200 gallons per person per day as a constant rate of use, and the aforementioned population estimates,[6] are shown in Figure 1.

Source and Treatment Capacity

It is estimated that yearly consumption for the urban sector is currently about 13.5 percent of water used consumptively in California.[7] If the supply remains constant until 2020, urban use would then require 20.5 percent of the total amount available for consumption. If the total available supply increases by 10 percent by 2020, urban uses would then require 18.7 percent of the total.

Another and perhaps more important set of estimates has to do with the operating capacity of municipal water systems. It is estimated that about 90 percent of Californians are served by municipal water systems having 200 or more service connections. Thus, including industrial use in all calculations will not seri-

Table 1

Water Use in California Cities
(Gallons Per Person Per Day*)

City	1975	1976	1977	1978	1979	1980
EBMUD	178	190	115	138	146	164
Fresno	264	258	204	217	243	243
Los Angeles	170	174	149	147	159	163
Marin Municipal	143	109	49	98	113	122
Modesto	345	330	293	304	332	327
Riverside	222	258	197	204	224	222
Sacramento	279	306	258	276	289	309
San Diego	178	193	180	173	175	185
San Jose	136	145	114	125	133	134
Santa Barbara	170	165	145	141	148	155

*Estimates developed by the City of Los Angeles Department of
Water and Power using information supplied by listed agencies
regarding total water sales and total population served.

ously bias aggregate estimates.[8] Further, it may be estimated that, overall, these
systems currently operate at 50 percent of capacity with 60 percent of capacity
being a safe upper limit considering peak demand periods and fire fighting emer-
gencies.[9] Using the project population growth rates, and assuming constant urban
use of 200 gallons per person per day, demand will reach safe hydraulic capacity
approximately by the year 2000, as shown in Figure 2. By the year 2020, according to the assumptions of this paper, system capacity will have to be increased by
27 percent.

IMPORTANT VARIABLES
Projected Population Growth by Region

Much has been made of California's shifting population patterns in recent
years. These include movements of population to the outlying parts of large
urban centers; more moderate growth of the older urban areas around Los
Angeles and San Francisco; comparatively rapid growth rates of the mid-size
metropolitan areas such as San Bernardino, Riverside, San Diego, Sacramento,
San Jose, and Fresno; and, finally, the high growth rate in many outlying rural or
semirural counties, although absolute numerical growth is often small.[10]

Anticipations are that several of these patterns will continue to characterize
California's future. However, projections indicate that the shifts will be subtle.

Figure 1

**Estimated Daily and Yearly Urban Use
for California for the Years 1980 to 2020**

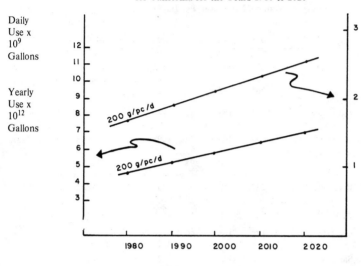

Figure 2

**A Treatment Capacity-Demand Crossover for
Urban Water Use**

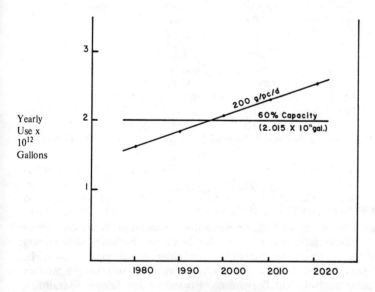

The five southern counties comprising the Los Angeles region are expected to receive 40 percent of the state's additional 12 million people between 1980 and 2020. When adding to these five counties four more in the southern portion of the state (Imperial, Kern, San Diego and Santa Barbara), it appears that 6.7 million, or 56 percent, of the state's growth in population will be in these areas.

Although the nine southern counties' share of the existing population is greater than the incremental share in the period 1980-2020, these counties will still continue to attract most of the state's additional people.

The very areas which in the past have relied heavily on imported water to sustain themselves will continue to do so in the future. In part, of course, the expected population growth implies a transfer of land from agricultural to urban uses, and this may relieve somewhat the pressures for additional water supply. However, much of the new population will be accommodated on vacant or nonagricultural lands or in already built-up areas involving a change from low to high density use. In the latter cases, the new populations will be in competition for water with established populations and agriculture. Even when urban uses replace agricultural uses in selected areas, more intensive cultivation of existing agricultural land follows, implying that more resources, including water, might be required to produce crops.

The eight counties around the San Francisco Bay Area are projected to attract an additional 1.4 million people. This growth, in comparison to the Los Angeles region, is modest. By themselves, Los Angeles, San Diego, and Orange counties are expected to add more people during the next forty years than the eight Bay Area counties together. Even if an expanded definition of the Bay Area region includes Sacramento, San Joaquin, and Santa Clara counties, the expected growth would still pale beside that of the Southern California region.

Some of the population growth in the Bay Area will involve conversion of farmlands to urban uses. Particularly in areas with heavy irrigation, urban water demands may be equivalent to farm demands. In counties expected to receive a major share of population growth, including Contra Costa, Solano, Sonoma, and Napa, the transfer of land to urban use will not necessarily, therefore, increase the net basic demand for water. However, land use succession in built-up areas, the absorption of nonirrigated range lands or development of vacant lands will also accommodate a significant part of population growth, and will thus compete with agriculture in demands for water. More intensive production on remaining farmlands presumably will also follow where economically feasible.

All together, the 22 counties indicated in Table 2 will receive close to 10 million or 83 percent of California's additional people. The remaining 2.1 million will be distributed in the remaining 36 counties. Many of these counties, especially in Northern California, have been exporters of water to the state's urban areas.

Even though residential population growth in many outlying counties involves a small number of people, cognizance must be taken of the growing seasonal and recreational populations in many parts of the state. Specifically, there is a growing number of "second homes." For basic domestic uses it may not make a great deal of difference whether water is consumed at the place of permanent residence or in a second home. However, aside from the fact that substitution is not complete, the populations owning vacation or second homes, and the residentiary populations which service them in scenic areas with recreational opportunities, may become powerful spokesmen opposing diversion of water to agricultural uses or the urban agglomerations elsewhere in the state. In counties in and around the High Sierras this conflict is likely to be intensified in the future.

Table 2

Projected Population Increases in California
1980-2020

	1980 Population	1980-2020 Increase
Southern California Counties		
Los Angeles	7,142,000	1,731,000
Orange	1,939,000	1,401,000
Riverside	627,000	480,000
San Bernardino	780,000	599,000
Ventura	503,000	576,000
Five County Total	10,991,000	4,787,000
Imperial	94,000	64,000
Kern	379,000	179,000
San Diego	1,804,000	1,558,000
Santa Barbara	299,000	124,000
Nine County Total	13,567,000	6,712,000
Bay Area Counties		
Alameda	1,111,000	190,000
Contra Costa	631,000	305,000
Marin	228,000	91,000
Napa	100,000	100,000
San Francisco	647,000	17,000
San Mateo	598,000	62,000
Solano	216,000	324,000
Sonoma	279,000	287,000
Eight County Total	3,810,000	1,376,000
Other Major Urban Counties		
Fresno	501,000	390,000
Monterey	295,000	224,000
Sacramento	750,000	396,000
San Joaquin	316,000	205,000
Santa Clara	1,275,000	669,000
Total	3,137,000	1,884,000
Rest of California	2,285,000	2,090,000
Total California	22,799,000	12,062,000

Household Formation and Housing

Reasonable projections which are carried out only to the year 2000 imply a continued aging of the state's population from about 30.8 years in 1980 to 36.0 in the year 2000.[11] About 79 percent of the added population will be above 18 years of age. This changing age composition implies further declines in average household size and a growing basic demand for housing units which exceeds population growth by a considerable margin. The 1970s already witnessed a decline in the number of persons per housing unit from 2.8 to about 2.6 and at the margin about

1.5 persons were added to California's population for every one housing unit added to the state's housing stock.[12] Declining household size was the result of several converging forces, including a shift in age composition and particularly a relative growth in those age cohorts prone to form and maintain their own households. Other factors were the rapid expansion of single or two-person households among unmarrieds, divorcees, and elderly. Basic demand was translated into effective demand by rising real incomes and increasing labor force participation by women supporting or expanding real income and wealth formation. These demand factors stand apart from the special circumstances of the late 1970s, including a strong investment demand for housing, the search for tax shelter with homeownership in the face of rapid inflation and supply constraints as reflected in growth controls.

The assumption is made here that the special circumstances of the late 1970s will be muted in the future and that historical relationships between housing expenditures, income, and wealth will be reestablished over the long run. Given these assumptions, an incremental population-to-housing unit relationship of 1.5 seems reasonable, at least until the year 2000. The growth in expected population, therefore, implies an average annual increment to the state's housing stock of close to 215,000 units, including mobile homes. Household size at the end of the century would approximate 2.2. A further assumption is that a major share (55 percent) of the additional units would be of the multifamily type with a large but indeterminate component being condominiums or planned unit developments. In other words, of the 4.3 million additional housing units in California to the year 2000, a little more than 2.4 million will be multifamily units and the remaining 1.9 million will be single-family or mobile homes. One outcome is that the share of single-family homes in the inventory would be further reduced from 62 percent in 1980 to 57 percent in 2000. Detailed projections of household formation and housing inventory developments beyond the year 2000 pose even more severe problems of imputation. It seems clear, however, that there will be further declines in household size and rising average age of the population beyond 2000.

Translation of the projected growth in population, households, and housing units into future urban water consumption presents complexities. Seasonal and annual variability in rainfall alone influence consumption behavior. Per capita urban use was sharply curtailed during the 1976-77 drought. Variations in household income, prices, household size, density of settlement, and the structure of local and regional economies also influence the use of water.[13]

Shrinking household size especially in recent years has created demand for additional housing units. Since moderate economies of scale in interior water use are present as household size increases, the opposite of this implies that per capita interior demand of, say, four persons living in two units versus one unit, would be slightly greater in the former case. Some portion of per capita residential water demand, therefore, varies with the number of persons in a housing unit, but some portion will be semifixed depending upon the characteristics of the housing inventory occupied by households. For example, four persons occupying two housing units with the same amount of irrigated landscaped open space surrounding the units would require twice as much exterior water than if these four persons occupied one unit. It seems reasonable, however, to assume that as household size shrinks the admixture of housing units by type would also change.

Precisely how changing household size and composition will combine to influence per capita water demand in the future is not totally clear. As the share of multifamily units in the housing inventory rises, the square footage of land per housing unit is likely to decline. Obviously this means less exterior space to maintain, with a reduction in water demand for gardening, pools, and other exterior purposes. However, expected savings in exterior residential water use realized because of high-density housing may be modified by an increase in open or common areas with landscaping, by the need to maintain vegetation for fire hazard reduction, and by diseconomies of scale in interior water use associated with smaller households.[14]

The impact of anticipated income and price changes on domestic water use will be important in affecting the outcomes. Real income growth would increase per capita water demand by inducing acquisition of water-using appliances and facilities, and increase demand for landscaped areas around homes. Relative price changes, however, may well overcome the effect of potential income increases. As the costs of energy to produce and distribute water rise, the delivered price of domestic water will also increase. Since much domestic water use is now discretionary, one would expect consumers to be sensitive to higher prices and reduce per capita consumption. Recent experiences give credence to the presumption that the prospects for substantial real income increases are dubious at best and that the demand-dampening effect of higher water prices may overcome any income growth effect.

Water Service and the Control of Urban Development

Traditionally, any developing discrepancy between the demand for potable water by California's growing municipalities and the available supply has been seen as a supply problem only, and has been solved by providing more supply. There is, of course, also the alternative solution of manipulating the demand for potable water. This demand can be expressed as the per capita consumption times the population. Either of these two factors can be influenced: the per capita consumption through pricing and conservation measures, or the population figure through the control of population growth. It is this last policy—managing the demand for potable water by population control measures, in general, and through the nonprovision of water in particular—which will be addressed here.

The past growth pattern of California's population is likely to undergo sizeable changes in future decades for at least two reasons: the provision of additional water becomes increasingly expensive at least in parts of the state, and the public sentiment about the merits of continued growth seems to be shifting. Increasing concern about the deteriorating environment finds its expression in major legislation at all levels of government and has, in particular, led to explicit growth control measures in several municipalities in California and other states. So far, the anticipation of a possible water shortage has not been a major motive—rather, it was the cost associated with extending water distribution systems and augmenting water supplies which contributed to the adoption of these measures. As the era of cheap and plentiful water comes to an end for an increasing number of municipalities, their citizens will be confronted with a reduction of their options: the continuation of relatively cheap water will mean either reclamation and conservation or control over urban growth. Otherwise, an increase in the cost of water is unavoidable.

Strictly speaking, except for the most unusual circumstances, there need not be, and there probably will not be, a serious water shortage emergency for at least two reasons. First, the urban population can function quite adequately with a fraction of its current per capita consumption. Second, supply of water can be significantly increased, and demand is likely to diminish, if the price of water is raised at an amount and at a pace similar to the recent increases in oil prices. Thus, the anticipated shortage of water in California will primarily be not a shortage of water per se but a shortage of inexpensive water. Municipalities which slow down population growth to reduce the growth of demand for water will actually secure the privilege of inexpensive water for their present citizens.

Since the control of growth is usually effected through zoning regulations and moratoria, it creates a shortage of housing. Therefore, housing costs in controlled-growth communities will go up, reducing the proportion of low income families. Furthermore, growth control will deter the influx or the continuation of growth industries and the jobs they create, and it will redirect population migration to municipalities with less exclusive regulations. If these municipalities are already experiencing the strain of their own growth, the additional population pressure will motivate them to adopt growth control measures too, leading to a general snowball effect.[15] Clearly, then, resolving the expected water shortage through population control at the local level means the manipulation of the geographic distribution of California's urban population, and, in turn, the distribution of economic activity, land values, transportation flows, and other related factors. Thus, the issue of anticipated water shortage which at first might appear as one of a limited natural resource and of local concern is in fact a political and legal issue and of statewide concern.

The Political Feasibility of Control Over Urban Growth

Because of past and present planning efforts, most Californians have not yet been confronted with expensive water bills or outright water rationing—or the possible alternative, which is regulating population growth. It is therefore exceedingly difficult to predict the outcome of future battles between those members of a community who will try to prevent the control of growth—land developers, renters, young couples looking for affordable housing, owners of undeveloped land—and those who will support it—environmentalists, taxpayer associations, homeowners. Once enacted, new policies on water prices, water allocation, and growth control will affect economic activity and thereby the job market, the cost of housing, and the choice of individual lifestyles, which in turn influence public sentiment about existing conditions and how they ought to be. Changes in public opinion will be reflected in subsequent elections for the legislative bodies in which these policies originated, thus starting a new cycle of the political process.

The evidence available is limited and inconclusive. If the broad support for Proposition 13 is any indication, the people of California, at least in the majority, are not in favor of continued tax hikes and increases in public expenditure as required by the next generation of new water supply systems. A number of local governments have successfully embarked on programs controlling the location and timing of population growth, primarily to protect the environment and to keep taxes down, but on occasion also to protect their available supplies of water.[16] However, many more local governments continue to allow for unconstrained growth and plan for corresponding augmentation of their water supplies.

The Legal Feasibility of Control Over Urban Growth

In reviewing the opinions of legal scholars and existing court rulings, it quickly becomes apparent that the control of growth by local governments represents largely new territory for the courts. For that matter, the whole notion of growth control is a fairly recent phenomenon in the United States, in direct opposition to its tradition of favoring growth. It is useful to distinguish between controls which try to channel growth in space and time (e.g., phased zoning) and those which establish an absolute ceiling (e.g., through an indefinite water hookup moratorium). Guidance of growth through open space zoning, urban service areas and subdivision regulations has been practiced more frequently, often motivated by concern over fiscal solvency, especially in municipalities experiencing rapid growth with its strain on public services.

The courts have generally upheld regulations controlling the rate and location of growth when they were designed to relieve financial pressure, or to preserve open space and the quality of the environment, provided they were embedded in a comprehensive general plan guided by the principles of "health, safety, morals or general welfare."[17] Some local policies delaying growth, but especially those stopping growth altogether, have been challenged on the grounds that they violate the fundamental right to travel, which includes the right to migrate and to settle.[18] Similarly, local governments might be disregarding the rights of third parties when they apply the principle of general welfare to the citizens of their community only, and have on occasion been lectured by the courts: "The general welfare does not stop at each municipal boundary. . ."[19] Keeping taxation low and the level of public services high have been considered by the U.S. Supreme Court as a legitimate desire, but insufficient as a reason to justify the burden which it puts on citizens elsewhere when they want to exercise their right to migrate and settle. To state the issue succinctly, how heavy a burden do communities have to accept to protect other people's rights to take residency within their limits? Or, to phrase it differently, do the citizens of a community have the right to keep others out "to defend privilege and restrict competition?"[20] Two examples may serve to illustrate the diversity of individual cases and court rulings.

To relieve the pressure on its public facilities and to preserve an element of its small town character, the City of Petaluma decided to reduce the rapid growth of its population. This was accomplished through the policy of issuing no more than 500 building permits per year. The district court dismissed the policy on the ground that it violated the fundamental right to travel. Although the court's decision was later overturned on formal grounds, the legality of the policy was never resolved by the courts.

When the Goleta County Water District approached the limits of its available water supply, it declared a water hookup moratorium, thereby, in effect, stopping further population growth. It could have stretched its supply through rationing or tried to augment it through an expensive water project, but it did not.[21] The court supported the moratorium because, in the words of the judge, "The fact remains that in our part of California. . .we eventually must run out of water and, consequently, stop further growth."[22]

To complicate matters further, in the opinion of at least one legal scholar, a water hookup moratorium is justified only after all other means have been exhausted, including all water conservation measures and the raising of construction funds to augment the supply.[23] Nevertheless, despite the confusing variety of professional opinions, it seems safe to conclude that local governments can control continued urban growth. Such control has already happened in several cases, and these may just be the beginning.

Domestic and Municipal Conservation

For many years it has been assumed that per capita daily use of water would increase for the United States in general and for California in particular. Reasons for the projected increase included lawn and garden irrigation, use of automatic dishwashers, use of automatic clothes washers, swimming pools, hot tubs, car washing, frequent baths, more clothes to wash, and so on. The idea of increasing per capita consumption seemed to be rooted in the notion of the 1950s that the population of the United States was inevitably becoming more suburban with a lifestyle growing increasingly affluent. More houses with larger lawns, more swimming pools, more automatic appliances, seemed not to be the American dream but rather the American reality. However, developments have not produced the increases once foreseen and the reasons for this phenomenon are not yet completely clear.[24] As noted above, new dwelling units may not be accompanied by larger lawns on the average. Automatic appliances may not have proliferated as much as forecasted and newer models may use water more efficiently. Pools and hot tubs may be beyond the financial reach of most people rather than becoming more common. In general, it may be hypothesized that the United States lifestyle is constricting rather than expanding, and people must learn to live with less rather than with more. If so, this general trend also influences urban water consumption and use.

Another factor is also involved. It is apparently assumed that people have become accustomed to an affluent consumptive life style and will not tolerate residential use levels lower than 100 gallons per person per day. The latter notion, however, has been fundamentally challenged by the Marin County experience during the California drought of 1977. Suburban Marin County is very affluent, in many ways the expectation of the 1950s come to pass. Yet the people of Marin reduced their average residential per capita use of water to about 35 gallons per person per day during summer 1977.[25] This figure, even though achieved during drought crisis, has challenged some basic assumptions of urban water supply planning. Marin County residents exceeded the rigorous goals of their county water district, demonstrating that affluent suburban residents can and will conserve.

If people can get by during an emergency with 35 gallons per day for residential use, can a planning figure of 100 gallons per person per day for normal urban use be seriously considered? Should it be 150 gallons per person per day? Perhaps 200 gallons per person per day is more realistic. The point is that estimates of daily per capita use moving from 200 to 300 to 400 gallons per person per day for urban use no longer seem valid as the basis of long-range planning. In fact, in the Pacific Northwest, the overall per capita daily use figure seems to have peaked and is now going down.[26] The meaning of this phenomenon, in conjunction with population changes and control over urban development, is explored in the next sections.

ALTERNATIVE FUTURES

Projections of Per Capita Daily Use

Competition for water in California is based to a considerable degree upon competing financial interests. Even if municipalities can count on adequate supplies of water for their future needs, water must be treated to make it fit for human consumption. Both federal and California standards for potable water require the construction and operation of expensive water treatment facilities, and although the quality of water varies greatly depending on its source, the necessary treatment may be more costly than the water itself. Thus, increasingly stringent requirements for better quality water constitute an additional financial burden. Directly or indirectly, the consumer has to pay the cost for water treatment, and as these costs go up they can have a dampening effect on the total amount of urban water consumption.

New major capital expenditures will be required as soon as the urban demand for potable water outstrips the current capacities of existing treatment plants. Using the expected growth of urban population and differing assumptions about future per capita consumption, estimates can be derived regarding when urban demand for water in California will exceed existing treatment capacity.

Figure 3 shows estimated yearly usage figures for all of California for the urban sector, assuming the California population growth projections cited earlier and usage rates of 100, of 150, of 200, of 250, of 300 and of 350 gallons per person per day. Also shown in Figure 3 is the estimated current safe capacity of the urban supply system. Figure 3 is very interesting for California as a whole, since it shows that estimated current safe capacity would not be exceeded even by the year 2020 if average daily per capita urban use were 150 gallons per day.

The result obtained, based upon an estimate of 200 gallons per person per day, has been in conjunction with Figure 1. The lines in Figure 3 representing 250, 300 and 350 gallons per day are above estimated current safe capacity. By the year 2020, usage at 250 gallons per person per day would exceed estimated current safe operating capacity by 1.179×10^{12} gallons. Analogous figures for 300 and 350 gallons per person per day are 1.818×10^{12} and 2.456×10^{12} gallons, respectively.

Since consumption figures vary widely during the course of a year and since treatment plants are expected to meet the demand even during periods of peak consumption, treatment plant capacity can be considered adequate if the year-round average production uses no more than 60 percent of the available capacity. Information for the East Bay and San Diego are found in Figures 4 and 6. In the case of Los Angeles, Figure 5, the 60 percent line has less meaning; this city has not yet completed its treatment facilities, and current plans call only for the construction of enough capacity to meet the current average consumption.

The data presented in Figures 4 through 6 represent rough estimates developed using information supplied by the three municipal water agencies and should not be viewed as anything more than the first approximations. For example, the population figures do not include undocumented immigrants, of which there may be 300,000 to 400,000 in Los Angeles alone. Clearly, the incorporation of figures of such magnitude would drastically alter the per capita consumption

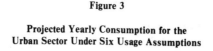

Figure 3

**Projected Yearly Consumption for the
Urban Sector Under Six Usage Assumptions**

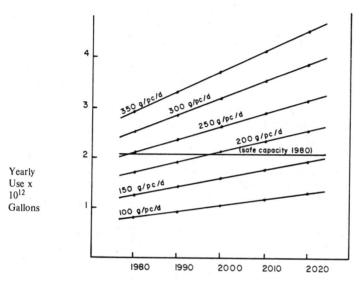

values. Also, there are no federal or state estimates for the future growth of these municipalities; the figures used here stem from the local planning departments and do not go beyond the year 2000; additional estimates to the year 2020 were obtained through simple extrapolation.

In addition to water consumption projections based on the current per capita consumption figures, projection curves assuming 150 and 250 gallons per capita per day have been included for comparison. Thus the graphs give an indication of a variety of possible outcomes depending on different assumptions about future per capita water consumption. For example, if we assume per capita consumption to remain constant, the City of San Diego will have adequate treatment capacity beyond the year 2020, but already faces inadequate capacity for peak demand periods. With constant daily per capita consumption, the East Bay area will have adequate treatment facilities for both average and peak demand until the year 2020. Los Angeles, on the other hand, does not currently meet prescribed water treatment requirements, and even the treatment facilities currently planned will only meet the average demand and only for the near future. However, should the city's demand for potable water continue to rise, the increased needs will be met through additional supplies of treated water purchased from the Metropolitan Water District of Southern California.

Regional and Sectorial Issues

Any attempt to assess realistically the future demand for and supply of urban water in California's regions must confront fundamental questions. Will the development and allocation of water resources by sector and region proceed

Figure 4

**Treatment Capacity-Demand Crossovers for
the East Bay Municipal Utility District**

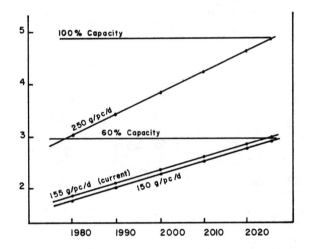

Daily
Use x
10^8
Gallons

Figure 5

**Treatment Capacity-Demand Crossovers for
Los Angeles**

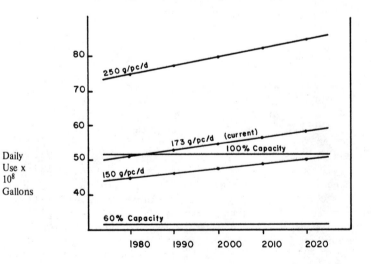

Daily
Use x
10^8
Gallons

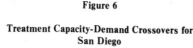

Figure 6

Treatment Capacity-Demand Crossovers for
San Diego

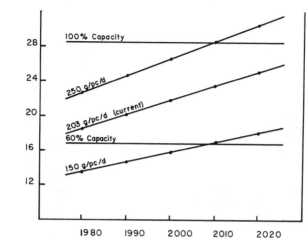

substantially on the basis of policies and practices of the past? In projecting the future, which of the many forces enhancing or impinging on water supply are to be treated as variables, and which are constraints? Are water policies and practices to be tools of general social and economic policies, or will general policies surrounding water demand and supply substantially shape the future of California's aggregate and regional economic growth and development?

Clearly, massive investment in water acquisition and treatment facilities and delivery systems, including transmission and distribution components to facilitate the movement of this resource from water-rich to water-poor areas, has been a linchpin of past policies in California. Assurance of a reliable, inexpensive, and high quality supply of water has been a primary concern in Southern and Central California. In part, facilities and systems were developed to meet projected future demands of growing urban populations with a growing appetite for water, and in part the facilities and system were tools of economic development policies. In the last decade alone, the transfer of a large amount of open land to agricultural use in the west San Joaquin Valley along the California Aqueduct near Interstate Highway 5 illustrates the regional economic implications of water policies.

The diversion of Colorado River water from California to the Central Arizona project in the 1980s will necessitate greater reliance on the State Water Project to serve Southern California.[27] The costs of delivering water via the State Water Project will rise considerably since the energy costs of pumping and distribution are expected to increase sharply. What impact higher costs will have on farmers and urbanites, and whether a significant dampening in water demand will result from higher water bills, remains to be seen.

Greater delivery of water from the State Water Project to Central and Southern California will be substantially determined by environmental as well as cost considerations. For the Delta region, the environmental implications of the Peripheral Canal project exemplify the type of public debate which is likely. The claims of areas and regions with potential for exporting water to metropolitan and farm areas will be more organized and forceful. In the past, population growth in these areas often was small because of significant out-migration. During the 1970s, however, a fourfold increase in net migration to California's nonmetropolitan counties was noted.[28] The immigrants comprise early retirees, those seeking a rural life style, second home owners, and workers serving local growth industries. These populations, together with environmentalists, may in the future join to oppose or delay the development of water resources for export to other areas. Contrary to the past when water projects were sometimes viewed as boosts to local economies, future responses will likely be less accepting.

Coming into sharper focus in the next decades will be the effectiveness of stretching water supplies by conservation or reuse, in contrast to historical approaches of investing in expansion of long-distance delivery syste..1s.[29] The large amount of capital required, high costs of capital, and high operational costs for developing new supplies will loom large in the deliberations. Moreover, the opportunities for expanding the supply by drawing on as yet untapped sources in Northern California have been substantially precluded by the Wild and Scenic Rivers Act of 1972 which protects six rivers (Smith, Klamath, Trinity, Scott, Salmon and Van Duzen) permanently, and one, the Eel River, until 1984, when hearings will be held to determine its status as a wild river.[30]

THREE SCENARIOS

Authors in this volume have been given the task of assuming three divergent future scenarios for water development in California, then to consider the policy implications of each for the issue at hand, in this case urban use. The first scenario assumes no major change in current policy and a continuation of current styles of crisis management—sporadic attempts at urban growth control and consumption penalties during periods of drought or when local demand begins to exceed supply capacity. The second scenario assumes further development of the water supply diversion, transportation, and storage facilities in California, but no new efforts at reallocation or redistribution. Specifically, it is assumed that the following projects will be built, yielding an additional two million acre-feet per year: Peripheral Canal, New Melones, Glenn Reservoir, Cottonwood Reservoir, Auburn Dam and Los Vaqueros Reservoir. Additionally, in the future, development of the Eel River and an enlarged Shasta Dam may be added to the water supply system. The third scenario assumes that legal, institutional, and organizational changes will be made that will support major efforts toward the redistribution and efficient use of water. Water pricing to encourage conservation, recycling, and reuse would form a significant part of scenario three, as would creation of a marketlike mechanism for transferring water among regions and sectors.

Developmental Control

Seven years ago the "California Water Plan—Outlook in 1974" considered the possibility of population growth control, though not for reasons of a potential water shortage. Instead it stated that the provision of water can be adjusted to the changing demands resulting from a possible control of growth, wherever and whenever it takes place.[31] In only seven years the issue has reversed itself: it is now assumed that there will be a shortage of adequately treated water, and the question is, should the control of population growth be one of the policies to cope with it, and what are these policies?

A vast variety of conditions and processes influences the growth of a community: physical conditions such as natural resources and climate, economic conditions such as employment opportunities and affordable housing, and conditions created by governmental action such as local taxes and public services. Since growth depends on many factors it can be manipulated in many ways. Local governments in particular have a wide range of tools at their disposal, and influence growth not only directly through the costs and benefits they generate for the individual citizen, but even more so indirectly through measures of land use control and their impact on the activities of the private sector. Each of these measures has its own degree of effectiveness and feasibility, and generates its own particular impacts.[32] Thus, local governments have the means to slow down growth or stop it altogether; for example, they are authorized by the California Water Code to declare a water hookup moratorium if the community is threatened by a water supply shortage. Likewise, any of the other means can be used for crisis management if they are judged as "reasonable," that is, if the means is appropriate for the end, and if the public welfare outweighs possible adverse impacts.[33] There are, of course, two alternatives to the growth control scenario which might be effective to head off a water supply crisis—water conservation measures and water supply augmentation through a capital improvement program, but these will be described subsequently.

By exercising control over the use of the land within its boundary, the local government has a powerful tool to regulate the amount, the spatial distribution, the timing, and the type and composition of urban growth in general and, thereby, the growth of the population in particular.[34] Land use control can be accomplished by regulation, contract, and acquisition. Regulation may be specifically accomplished by taxation, zoning, and control by permit. Taxation constitutes a "soft" type of regulation; among its drawbacks is relative uncertainty about effectiveness. Its performance seems to be particularly poor in areas experiencing rapid growth.

Among the various zoning mechanisms, those of agricultural and resource zoning have been widely applied, but their use for the control of population and thereby water consumption is at least questionable, because they were neither designed nor intended for this purpose. Most land use controls have a negative equity impact, distributing their social costs and benefits rather unevenly over the community. This is particularly true for large-lot zoning in residential areas. Whereas it may not be intended to function as an exclusionary, discriminating device, it tends to have this result and may therefore not survive a challenge in the courts. Phased zoning and subdivision, on the other hand, gives the government considerable latitude not only to exercise control over urban growth in space and time, but also to implement many other components of its general plan.

Refusal to grant permits for additional water connections, or declaration of a water hookup moratorium, is the policy most directly aimed at preventing an increase of water consumption. Whereas the nonprovision of water is a highly effective tool, it brings about an immediate freeze of the existing land use pattern, a pattern which might not be optimal and might, in fact, differ significantly from that envisioned in the general plan (for example, for this reason Santa Barbara County is now considering replacing the Goleta water hookup moratorium by a system of land use regulations).[35]

The single most troublesome issue associated with developmental control is its uneven equity impact both within and without the community. Governments at all levels are charged with the task of fostering and promoting the well-being and welfare of all citizens, not just those who live in a particular municipality and own a home. It is the obligation of government to try to increase opportunities for all of its citizens, and ease in taking advantage of them. Preliminary research indicates that growth control has the opposite effect: since it tends to increase property values and housing costs, it will therefore redistribute income from renters and young families to property and homeowners, and it will keep out future citizens altogether except those who can afford it.[36] To dampen these effects, any growth control policy should therefore include provisions for low and moderate cost housing. Furthermore, to withstand legal challenges and to contribute to the overall welfare of the community, it should be part of a comprehensive general plan— temporary moratoria and interim zoning provide local governments with the time they may need to revise their long-range plans.[37]

The current climate for the funding of major public projects is unfavorable and might continue for years to come. Municipalities and water districts with limited local and regional water resources not presently connected to any of the large state water transfer networks might be the first to run out of water. At least for them, the management of limited water supplies through growth control is a serious policy alternative whose time may have come.

Increasing the Supply

Until recently, the dominant policy stance regarding demand for water by the domestic and municipal sector was to increase supply to meet increasing demands from a growing population. The basis for this policy seems to have been an "open frontier" outlook, coupled with a reliance on high technology to make available that which is needed for a satisfying and meaningful life. A notion here was that people have a right to purchase at a moderate price all the water they wish to use for daily living. Important values were, and still are, embedded within this policy. California is a state of high technological development, and in fact would not have developed the way it has, were it not for vast interbasin transfers of water to agricultural and urban areas. Thus a reliance upon technology for development has been fundamental to California's growth and productivity. California represents a future-oriented ideal residence for many, where the "good life" can in fact be realized. People maintain hope in believing that they too can have comfortable homes, large green lawns, and gardens with pools, fountains and other water-related amenities. They have tended to believe that water as a public utility should be made available to all at the most inexpensive price possible. Water districts should not be allowed to make unreasonable profits because they have gained control over a life's necessity.

In opposition to these expressed or assumed values are other important values. The cost of constructing and operating water collection, storage, treatment, and distribution systems escalates with inflation. Providing *more* water per person per day for a population that is itself growing, yields incredibly high estimated construction and operating costs. Apart from the issue of expense, a second issue has to do with further development of California's rivers. There are intangible, yet fundamental, values associated with wilderness, wild rivers, and nature in its unspoiled state. A future in which all rivers are a series of dams and reservoirs seems unthinkable. A third important issue revolves around allocation for individual or society-wide needs. If the municipal and domestic sector demands more water, it must take from agriculture and industry, even while our growing population needs more food and our economy needs to become more productive. Each individual personally consuming more water in pursuit of the good life may, in fact, make the good life less attainable for all by lowering general agricultural and industrial production. Finally, if more water is for domestic and municipal use in developing urban areas, less water will be available in the basins from which it is taken. Much has been written regarding whether the urban development of the San Fernando Valley was more important than the agricultural development of the Owens Valley. Presently the issue seems to be maintaining the rurality of northwestern California versus further agricultural and urban development in the south.

Thus the values inherent in increasing water supply to meet increasing demand—technology, the good life, inexpensive necessities—come into conflict with other values—the cost of increasing supply, wilderness, agricultural and industrial productivity, and interbasin transfer inequity. It appears that values opposing further large supply increases are becoming more dominant.

Conservation and Reuse

Another way of dealing with demand is conservation, or the "efficient" use of water. In the past, conservation has not been considered as a serious policy option, apparently because water was seen as a necessity, and because conservation programs were seen as ineffective. Reuse programs may not have been seriously considered because of perceived health agency and public opposition to domestic and municipal reuse of water reclaimed from sewage. But perhaps the most important reason that conservation has not been pursued with enthusiasm by water agencies is that their income depends upon sales, and if less is used, less income will be received. While conservation may be a laudable societal goal, it may mean reduction of water agency income. These reasons for the unpopularity of conservation and reuse need to be more carefully examined.

Water is certainly a necessity for life; however, the average person probably ingests less than two gallons per day in food and drink. Further, it is estimated that, in most households, about half of water consumed is used for exterior purposes such as lawn irrigation; inside the house, about 25 percent is used just for toilet flushing.[38] Upon careful consideration, therefore, it may be estimated that the amount of water actually required for daily life is much less than 200 gallons per person per day. The Marin County experience again is striking proof: although Marin lawns turned brown in the summer of 1977, people lived with no serious problems and in fact conserved water with such vigor that they exceeded the stringent goals of their own water district.[39]

It is thought that people are not motivated to conserve, their general disposition making conservation programs both unpopular and unsuccessful. This idea is contradicted by recent trends in water use[40] and by conservation results in water districts around the San Francisco Bay.[41] Daily per capita water use is going down even in western areas where drought has not been recently experienced and conservation programs have not been initiated.[42] In addition to Marin County during 1977, people of the Bay Area also conserved more, that is they used less, water than recommended by their water agencies.[43] Such zealous efforts to conserve actually created an embarrassing double bind for certain water districts which wanted to encourage conservation but also wanted to avoid financial crises. These examples indicate that people can and are willing to conserve more than previously believed. It may take time to get exterior vegetation transferred to native drought-resistant plants and to change appliances and interior plumbing in order to conserve water; however, once these changes are made they lead to reduced water use over the long run with little additional expense or effort required.

Recent developments also show that health agency and public opposition to domestic and municipal reuse of reclaimed water is declining. The California Department of Health Services has approved use of reclaimed water for domestic lawn irrigation in Irvine, with other projects in the planning stage.[44] Further, recent public opinion research shows clearly that the public is overwhelmingly favorable toward using reclaimed water for domestic lawn and garden irrigation and also for park, playground, golf course, and greenbelt irrigation.[45] Such irrigation projects will incur the considerable initial expense of constructing a second, or dual, water system. However, since half of domestic and municipal water use is for exterior purposes, and since the half used for interior purposes is potentially reclaimable, use of reclaimed water, while not directly increasing supply, can potentially reduce demand for potable urban water up to 50 percent.

Finally, the possible financial disincentives to water districts for promoting conservation must be considered. With most rate structures, if people use less, they pay less. If conservation occurs, the water agency receives less income; conservation is thus obviously not in the financial interest of the agency. Many water agencies still use declining rate structures which encourage use since lower rates are paid per unit consumed above and beyond specified minima. Inclining rate structures, however, are receiving more attention. This rate structure actually charges *more* per unit of use beyond specified minima. The interesting feature of this rate structure is that it encourages conservation while also helping to preserve reasonable income levels for water agencies. Careful economic studies are being done[46] to investigate these matters further, but it appears that rate structures that encourage conservation may not necessarily reduce overall income for water agencies.

Certainly the potential for water conservation is also present in agriculture.[47] It has been argued that runoff of excess water in irrigation will replenish underground water basins or flow into rivers nearby and, therefore, be again available; this notion, however, is not necessarily correct. Much of the runoff cannot be recovered, and the current pricing and allocation system offers insufficient incentives to conservation. Given the current share of water used in agriculture, a 10 percent saving via conservation methods and proper pricing could reduce water consumption equivalent to or greater than a 50 percent saving in the urban sector.

Pricing structures to encourage efficient water use in California could reduce conflict between sectors and also between water-importing and -exporting regions of the state. Further, and also important, Figures 2 through 6 of this chapter show that urban conservation can have a more dramatic impact than previously believed. Given such reduction in water use, many agencies and municipalities may not need to enlarge the capacity of their water systems during the remainder of this century. Public funds not spent to enlarge capacity might better be used to upgrade treatment facilities for water and wastewater. At present for California, urban water quality, not quantity, should be the major policy determinant.

REFERENCES AND NOTES

1. California Department of Finance, *Population Projections for California Counties 1975-2020 with Age/Sex Detail to 2000,* Series E-150, Report 77-9-3 (Sacramento: December 1977).
2. U.S. Census Bureau, *Report 80 E-1* (Washington, D.C.: Department of Commerce, 1980).
3. *Population Projections for California Counties 1975-2020 with Age/Sex Detail to 2000.*
4. East Bay Municipal Utility District, *Fact Sheet for 1980* (Oakland, California: 1981).
5. California Department of Water Resources, *Water Conservation in California,* Bulletin 198 (Sacramento: The Resources Agency, May 1976).
6. *Population Projections for California Counties 1975-2020 with Age/Sex Detail to 2000.*
7. *Water Conservation in California.*
8. Department of Health Services, Environmental Health Branch, Social Environmental Health Programs Section, *Small Water Systems Program Status Report* (Sacramento: January 1979).
9. E.W. Steel, *Water Supply and Sewerage* (New York: McGraw-Hill, 1960, Fourth Edition).
10. "Population Changes in California Counties 1970-1978," *California Real Estate Indicators* (Los Angeles: University of California, Graduate School of Management, Spring 1979), and "California Population Shifting," *California Real Estate Indicators* (Los Angeles: University of California, Graduate School of Management, Fall 1977).
11. *Population Projections for California Counties 1975-2020 with Age/Sex Detail to 2000.*
12. "Changes in California Housing Inventory," *California Real Estate Indicators* (Los Angeles: University of California, Graduate School of Management, Spring 1980).
13. Metropolitan Water District of Southern California, *Water Supply and Demand Data: MWD and Other Service Areas* (Los Angeles: June 1979).
14. *Water Supply and Demand Data: MWD and Other Service Areas.*
15. Nelson Rosenbaum, "Growth and Its Discontents: Origins of Local Population Controls," in Judith May and Aaron Wildavsky, eds., *The Policy Cycle: Sage Yearbooks in Politics and Public Policy,* Vol. 5 (Beverly Hills, California: Sage Publications, 1978).
16. Robert A. Johnston, "The Politics of Local Growth Control", *Policy Studies Journal,* Winter 1980.
17. Village of Euclid v. Ambler Realty Company, 272 U.S. 365, 395, 1926.
18. R. Fielding, "The Right to Travel: Another Constitutional Standard for Local Land Use Regulations?" *The University of Chicago Law Review,* 39 (1971-72).
19. "Phased Zoning: Regulation of the Tempo and Sequence of Land Development," *Stanford Law Review,* 26 (1974).
20. Bernard J. Frieden, *The Environmental Protection Hustle* (Cambridge, Massachusetts: M.I.T. Press, 1979).
21. Richard M. Golden, "The Thirst for Population Control: Water Hook-up Moratoria and the Duty to Augment Supply," *Hastings Law Journal,* 71 (1975/76).
22. Notice of Intended Ruling on Demurrer and Motion to Strike, April 11, 1974, *Pomatto v. Goleta County Water District,* Santa Barbara, California Superior Court: No. 101404 filed Oct. 26, 1973.
23. Golden, "The Thirst for Population Control: Water Hook-up Moratoria and the Duty to Augment Supply."
24. D.W. Browne, G. Minton, and C. Barnhill, "Forecasting Water Demand in the Pacific Northwest," *Journal American Water Works Association* 72(1980): 506-507.
25. W.H. Bruvold, "Residential Response to Urban Drought in Central California," *Water Resources Research* 15(1979): 1297-1304.
26. Browne, Minton, and Barnhill, "Forecasting Water Demand in the Pacific Northwest."
27. R.N. Blanche et al., *The Metropolitan Water District: The Institution and Water Supply Planning* (Los Angeles: University of California, School of Architecture and Urban Planning, June, 1981).
28. Willard T. Chow, "Planning for Metropolitan Growth in California," *Town Planning Review,* Vol. 52, Number 2, (1981).
29. Blanche et al., *The Metropolitan Water District: The Institution and Water Supply Planning.*
30. Frank Stead and Walt Anderson, "The California Water Plan: Onward and Upward," *Cry California,* Summer, 1976.
31. California Department of Water Resources, *The California Water Plan, Outlook in 1974,* Bulletin No. 160-74 (Sacramento: The Resources Agency, November 1974).
32. R.A. Johnston, "Open Space Protection Through Land Use Controls: A Review of Methods with California Examples," in *Roots of Productive Conservation: Economics, Ethics, Ecology,* Proceedings of the Annual Conference of the Soil Conservation Society of America, 1981. Also, R.A. Johnston and S.I. Schwartz, *Public Mechanisms for Controlling Land Conversion in California,* Institute of Governmental Affairs, Research Report No. 32 (Davis: University of California,

1976), and Seymour I. Schwartz et al., *Controlling Land Use for Water Management and Urban Growth Management: A Policy Analysis,* Water Resources Center, Contribution 180 (Davis: University of California, 1979).

33. G.C. Rhea et al., *California Land Use Primer* (Stanford, California: Stanford Law School, 1973).

34. M. Cranston et al., *A Handbook for Controlling Local Growth* (Stanford, California: Stanford Law School, 1973).

35. B. Ramsay, "Control of the Timing and Location of Government Utility Extensions," *Stanford Law Review* 26(1974): 945.

36. Seymour I. Schwartz et al., *The Effect of Growth Management on New Housing Prices: Petaluma, California,* Institute of Governmental Affairs (Davis: University of California, July 1979), and Robert A. Johnston, Seymour I. Schwartz, and William S. Hunt, *The Effect of Local Development Regulations on Single-Family Housing Costs,* Institute of Governmental Affairs (Davis: University of California, 1981).

37. *Open Space Zoning Handbook* (Sacramento: California Assembly Select Committee on Open Space Lands, 1973).

38. *Water Conservation in California.*

39. Bruvold, "Residential Response to Urban Drought in Central California."

40. Browne, Minton, and Barnhill, "Forecasting Water Demand in the Pacific Northwest."

41. Bruvold, "Residential Response to Urban Drought in Central California."

42. Browne, Minton, and Barnhill, "Forecasting Water Demand in the Pacific Northwest."

43. Bruvold, "Residential Response to Urban Drought in Central California."

44. W.H. Bruvold, "Community Evaluation of Adopted Uses of Reclaimed Water," *Water Resources Research* 17(1981): 487-490.

45. W.H. Bruvold and J. Crook, "Reclaiming and Reusing Wastewater," *Water Engineering and Management* 128(1981): 65-71.

46. S.H. Hanke, "Pricing as a Conservation Tool—Economist's Dream Come True?" in D. Bauman, D. Dworkin, and D. Holtz, eds., *Municipal Water Systems: The Challenge for Urban Management* (Bloomington: Indiana University Press, 1979).

47. Blanche et al., *The Metropolitan Water District: The Institution and Water Supply Planning.*

CHAPTER IV

INDUSTRY

by

Michael B. Teitz and Richard A. Walker

ABSTRACT

The industrial demand for water cannot be separated from the general growth of population and urbanization in California during the coming decades. Nonetheless, industrial and commercial activities account for more than three-quarters of employment and almost 85 percent of income in the state, and their performance will shape the investment climate and affect economic development and migration.

Although adequate water supply is by no means assured for industry everywhere, its role is ambiguous. On the one hand, the threat to the state's economic climate posed by potential water shortages will require that government and the private sector support measures to maintain an adequate supply, as they have done for many years. On the other hand, the rising cost of new water projects, the competition for state funding in a period of need for reinvestment in urban infrastructure, and the undoubted capacity of industry to outbid, if needed, almost all other users for water, all suggest that industry may best be served by an incremental change toward a partial market approach to water allocation in the medium term future. Such an approach is supported by the fact that most industrial water demand will occur in conjunction with urban and residential development. Competition for future supplies is likely to shape up between agriculture, urban users (including industrial and commercial), and conservation, rather than between industrial users and the rest. Those sectors with especially high demands, for example primary energy, are likely to make their own supply arrangements and seek improved conservation measures in the face of rising costs and local shortages of water.

INDUSTRIAL DEVELOPMENT AND WATER DEMANDS

The creation of new employment and income in private sector manufacturing, transportation, trade, and services will fundamentally shape California's development in the next twenty years. Together, these broad groupings of economic activity account for over 75 percent of total employment and 84 percent of gross income in the state. Their performance establishes the environment of corporate and individual opportunity that determines investment and migration. Although agriculture and government are also critical to the state's economy and management, nonagricultural private and quasi-private sector activities are likely to be the dominant influences on California's future.

Adequate water supply in California is by no means a certainty at all times and places. Therefore, the possibility that insufficient water might affect the economic position of California's leading sectors deserves careful evaluation as the state experiences unemployment problems and threats of worldwide competition for its products. Recently, state government has taken an active role in responding to industrial changes, for example, plant closures, and in planning for the future competitiveness of California's industries. Although water has not been an explicit part of that discussion, the necessity to maintain a "positive economic climate" for investment suggests that any threat to water supplies for industrial growth would be an important concern for development interests in the state and, through them, to state government.

Water's role in industrial development is enigmatic. On the one hand, water is a necessary input for virtually all economic activity and an absolute requirement for some specific industries.[1] Under conditions of extreme shortage, economic activity may be impossible. The amount of water required in industry is in most instances small compared with agriculture or residential use, and its costs are small relative to the cost of labor, raw materials, capital, or marketing. Water is widely available in the quantity and quality suitable for industrial purposes; therefore it is normally not a major consideration in the decision to invest or to locate economic activity in a particular place.

The demand for water for industrial purposes cannot, however, be separated from the larger issue of urban development. There are many arguments about the "chicken-egg" relationship between population growth, especially that due to immigration, and industrial development. It is sufficient to note here that one implies the other, with only rare exceptions. Thus, if we discuss industrial water demand in the broad sense, that is, including the tertiary sectors, we imply a complementary demand for residential uses. Conflicts over water use generally pit urban, agricultural, and conservational interests against each other, rather than focusing on industrial and commercial activities per se.

The following discussion suggests that industrial dependence on water in California is not a particularly worrisome factor in the economic development of the state. Nonetheless, present water policy may not be the best way of serving industrial needs and may actually work against industrial interests if creation of massive, uneconomic water supply facilities imposes heavy subsidy burdens. Since industry and other urban uses can normally outbid agriculture for water supplies, much as a bank can outbid all other uses of urban land, movement toward a partial market approach to water allocation probably represents the wisest course for urban water supply in the medium term future.

PATTERNS OF INDUSTRIAL WATER USE IN CALIFORNIA

In this section of the paper, we examine industrial water use in the aggregate, by sector and by location.

Definitions

Industry is here defined as all nonagricultural economic activity, except for government enterprise, utilities, residences, and municipalities. Thus, it includes mining (Standard Industrial Classification category 10-14), construction (SIC 15-18), manufacturing (SIC 19-39), transportation and communications excluding utilities (SIC 40-49),[2] trade (SIC 50-59), finance, insurance and real estate (SIC 60-69), and services (SIC 70-89). Government (SIC 91-93) is a special category for which we include data but, conventionally, treat separately from the private sector. Time series data on water utilization is difficult to find and subject to definitional problems. In particular, it is not always clear whether water use information refers to total withdrawals, including water passed back into the system for reuse elsewhere, or to final consumption of water.[3] In addition, it is difficult to quantify levels of seriously polluted waste discharge by industrial sectors over time. Thus, the discussion draws eclectically on such data, including partial series, as exist.

Industrial Water Use in the State

In contrast to its role in generating income and employment, industry uses only a small share of water in California. As shown in Table 1, all industrial, residential, and governmental use in 1976 amounted to less than 6 million acre-feet, or about 14 percent of the total. Residential use accounted for at least 8 percent, leaving no more than 6 percent devoted to industrial uses. Manufacturing, the largest single industrial subsector, accounted for about 2 percent of the state's total water use. The remaining 86 percent went to agriculture. While using only 6 percent of the water, however, industry generated 84 percent of gross state income and 76 percent of total employment. Of the remainder, government accounted for 12 percent of gross income and 19 percent of employment, and agriculture 3 and 5 percent respectively.

Table 1

**California Income, Employment, and Water Use
by Sector, 1976**

Sector	Gross State Income (Billions)		Employment (Thousands)		Water Use (Thousands of Acre-Feet)	
	Total	Percent	Total	Percent	Total	Percent
Agriculture	5	3	451	5	34,460	86
Mining	2	1	24	0	318	1
Construction	8	7	402	4	12	0
Manufacturing	41	22	1,696	18	950	2
Transportation, communications, and utilities	16	9	489	5	46	0
Wholesale and retail trade	29	16	2,128	23	370	1
Finance, insurance and real estate[a]	27	14	516	6	3,641	9
Services	30	16	1,841	20	41	0
Government	23	12	1,733	19	230	1
Total	181	100[b]	9,282	100	40,064	100

[a]Largely residential water use.
[b]Percentages may not add to 100 owing to rounding.

Source: California Department of Water Resources, *Measuring Economic Impacts,* Bulletin 210 (Sacramento: The Resources Agency, 1980), Table 3, p. 12.

These crude sectoral estimates need to be interpreted with care, especially as regards withdrawals versus final consumption, the linkages between industry and agriculture, and the relationship between industry and urbanization. Nonetheless, the overall picture suggests that conflicts over the industrial use of water are most likely to focus on either (1) institutional difficulties in obtaining agricultural conservation and transferring water from agricultural to industrial/urban use, or (2) problems in developing incremental water supplies for industrial development in areas of the state where such transfers are not technically feasible.

There can be no doubt that if a water market existed in the state, industry would have the capacity to outbid other users. In 1976, for example, the manufacturing sector had about $43,000 in sales per acre-foot of water used. For agriculture, the corresponding figure was $145 in sales per acre-foot, almost 300 times less. No branch of agriculture can compare with any nonagricultural use in value added per unit of water (see Table 3). To ensure supplies, industrial users could pay substantially higher water prices without fundamentally distorting their cost structure.

No use of water, including industrial, is inviolate, of course. Industrial water demand is subject to modification, i.e., is price-elastic and responsive to quantity shortages, and may be altered by changes in processes and behavior due to technological progress or regulation. In fact, the potential for industrial water conservation is substantial. As evidence of adaptation in water demand, it is striking that between 1957 and 1970 the use of water by the manufacturing sector remained constant despite a large increase in total output.[4] Reduction in heavy use sectors offset rising demands in others. However, pollution control efforts rather than shortages or rising costs are likely to be the most important reason for recycling and increased use of reclaimed water across a variety of sectors.

Sectoral Variation in Water Use

Within the broad industrial categories discussed here, there is substantial variation in the absolute amounts of water used and its relative importance as an input to production. Table 2 lists the top nine industrial water using sectors in 1976. This table is unusual in that it includes primary sectors (petroleum extraction), secondary sectors (chemicals), and tertiary sectors (retail) together. Clearly, the way in which sectors are defined will affect their rank. We have chosen to stay at the 2-digit SIC code-level of classification to ensure some degree of comparability.

Retail trade is, somewhat surprisingly, the largest sectoral user of water. This points up an important feature of industrial water use: most is not "process" water, but people-serving, air-conditioning, and landscape-irrigating in purpose. Retail trade uses a large amount of water because it employs very large numbers of people (over 1.6 million person-years in 1976), must provide services for a far greater number, and is highly disaggregated, mainly consisting of very small units, tightly linked to the distribution of population and housing in the state.

With the exception of retail trade, heavy water use in California is concentrated at the primary processing end of the production spectrum. Among manufacturing industries, food processing, with canned and frozen foods the main component within it, is the largest single consumer. Other major manufacturing sector users are paper, petroleum refining, chemicals, lumber and mill products, and stone, clay and glass products. Petroleum and natural gas are the largest users

Table 2

Nine Major Industrial Water-Using Sectors
in California, 1976,
by Absolute Level of Water Use

Rank	Sector	Water Use (in Acre-Feet)	Percent of Total State Water Use	Percent of Industrial Water Use*
1	Retail trade	358,785	0.9	18.2
2	Food processing	281,763	0.7	14.3
3	Petroleum extraction	185,667	0.5	9.4
4	Paper manufacturing	170,773	0.4	8.7
5	Petroleum refining	141,893	0.4	7.2
6	Chemicals and allied products	75,771	0.2	3.8
7	Lumber and mill products	70,759	0.2	3.6
8	Natural gas and natural gas liquids	60,769	0.2	3.1
9	Stone, clay and glass products	42,824	0.1	2.1
Total Nine Largest Sectors		1,389,004	3.6	70.4

*Total use less agricultural and direct residential.

Source: Adapted from California Department of Water Resources, *Measuring Economic Impacts,* Bulletin 210 (Sacramento: The Resources Agency, 1980), Table 17. Sectors combined to form 3-digit SIC equivalents.

in the primary extractive sectors. If extraction is combined with refining, petroleum processing as a whole exceeds food processing in total water demand. Together, these nine sectors account for over 70 percent of all industrial water used in the state. No single 2-digit sector, however, takes as much as one percent of total water demand in California (see Table 2).

Total water use by sector is, to some degree, misleading since it depends both on the intensity with which the sector uses water in its production processes and on the level of output of that sector within the state. One measure of the intensity of water use, value of output per acre-foot of water, is shown in Table 3.[5] The lower the value of output per acre-foot, the higher the intensity of water use in the sector, regardless of the scale of production. Where the intensity is high, as in agriculture, use will be very sensitive to the cost of water unless demand for the product is highly price-inelastic (an unlikely circumstance for agricultural products); where intensity is low, as in light manufacturing, a sector is likely to be less sensitive to water cost and able to bid up the price in conditions of scarcity.

The striking feature of Table 3 is the great range of value of output per acre-foot of water used across sectors. The difference between the highest (advertising) and the lowest (rice) is more than six orders of magnitude. Heavy manufacturing and extractive industries are typically 10 to 100 times higher in their output-value-to-water-use ratios than agriculture. More important, medium-to-light manufacturing and services, which are the leading edge of industrial growth in the state, are anywhere from 100 to 100,000 times higher in value-to-water-use ratios than agriculture. These are powerful differences. They reinforce the importance to the state of a reliable supply of water for urban-industrial purposes and the potential cost of failure to secure such a supply. They also suggest that transfers of water between sectors, especially out of agriculture, may be an economically efficient response to a condition of tightening and high cost supply.[6]

Location of Industrial Demand

Thus far, the discussion of industrial water use has dealt with the problem at the statewide and sectoral levels only. This does not do justice to the complexity of industrial development and water supply. Industrial water problems are both intensified and mitigated by the uneven locational distribution of demand and supply (see Table 4). The concentration of almost two-thirds the state's population and production in the southern portion of the state means that large absolute quantities of water must be moved from wetter areas to meet current and future demands for urban-industrial water. Neither the Los Angeles basin nor the San Diego area can be self-sufficient at current levels of development. The same is true of the Bay Area. The most intense recent development, in Santa Clara County, has occurred in an area that has previously relied on groundwater and needs to secure a reliable external supplemental supply.

Some of the largest industrial users of water are not, however, located in the major coastal urban areas. A large portion of petroleum and gas extraction is located in the San Joaquin Valley; food processing takes place throughout the Central Valley as well as in the cities; lumber, milling and paper manufacturing are largely concentrated in the northern portion of the state; and mining and quarrying are normally rural activities.

Industrial Water Supply

Presently, industry must secure its water either from (1) public authorities, either special districts or municipal systems, or (2) self-supply under private water rights or municipal systems.[7] Industries that depend on the latter receive water from a handful of public agencies: member units of the Metropolitan Water District of Southern California, the Los Angeles Department of Water and Power, East Bay Municipal Utility District, the City and County of San Francisco, Sacramento Municipal Utility District, Fresno City Water Department, Contra Costa Water Agency, and the municipal water departments of a few other cities.[8] These authorities secure water either by locally developed systems and water rights or via contracts with the state or federal governments. Additional public water supply development is at this stage dominated by state and federal projects, such as the proposed Phase II of the State Water Project and the San Felipe and Auburn units of the Central Valley Project.

Access to existing suppliers and their distribution systems is normally an advantage in industrial locations but can be done without either through self-supply or the creation of new public service districts. Large-scale industry has traditionally not been as dependent on public water supply systems as smaller urban users. Private development of wells and direct extraction from water courses is common. Self-supply in industry is close to 50 percent statewide.[9] Also,

Table 3

Output Value and Water Use in Selected Crops and Industries, 1977

Sector	Value of Output (Millions of Dollars)	Water Use (Thousands of Acre-Feet)	Value of Output per Acre-Foot
General Manufacturing and Services (Light Water Users)			
Finance and insurance	$11,573	4.6	$2,515,870
Communication equipment	4,650	4.9	948,979
Advertising	4,649	0.4	11,647,500
Motor vehicles	4,572	4.6	993,913
Air transportation	4,480	1.5	2,986,666
Textile products	4,177	6.2	673,710
Electronic components	3,781	8.0	472,625
Largest Water Using Industries			
Retail trade	$24,255	358.8	$ 67,600
Petroleum/wells	2,932	185.7	15,788
Wholesale trade	12,214	117.0	104,393
Paper and paperboard	2,848	170.8	16,674
Petroleum refining	11,026	141.9	77,702
Canned and frozed foods	6,951	113.2	61,404
Logging and sawmills	2,046	63.37	32,286
Natural gas	333	60.76	5,480
Sugar	959	41.83	22,871
Industrial chemicals	1,892	37.72	50,159
Stone, clay and quarry	411	26.94	15,256
Cement and concrete	1,135	23.26	48,796
Aircraft	9,081	14.6	621,986
Chemical and mineral mining	145	19.21	7,548
Agriculture (Largest Water Using Crops)			
Hay and pasture	$ 794	11,350	$ 70
Cotton	833	4,677	178
Rice	161	3,521	46
Noncitrus fruits	1,344	3,451	389
Vegetables	1,388	1,972	704
Corn	181	1,691	107
Wheat	229	1,350	170
Sugarbeets	192	1,110	173
Barley	157	1,049	150
Almonds	182	841	193
Citrus	430	820	524
Walnuts	109	646	169

Source: Data drawn from DWR Bulletin 210 (see Table 2); calculations by authors.

for many industrial uses quality requirements are moderate, but it has been estimated that as much as 45 percent of water used in manufacturing is brackish. Manufacturers are not averse to use of reclaimed water of adequate quality; the use of internal recirculation systems has risen greatly during the past 20 years. Even where water of very high quality is required, as in electronics, the small quantities involved in relation to value of product make on-site purification or specialized purchases economical for firms.

Table 4

**Employment in Major Metropolitan Areas
in California, 1979**

Standard Metropolitan Statistical Areas	Civilian Employment	Percent of State Total
Los Angeles-Long Beach	3,303,000	32.1
San Diego	682,800	6.6
San Francisco-Oakland	1,507,600	14.6
San Jose (Santa Clara County)	669,900	6.5
Orange County	1,019,300	9.9
Riverside-San Bernardino	533,100	5.4
Sacramento	427,000	4.1
Fresno	243,000	2.3
Total 8 Largest SMSAs	8,385,700	81.5
Total California	10,285,000	100.0

Source: *California Statistical Abstract,* 1979.

Self-supply and treatment is not, however, a viable option for most service activities, which are generaly small in scale and tightly locked into the urban and residential structure. For these sectors, which have been the fastest growing in the state's economy, reliance on municipal water systems is critical. They require stable public supplies of high quality fresh water.

The cost of publicly supplied water to industry depends on several variables, including cost and quality of the input source. By far the largest component of urban supply cost, however, is the expense of building the distribution system. Nationally, the latter makes up roughly one-half of all costs of public water. The expense of delivering in urban areas means that, of necessity, urban users pay more per unit of water than farmers. This difference is typically compounded by price discrimination and subsidy policies of virtually all public agencies from the federal Bureau of Reclamation to local water districts.[10]

An important counterpart to industrial water supply is waste disposal. Resource extraction and heavy manufacturing generate wastewater containing heavy metals, salts and exotic chemicals that are frequently resistant to (and damaging of) conventional treatment systems. This problem cannot be covered within the scope of this paper, but both in cost and technological demands, it may prove to be more difficult than the provision of usable water in the first place. And, as shown by recent discoveries such as the widespread contamination of drinking water wells in the San Gabriel Valley by trichloroethylene, an industrial solvent, failure to solve the pollution problem can worsen the problem of water supply.

FUTURE DEMAND FOR WATER BY INDUSTRY

The future of California's economy is bound up with the development of the U.S. and world economy in which California is now a significant component. Prospects for the U.S. in world markets and in industrial innovation over the coming years are murky. Recent trends indicate a slowing rate of investment and productivity, signs of an aging economy. The key growth sectors of the 20th century, especially the automobile industry, are in disarray, and may have difficulty in staging more than a partial recovery. It seems unlikely that they can again become the dynamic driving forces in the economy that they were. On the other hand, the U.S. still holds a narrowing lead in high technology industries, particularly semiconductors and computers, which promise to provide the lead momentum for the immediate future. And nascent industries, such as genetic engineering, will certainly contribute to economic growth if they turn out to have the strength that is predicted. California, on balance, stands to gain absolutely and relatively from these trends.

Over the past 30 years, the state has evolved from an important but peripheral part of the U.S. economy, to a national and international leader in major industrial sectors, notably electronics and advanced technology. The state's traditional role as an exporter of agricultural products is also likely to continue in the future as world demand for food grows. It is unlikely, however, that the decline in the proportion of employment and income generated by agriculture in the state will be reversed. Rather, the vitality of the state's economy will rest upon its capacity to maintain investment and innovation in leading industrial sectors, and in its capacity to generate new forms of consumer demand and services.

California has gained population and economic activity from the westward and southward national migration that has continued at varying rates for more than a century. As the state becomes more urbanized and conscious of the external costs of growth, increasing opposition to development and regulation of its forms may be expected. The results are likely to be relocation of growth rather than its absolute diminution. In the process, urbanization is likely to continue at a rapid pace in the Central Valley and more peripheral parts of the Southern California metropolitan areas. Elsewhere, growth will not stop, and it will require an effective water policy. Projections of future water demand are problematic, at best. They require speculative assumptions about levels of economic activity and population growth, and, just as importantly, quantity and price conditions in water supply. Water has traditionally been priced below its marginal cost and delivered cheaply. Since new supplies will be much more costly than in the past, projections of demand should not simply reflect past behavior based on low prices. In assessing future industrial water demand, therefore, we will focus on alternative scenarios of supply conditions.

Assumptions on Population Increase

Growth in population is the conventional starting point for water demand projections. Over the 40 year period from 1980 to 2020 many futures are possible. In the absence of catastrophe, the demographic structure of the state's population and its attraction for domestic and international migrants indicate that substantial growth is probably inevitable. How much depends upon the assumptions selected. Estimates by the California State Department of Finance suggest the following range:

1980	2000	2020
23.5 *million*	29.3 *million*	34.9 *million*

These figures are primarily based on extrapolations of present demographic trends. They assume no major obstacles to growth, although both water and housing supply have been suggested as potential constraints that could significantly lower the final total.[11]

Over 40 years the probable error in these estimates is quite large. If we accept a 49 percent increase by 2020 as a reasonable guess, what does such population growth mean for industry? It is reasonable to expect production and income to grow somewhat faster than population. A modest 2 percent per year growth rate in income per capita would imply growth in gross income over the period by 221 percent. In round terms suitable to the reality of error in a 40 year projection, this amounts to roughly a doubling of output. What does this, in turn, imply for industrial water demand? The answer depends upon our assumptions about the composition of production, water supply, and price.

We will consider supply variables by means of three broad scenarios:

(1) *No Project Scenario:* No major institutional or legal changes occur; supply changes only marginally.

(2) *Development Scenario:* Development of further water supplies occurs through a series of projects without major institutional shifts. Projects may include the Peripheral Canal, the filling of New Melones, Glenn Reservoir, Cottonwood Reservoir, Auburn Dam, and Los Vaqueros Reservoir.

(3) *Reallocation Scenario:* Reallocation of water is pursued as an active policy with major changes in law and institutions providing defined and separable property rights in water; no major increase occurs in supply; and development of a marketlike system for sale and exchange of water among willing parties takes place under state sponsorship and regulation.

No New Project Scenario

Without any new surface water storage projects by the state or the federal government, aggregate water supplies will not expand markedly from the approximately 40 million acre-feet now withdrawn annually in California. Indeed, they may decline due to groundwater overdraft and loss of Colorado River water to other states. If we assume that industrial water demand grows proportionately to growth in output, it will about double by the year 2020, to approximately 3.2 million acre-feet. If accompanying residential and public use increases by just 50 percent (the predicted rate of population growth), nonindustrial demand will rise from about 3.6 to 5.4 million. All together, the urban sector will require an additional 3.4 million acre-feet. Given this prospect, four alternatives (or combinations thereof) present themselves for industry:

(1) *Industry develops more supply on its own.* Since industry already secures a large percentage of its water on its own initiative, blockage of public water supply expansion would undoubtedly spur firms to develop further means of self-supply. Except in coastal areas, it will be quite difficult to secure surface water rights. Therefore, the likely course will be for industry to pump groundwater. Because of its greater capital resources, industry can almost always outcompete other groundwater users by driving its wells deeper. Conflicts between industry and farmers over such competition is common. The difficulty with this solution is that groundwater overdraft will be worsened in many parts of the state.

(2) Industry reduces the intensity of water use. We can be reasonably sure that the conditions of industrial demand will not remain constant under any circumstances. Changes in industrial water use may come about for any of the following reasons:

First, intersectoral shifts in economic activity will take place. The trend of the past 20 years towards a higher proportion of output in services and highly technical manufacturing will probably continue, with some slowing in rate. This will reduce industrial water demand per dollar of GNP because these sectors use less than traditional heavy industry. Evidence of the shift will be quite variable from place to place, however.

Industries will manifest a wide range of patterns in output growth and water use. For example, decline in the resource base of California's timber industry suggests a reduction in water demand as production shifts out of state. Similarly, the demand for canned fruits and vegetables has not been strong recently and this industry may continue to show poor growth. On the other hand, as oil fields become less productive and flow enhancement processes are increasingly necessary, water use will probably rise, as such fields are unlikely to be abandoned in the present climate of oil demand.

Second, technical change within industrial sectors may reduce water use even as sectors grow. Because demand is concentrated, improvements in water use efficiency in a few high-use sectors can offset overall demand expansion due to rising outputs. For example, the aggregate stability in manufacturing demand for water between 1960 and 1970 was due almost entirely to a 68 percent decrease in water intake in the wood products industry.[12] This decrease is largely attributable to technological change in the use of water in storage and preservation of logs. One cannot be sanguine about the course of technical change, of course. For instance, the petroleum industry has been quite resistant to change in its oil recovery practices despite attempts at regulation stemming from concerns over contamination of groundwater by injected brines.

Third, locational shifts may increase water use, if, as seems likely, the southern part of the state continues to grow more rapidly than the north, and industry continues to decentralize from the coastal cities into the interior. Higher demands for landscaping and air conditioning can be anticipated, compounded by fashions in industrial and office parks and enclosed shopping centers. This might be offset by greater access to self-supply in the Central Valley or by non-process-related practices such as shifting to electric air-conditioning (which has other problems from the standpoint of energy demand) and toward landscaping with more xerophytic plants.

Fourth, industry will have to respond directly to price and quantity signals in water supply. The inevitable price increases and periodic supply shortages which a No Projects Scenario holds in store will put pressure on industry to adopt innovations in water using practices. That industry has the capability of responding to such constraints is certain. For example, as a consequence of the severe drought of 1976-1977, East Bay Municipal Utility District reported a *permanent* cutback in industrial demand between 1975 and 1980 of 17 percent.[13] In another case, significant demand reductions were achieved when the City of Santa Monica recently switched from a declining block to flat rate structure; one factory achieved 60 percent savings.[14]

In sum, the prospects for marginally reduced water intensity in industry and allied urban sectors are probably good, especially as economic signals begin to be felt. But significant reductions will require more dramatic crisis conditions and coordination by government bodies, if the experience of the recent drought is any indication.[15]

(3) Industry suffers restrictions on its growth due to water supply shortages. We find this to be a rather unlikely outcome, for several reasons previously mentioned: the minor role water plays in most industrial processes, the relative capability of industry to respond to supply signals, and the proven cutbacks by industry in selected circumstances. The biggest obstacle to industrial growth from water shortages would likely be constraints on water hookups for new housing development, which could affect labor markets via rising housing costs. It is unlikely, however, that water supply would be allowed to act as a serious growth inhibitor for long.[16] The balance of economic and political power in the state undoubtedly rests with industry and the cities. Although this power is rarely mobilized against agriculture, for a variety of reasons, in a crisis situation it is virtually certain that *ad hoc* measures to shift supply from agriculture to urban water users could be instituted.

Nonetheless, it is by no means clear that perceptions match realities among urban constituencies, who generally do not understand the patterns of water utilization and political power in the state. Economic crisis or even fear of growth slowdowns might well precipitate sharp reactions favoring renewed water project development on a crash basis. Business leaders will probably support such action, as they have in the past. Business typically dislikes uncertainty, as would be likely owing to water supply shortages, and the threat of government regulation, as would be necessary in a supply pinch. The construction and real estate sectors would almost certainly find any supply limitations or forced changes in housing practices distasteful. Some sectors of business closely linked to agriculture will oppose any policy that works to the disadvantage of the latter. Finally, new water projects will be favored by many because of the hydroelectric power and construction jobs they promise.

(4) Industry and urban users receive water from agriculture. If a full 3.4 million acre-feet of water were diverted from agriculture to supply urban-industrial users, the latter's share of the state total would increase from 13 to 22.5 percent and agriculture's share would fall from 86 to 76 percent.[17] Such a major transfer out of agriculture would probably not be legally or institutionally possible under existing arrangements. In some cases, such as the State Water Project, urban contractors have priority over agricultural contractors for firm water supplies, although this priority has never been asserted. Indeed, large amounts of unused water have been transferred to San Joaquin Valley growers each year. In the case of the Lower Colorado River Storage Project, on the other hand, priority goes the other way under an agreement signed fifty years ago. (This would be politically difficult, but not impossible, to change.) In still other circumstances growers and rural irrigation districts have secure water rights that could not be taken away without a major legal upheaval.

It may happen, however, that some agriculturalists will have a surplus which they would willingly part with in the not distant future. This may come about as energy prices force up the cost of pumping for both groundwater and surface water systems (see Chapter V). As water prices go beyond $50 or even $100 per acre-foot in some farm areas, it will not be profitable to grow many currently profitable crops (see Table 3). Even so, the institutional barriers to transferring this water from agriculture to urban users will remain.

These considerations concerning the No Project Scenario strongly indicate that a do-nothing policy in water resources is not in fact possible. It will inevitably create conditions of shortage that require a response. In part that response will consist of private decisions to conserve. Although the No Project Scenario is unlikely to restrict urban-industrial growth significantly, it will be attacked on the ground that it will have such an effect. The state will then surely be forced to respond, due to the need for coordinated action.

Ultimately, the No Project strategy would do no more than defer hard choices about allocation of water sources that must be made as growth takes place. Under the pressure of crisis conditions, moreover, rational policy choices will be difficult to make. The No Project policy is not therefore an appealing one for California. That leaves two positive policies to be considered.

Development Scenario

Supply expansion is a policy with several cost dimensions, including direct construction costs and environmental costs, which cannot be addressed here. It is often assumed, however, that whatever its other shortcomings, full development will at least solve the water shortage problem; that is, it will bring supply and demand into equilibrium at prevailing prices. Acting on such an assumption, industrialists may, in light of the political implications of the No Project Scenario, support development of more storage facilities in the hope that conflict, restraints on growth, and/or forced innovation can be avoided. They are likely to be disappointed, however.

As noted previously, the industrial sector will require an additional 3.4 million acre-feet by the year 2020, ceteris paribus. If all new water projects currently envisioned are constructed in this time, they will generate no more than 3 million acre-feet of new yield. In other words, even under the full development scenario, *projected supply increases will not be sufficient to cover industrial-urban growth, let alone allow for expansion of agricultural water use.*

Of course, industrial water demand may not grow at the same rate as output, as indicated previously. If that is the case, then conflicts will be reduced. But if agriculture absorbs another 2 to 3 million acre-feet of water per year by 2020, conflict cannot be eliminated. Even under the most optimistic conditions, industrial and urban water saving is unlikely to make up the difference, as it would require cutbacks in use in the range of 40 to 60 percent.

Again we are faced with the hard question of how water should be allocated between, as well as within, the urban and agricultural sectors. Building new projects does not relieve the citizens of California from the need to have a positive policy concerning the end-uses of water. Some form of efficient and fair system of water distribution is still required.

Before proceeding to a consideration of the Reallocation Scenario, however, the issue of the costs and benefits of new projects must be addressed, since some new development may be considered under either scenario. From industry's point of view, there are several reasons why new supply projects are a financially unattractive means of securing greater supplies for the industrial-urban sector.

First, such projects have become extremely costly because the best dam sites in terms of proximity, storage capacity, and hydroelectric generating capacity have already been developed. For example, the State Water Project has capital costs of about $45 per acre-foot north of the Tehachapi Mountains.[18] Estimates of the capital cost of additional water run as high as $350 per acre-foot.[19] Add to this, pumping costs will soon rise to $25 to $35 per acre-foot north of the Tehachapis and more than twice that south of the mountains, in metropolitan Southern California (see Chapter I). Supply development does not mean cheap water.

Second, industry, and urban consumers in general, are apportioned a small share of total project yield, compared to agriculture. Most water projects are over-kill as far as industry is concerned. For example, the Metropolitan Water District of Southern California has firm water entitlements to only about one-half million out of 4.5 million acre-feet supplied to California from the Lower Colorado River Storage Project, and one million of the 2.3 million acre-feet supplied by the State Water Project—it currently takes only about two-thirds of this share, yielding the rest to Kern County. It would get half of the water from new additions to the State Water Project, as well.

Third, urban-industrial users currently underwrite low cost agricultural water. For example, the Central Valley Project, which delivers 5 to 6 million acre-feet per year to agriculture, has had difficulty paying even its operation and maintenance costs, so low is its cost recovery from user charges. Repayment of capital costs is by hydroelectric revenues and transfers from the federal treasury—costs which urban dwellers pay via higher electricity rates and income taxes. The State Water Project currently involves substantial financial transfers from the rate and taxpayers of the Metropolitan Water District of Southern California to San Joaquin Valley irrigators, because the MWD turns over several hundred thousand acre-feet of "surplus" water a year to agriculture on which it still pays the fixed costs.

Fourth, the proposed expansion of the State Water Project will be financed by means of revenue bonds, which will form a large part of the new bonded debt of the state. California can take on only a limited burden of debt, so these bonds compete for available capital with other kinds of bonds that benefit industry and urban development, such as industrial parks, pollution control investments, and municipal water and sewer systems. Moreover, if the State Water Project experiences any difficulties in repayment by contractors—owing perhaps to demand cutbacks in the face of rising water prices—its revenue bonds will be difficult to sell and California's bond rating, which determines the cost and ease of borrowing, could be jeopardized.

Reallocation Scenario

The most rational policy from industry's perspective would be to reallocate presently developed water supplies. A transfer of roughly 5 percent of agricultural water used in California would amount to a doubling of water available for industrial customers; a transfer of 11 percent would mean a doubling of water available for *all* urban uses. Under the Reallocation Scenario, the water demands of industry and attendant urbanization would be met principally by transfer of 3.4 million acre-feet of presently-developed water supplies from agriculture to urban users. This amounts to approximately a 12 percent decrease in agricultural water use intensity, correspondingly more if irrigated farm output were to expand. This does not appear to be an unachievable figure, compared to the 17 percent permanent reduction of industrial water use in the East Bay service area in only five years.

In fact, the degree of water transfer is likely to be much lower than the above figure of 10 percent of all developed supplies. That figure, arrived at by the simplest arithmetic, represents an upper bound. More sophisticated calculations of marginal transfers from the lowest to highest efficiency uses arrive at a total of less than 3 percent shift in total water use (see Chapter VIII).

A Reallocation Scenario is preferable to the No Project Scenario because it reduces business uncertainty and eliminates a possible growth crisis due to supply shortages. Reallocation is preferable to Full Development for reasons of cost effectiveness. Furthermore, *reallocation is unavoidable in either case, so it is better to consider a positive and creative policy now rather than later when a crisis hits.* Three further arguments can be made in its favor.

First, transfer of water between economic sectors can serve the general social good. That is, where a presumption can be made that market valuations are a good measure of social worth, social welfare is served by the efficient allocation of resources to economic uses where their contribution to production (marginal product) has the highest value. One need not accept a full-blown version of welfare economics in order to apply this principle. *At the margin* water is being applied to uses with a lower value-added per acre-foot in agriculture than in industry, principally due to lower returns on agricultural than industrial products (see Table 3). Other sources of inefficiency are losses in transit, low efficiency in application, a high rate of water use by crops, or low returns on certain products. Thus *both* physical and economic efficiency are involved. And this applies chiefly to the marginal percent of uses, not the bulk of perfectly reasonable and beneficial applications of irrigation water. If only a 20 percent cutback in the lowest valued crops (per acre-foot of water applied)—hay and pasture—were achieved, the amount of water would nearly equal the yield of Phase II of the State Water Project. A 5 percent cutback would exceed the yield of the Peripheral Canal alone.

The second argument for transferability is that it is cheaper for industry (and other urban uses) than other possible sources of water. For example, Colorado River water now being sold for under $5 per acre-foot to the Imperial Valley could be purchased for from 15 to 70 times its present price and still be competitive with water generated by the various new supply augmentation projects on the drawing board.

Conversely, a grower who could sell water acquired at low prices would stand to make a healthy profit. Saleable water would become available either through conservation measures (more efficient transfer and application), altered cropping patterns (shift from more to less water intensive crops), or withdrawing land from production of irrigated crops. Each of these alternatives normally has a cost associated with it. But the revenue to be gained from the sale of water will frequently exceed the cost of generating a salable surplus through purchase of better irrigation equipment, lining irrigation ditches, or foregoing revenues on idled land.

For example, the average value of output in hay and pasture per acre-foot of water applied is only $70 (see Table 3). Urban users could pay more than this per acre-foot and still the water would cost less than from all but one of the units of the proposed expansion of the State Water Project—and considerably less than the average cost of water from the whole of Phase II of the State Water Project, which has been estimated to be $225 per acre-foot. Meanwhile, farmers will make more by *not* growing alfalfa (which also has other input costs) than by growing it.

The possibility of financial gain to the growers under a reallocation scheme is of crucial importance. Abstract considerations of "social welfare gain" are of little use in generating political support for water transfers. To be politically viable, a reallocation strategy must also be essentially *marginal* involving no more than 20 percent of the farm total over the next 50 years, and occurring through carefully regulated trading, in limited circumstances and for restricted purposes. This would allow smooth growth and change in the state's industrial base without serious disruption to agriculture. If, on the other hand, reallocation were taken to mean a full "market solution" applied to all presently-held water rights and contracts, its impacts would be unpredictable and its political palatability would be nil. The ultimate success of a reallocation policy will depend upon whether it is perceived as a gradual or radical change.

CONCLUSIONS

We support a proposal for limited market transferability of water in the State of California. It is, we believe, the best method of dealing with the problem of supply shortage and conflict between sectors over the distribution of water resources.

Any reallocation of water resources, however, must occur at the margin, beginning from the present base. This requires, first, certainty of tenure, or firm property rights. Second, *there can be no permanent forfeiture of rights through sale of surplus water*. Transfer must be defined as a "reasonable, beneficial use" and take place on a periodic basis. In addition, one must have rights over "salvage water," saved by conservation measures. At the same time, other users must be protected. Normal unrecovered excess water (unconsumed) needed by downstream users for streamflow protection and groundwater recharge must be left in place.

If supply augmentation becomes necessary in the future, the state must still plan the size of new additions and the distribution of new water among competing claimants. This cannot be done simply by the market. First, allocation of new rights would be a highly charged issue. Second, the changing cost curve of supply means that past demands based on past costs are not a good measure of future demands. Third, water supply investments are notoriously "lumpy," so there is no possibility of marginal adjustments in output.

A "true" water market would allow for the possibility of permanent transfer and alienation of rights. This is not our suggestion. Water is too essential in California to go simply to the highest bidder. Indeed, our Reallocation Scenario would not eliminate existing subsidies to certain water users, especially irrigators. It merely tries to improve the efficiency of water use given initial positions and financial discrimination, by enlisting the profit-seeking tendencies of present users. Under a modified water market system, industry would benefit without great injury to agriculture.

REFERENCES AND NOTES

1. For discussions of water's role in industrial location see Charles Howe, "Water Resources and Regional Economic Growth in the U.S., 1950-1960," *Southern Economic Journal,* 34:4, 477-489; Allen V. Kneese, "Economic and Related Problems in Contemporary Water Resources Management," *Natural Resources Journal,* 5(1965):2, 236-258; Robert Estall and R.O. Buchanan, *Industrial Activity and Economic Geography* (London: Hutchinson and Co., 1961), pp.

147-156; John McGregor, "Water as a Factor in the Location of Industry in the Southwest," *Southeastern Geographer*, 10(1970):1, 41-54.

2. Electric utilities in particular are excluded because they are treated in Chapter V, and because data is unreliable for this sector.

3. Data from the California Department of Water Resources generally refer to water withdrawn and not to consumptive use. See Tables 1-3.

4. California Department of Water Resources, *Water Use by Manufacturing Industries in California, 1970*, Bulletin No. 124-2 (Sacramento: The Resources Agency, 1977).

5. Note that the industrial categories in Table 3 are not identical in definition to those of Table 2. Note also that a better measure of water intensity, for which commensurate data were not available, would be value added per acre-foot of water.

6. Considerably more information would be needed on cost structure, input-output relation growth dynamics, and social valuation, before concluding that such transfers are necessarily the best policy, however.

7. Industrial firms are usually the largest single consumers from public systems.

8. There are very few private water utilities; San Jose Water Works in Santa Clara County and California Water Service Company, which serves areas scattered around the state, are two notable exceptions.

9. *Water Use by Manufacturing Industries,* op. cit.

10. M. Storper and R. Walker, "Urban-Rural Subsidy in Financing the State Water Project," unpublished manuscript.

11. L. Kimball and D. Shulman, "Growth in California: Prospects and Consequences," *Public Affairs Report,* 21(1980):5.

12. *Water Use by Manufacturing Industries,* op. cit., p. 21.

13. Officials of EBMUD, personal communication, August 15, 1981.

14. Testimony of Chris Reed, member, Santa Monica City Council, before the Assembly Committee on Water, Parks, and Wildlife, Los Angeles, December 2, 1981.

15. William Bruvold, "Residential Water Conservation: Policy Lessons from the California Drought," *Public Affairs Report,* 19(1978):6.

16. See Richard Walker and Matthew Williams, "Water from Power: Water Supply and Regional Growth in the Santa Clara Valley," unpublished manuscript, Department of Geography, University of California, Berkeley, 1981.

17. The difference from 100 percent is made up by government water use.

18. M. Storper and R. Walker, "Urban-Rural Subsidy . . .," op. cit.

19. The urban consumer's water bill will not increase proportionally to the increased cost of new water because of mixing old and new supplies and the large component of fixed capital in the treatment and distribution system.

CHAPTER V

ENERGY

by

Mark N. Christensen, Glenn W. Harrison, and Larry J. Kimbell

ABSTRACT

Increasing prices for energy are affecting costs of water supply/disposal and aggregate levels of demand. Prices for gas and electricity, which reflect average rather than marginal costs of new supplies, will rise more than will prices for petroleum products.

Future demands for water used in energy production should be less than 1.5 million acre-feet per year. If demands for energy continue to decline, then derived demands for water-for-energy will also decline, and vice versa. At any given quantity and quality of demand for energy, alternative mixes of supply technologies can vary by a factor of three in the amounts of water required. Public policies that influence choices of energy supply technologies, therefore, have strong implications for future demands for water.

In the municipal and industrial sectors, rising costs of water will have small economic impact but will restrain demands for additional supplies. Most affected by higher costs of water will be those sectors of agriculture that depend on large quantities of low cost water—hay and pasture, cotton and rice, which together account for about 45 percent of water consumed in California.

Future demands for water will depend not only on costs of energy/water, but also on changing costs of other factors of production—capital, labor, other resources, environmental necessities (e.g., clean air). No existing method of forecasting future demands adequately accounts for the direct, indirect, and induced demands for all critical resources in a complex interdependent economy.

Environmental externalities that are resistant to internalization as costs or to regulatory control are now central to policy for both energy and water. On some time scale those externalities will constrain economic activity through either (1) self-imposed constraint on consumption or (2) degradation of the environmental systems that support production. Critical uncertainties concern the scale and rate of change of externalities.

Future demands for water will be affected by factors that resist quantification, including changing lifestyles, attitudes toward government, national and international circumstances. Quantitative methods of forecasting demand are useful as "if..then..." constructs; factors not captured in the models, however, will have large impacts on future demands. Selection of any particular quantity of water as a basis for planning turns on subjective preferences or prior commitments.

Economic effects of alternative supply scenarios are critically dependent on the extent to which other factors of production can be substituted for water. If substitutability is high, then large changes in water usage can be generated by small changes in relative prices of factors, and vice versa. Careful study of sector-specific substitutability is clearly important to development of water policy. Enough is known about substitutability, however, to indicate that existing water supplies could be used more productively if there were means of reallocating water from lower-valued to higher-valued purposes (as measured by value added in the course of using water in productive processes). Small reallocations of present supplies could achieve large improvements in economic efficiency.

Existing water law virtually prohibits reallocations, even where they would be of mutual benefit to potential buyer and seller as well as to society at large. Existing law emphasizes security of tenure to preexistent rights, regardless of the social value of existing use. That constraint forces water supply organizations to seek additional supplies through construction of new and very expensive supply projects, rather than through reallocation of much cheaper existing supplies used for low-valued purposes. Institutional changes are required for more efficient use of California's water resources.

WATER AND ENERGY

In the process of long-range planning for water in California, energy enters as a significant factor in three very different kinds of ways. First, the processes of extracting and processing energy in various forms consumes water, and that consumption is a factor in the competition for water. Second, energy is used in moving and treating water, so the prices of energy affect the costs of supplying and using water. Third, rising prices and changing forms of energy resources are inducing changes in patterns of economic activity, thereby indirectly affecting future demands for water. All three of these matters are discussed in the following section. Subsequent sections of this paper consider alternative scenarios for water development, and provide conclusions.

IMPORTANT VARIABLES: PRICES, USES, CIRCUMSTANCES

In this section we seek to identify and describe the more important variables under categories listed below, and to identify some important interactions among them. The factors that we examine are: (1) prices of energy; (2) water used in energy production; (3) energy used in water supply; (4) the interdependence of water and energy use in the California economy; and (5) changing circumstances, especially rising marginal costs, externalities, and domestic and international contexts.

Prices of Energy

Prices paid for energy will substantially affect costs of water and overall patterns of production and consumption in the years ahead. Long-range planning for water is necessarily rooted in some expected schedule of prices. Our expectations of prices for energy are based on consideration of factors that have affected prices in recent years.

The cost of producing energy in the United States began to rise in the 1960s, after having fallen for many previous decades.[1] Those increases in costs appeared in many different aspects of the production system: costs of exploration and development began to rise; producers and consumers began to pay for real costs that had previously been treated as "external" to their transactions (e.g., health and safety of workers, air and water pollution, collective risks of dam safety and nuclear power plants); productivity and economies of increasing scale began to level off while wages continued to rise; and costs of capital began to rise. In 1970 production of oil in the United States peaked and began to decline, while consumption continued to increase rapidly, as did imports of oil. Starting in 1973 the Organization of Petroleum Exporting Countries (OPEC) took advantage of these circumstances to initiate a series of dramatic price increases for oil. Since that time the world has been looking for new sources of energy as alternatives to OPEC oil in particular, and, in the longer term, to oil in general.

There appears to be a wide variety of alternative sources of energy that can be produced economically in large quantities when petroleum is priced in the range from $25 to $50 per barrel (all discussion of prices here is in terms of 1981 constant dollars). The costs of production of, and competition among, those substitute or "backstop" sources of energy will in the longer term determine the level of energy prices.

Prices paid for energy, however, depend not just on costs of production but also on the relation between levels of supply and demand. If world demand for petroleum grows faster than new sources and competition for liquid fuels can be developed, then OPEC will have a rather free hand in setting oil prices. If world demand for oil should continue to decline as it has for the last year or so, then world prices should move downward. Conventional wisdom expects world demands for oil to increase, but at $35 per barrel of oil, it is so much cheaper for users of oil to invest in ways to save a barrel of oil than it is to buy a barrel, that demands may decrease even while population and economic activity increase. Potentials for saving energy through investments that are cost-effective at prices of $35 per barrel are very large—on the order of 30 to 50 percent of current United States consumption.[2]

The hand of OPEC is also weakened by development of substantial new sources of oil production (e.g., Mexico). Demands for OPEC oil in particular have recently declined. If they should continue to decline in response to continuing conservation and new, non-OPEC sources, then current OPEC price levels can be sustained only by substantial cuts in OPEC production. The floor under any prospective decline in OPEC prices is formed by the costs of alternatives to OPEC oil. Those costs are now probably in the range of $15 to $25 per barrel (1981 prices)—and rising.

Petroleum so dominates markets for energy that prices for other, competitive fuels change in response to changes in oil price. We expect that relationship to persist at least until the year 2000 and probably beyond. Our expectations for prices of various fuels are listed in Table 1. We consider two alternative projections. If potentials for efficiency are achieved, prices should be toward the lower end. If conservation is less effective and/or if costs of producing synthetic fuels are toward the higher end, then prices should be higher. These projections assume present environmental regulations. Many real costs of energy production are still not internalized (e.g., damages to aquatic ecosystems, acid rains, carbon dioxide in the atmosphere, nuclear wastes and residue, prospects of nuclear proliferation and/or terror). If these costs, and the externalities of large-scale synfuels production, should be more fully internalized, then costs and prices could rise even above the high projection.

In the nearer term, any large-scale disruption of the supply chain from the Persian Gulf could send the price of oil and all other forms of energy far above the high-range projection. Vulnerability is built into the fact that the U.S. imports

Table 1

Assumed Prices for Energy in 2020

Assumed prices for energy in 2020, at point of end use. Prices include costs of extraction, processing, transportation, environmental controls during those stages, and royalties. Prices exclude costs of conversion and environmental control at point of end use. All prices in constant 1981 dollars.

Energy Type	1981 Price[a] $/Unit	2020 Price $/Unit Low	High	2020 Price $/MBtu[f] Low	High
Hydrocarbon					
Crude oil (and synthetic liquids in future price to refiners)	$33.40/bbl[b]	$25/bbl	$50/bbl[e]	$4.30	$8.60
Natural gas (and syngas in future years)	$4.07/mcf[c]	$4/mcf	$10/mcf	$4.00	$10.00
Coal (12,000 Btu/lb)	$1.35/mBtu[d]	$60/ton	$120/ton	$2.50	$5.00
Electricity	$0.05/kwh	$.08/kwh	$.15/kwh	$10.00	$23.00
Solar heat Passive				0	$2.00
Active				$5.00	$10.00

Notes: (a) Source: Monthly Energy Review, EIA/DOE, April 1981.
(b) Refiners composite (domestic and imported) acquisition cost, January 1981.
(c) Average residential price, mcf = thousand cubic feet.
(d) Average price delivered to electric utilities, all ranks of coal. 2020 prices are for high rank coals at 12,000 Btu/pound.
(e) Prices of synthetic liquids will probably be near or about $50/bbl.
(f) One Btu is defined as the quantity of energy (heat) directly required to raise the temperature of one pound of water one degree Fahrenheit; mBtu is million British thermal units.

nearly 40 percent of its petroleum, and free world oil supplies are highly concentrated in the Persian Gulf region. Political instabilities (such as occurred in Iran), active war (now going on between Iran and Iraq), or potential extension of influence by the Soviet Union in the Gulf region could lead to a prolonged and serious disruption of free world oil production. The impacts that petroleum shortfalls of various magnitudes are expected to have on the U.S. and California economies have been analyzed.[3] It is estimated that a 6 percent shortfall would produce a pause in growth or a mild recession; a 12 percent shortfall would produce economic disruption roughly similar to a moderate recession; and a 25 percent shortfall would impact the U.S. and California economies like a severe recession, such as that of 1975. Finally, estimates are that a 40 percent shortfall would produce results comparable to the Great Depression of the 1930s. A 6 percent shortfall is viewed as more likely than the more serious shortfalls—a 40 percent shortfall would require a complete shutdown of the entire Persian Gulf. It is not unlikely that there will be at least some disruption of supplies from the Persian Gulf during the next two decades.

Prices for electricity and natural gas are influenced not only by prices of petroleum but also by the practices of utility regulation, especially "average cost pricing" and rate structures. Consumers do not experience the full cost of new sources of energy, but rather are charged a price that reflects a composite average of old, cheap sources and new, expensive sources. Only the well-informed user foresees the inevitable price increases that must come as old, long-term contracts for fuels at low prices gradually expire, to be replaced by new contracts for fuels at much higher prices. In the meantime, many users of electricity have invested in equipment and facilities on the basis of present, unrealistically low prices for electricity. ("Average-cost" pricing of water likewise obscures the real costs of new sources of supply.)

Regulatory bodies are moving to influence demands by changing rate structures. Traditional policies and practices were developed during the decades when costs of electricity and gas were falling and expansion of the supply system brought benefits (more energy at lower prices) to almost everyone. Under those circumstances, "declining-block" rate structures gave lower prices per unit for larger quantities used, encouraging increased demands and discouraging industrial co-generation (which uses fuels much more efficiently to produce both electricity and steam for industrial processes). Now that costs of new supplies are rising, and expansion of the supply system brings higher costs (and more obvious environmental impacts) to all users, regulatory policies are changing. Both the California Energy Commission and the California Public Utilities Commission are working to restrain growth of demands and to diversify supplies in a variety of ways. Policies are in a state of flux, but users of electricity and gas are not likely to see again the kind of rate structures and (low) price incentives they were used to when marginal costs of new energy supplies were falling.

"Peak-load pricing" for electricity is now being considered by the California Public Utilities Commission and being used experimentally by Pacific Gas & Electric Company for agricultural users. The costs of producing energy during times of peak demands is greater than the cost during times of average demands, so charging extra for electricity used during peak periods has a certain logic. The time of peak load is summer; electricity for irrigation pumping constitutes 11 percent of summer peak load.[4] Peak-load pricing of electricity significantly increases the costs of irrigation, as presently practiced, and encourages pumping on off-peak hours.[5] The Public Utilities Commission is also encouraging utilities to experiment with radically new kinds of activities, including investments on "the customer's side of the meter" (i.e., in conservation) because under present circumstances it is cheaper to save a kilowatt hour than it is to produce one.

Changing rate structures for energy have substantial implications for users of large amounts of water. In addition to those specific impacts, more general considerations are also important to note: changing circumstances (e.g., increasing marginal costs of energy) are inducing major changes in long-standing public policies and practices that previously encouraged demand, and development of additional supplies. In the course of those changes, utility companies are being radically reformed as institutions. Rising marginal costs of water may presage comparable changes in institutions that supply water.

Water Used in Energy Production

Use of water in production of energy is presently a marginal concern in terms of both quantity of water used, and the effect of costs of water on costs of energy production. Freshwater used in producing energy (thermal electric generation; extracting and processing oil and natural gas) amounted to about 1.1 million acre feet (MAF) or 3 percent of developed water supplies in 1976; for comparison, the hay and pasture sector of agriculture used 11.3 MAF, or 28 percent of the total.[6] Nevertheless, there is substantial concern about prospects of increasing demands for "water-for-energy," both because many new sources are more water-intensive than existing sources, and because demands for energy are generally expected to increase.

Only a few years ago there was serious and pressing concern over requirements of water-for-energy.[7] Rapid increases in demand for energy were forecast, especially for electricity; utilities felt an urgent need for many more large power stations. Coastal sites for new power plants were constrained by requirements for coastal protection and seismic safety, so that new plants were expected to be located inland, competing for limited supplies of freshwater. Many of the newer energy technologies are substantially more water-intensive than the technologies they replace. Nuclear power and some forms of geothermal power are less thermally efficient than fossil fuel power plants, and therefore require more cooling water per kilowatt hour of electricity produced. Enhanced oil recovery requires more water than does primary production. A large tar sand or synthetic fuels industry, if it should develop in California, would generate large demands for water. An energy system that is dependent on large quantities of freshwater would be vulnerable to shortfalls during droughts. Finally, a number of environmental consequences of the new technologies, especially their impacts on aquatic ecosystems, are not well understood.

The effects of various mixes of energy supply technologies and levels of demand have been analyzed by John Harte,[8,9] who showed that the requirements for water to meet any particular level of demand can vary by a factor of 2 or 3,[10] depending on the particular mix of supply technologies adopted: nuclear and geothermal electricity and synthetic fuels are particularly water-intensive; wind-electric generation, passive and active solar heating and cooling, and more efficient uses of energy require little or no water. State and federal energy policies can have a strong influence on the mix of supply technologies that is in fact adopted. Energy policy, therefore, will have a strong impact on future requirements of water-for-energy.

While long-term concerns remain regarding water requirements for energy, the immediacy of those problems has vanished in the last three years. The major utility companies of the state have canceled or postponed all plans for major, new in-state power plants; those cancellations stem from the fact that anticipated increases in demand have not developed and forecasts of future increases have been drastically lowered. Reinforcing the changing pattern of private consumption, the Public Utilities Commission and the Energy Commission have developed a long-range strategy and are acting in concert to (1) place conservation at the heart of the long-range strategy for energy, and (2) encourage a diverse array of new energy sources, of which some important types require either no water (wind-electric) or small incremental amounts of water (industrial co-generation, small-scale hydro-power at existing dams).[11]

While debate on energy policies for California has been bitter and divisive for a number of years, a new and very different perception of the problem and tentative consensus on general directions for both private choices and public policies has emerged. Given the magnitude of the implications of that change, the shift has come about in a remarkably short time. With a slow rate of increase in demands and emphasis on diverse sources (in smaller increments that have short lead times to put in place), supplies can be adjusted to demands as they develop. The former strategy (increases in supply in large increments to satisfy rapid increases in demand) required major political and economic commitments (e.g., power plant siting) to be made decades in advance. It was then thought that a set of inexorable and inevitable increases *must* be planned for. It is now clear that there has never been an adequate methodology for long-range forecasting of demands—that the seemingly urgent imperatives of those anticipated increases in demand reflected the conventional wisdom and subjective preferences of the experts and institutions doing the planning, rather than the actual dynamics of the economy and society. Long-range planning for water, rooted in long-range forecasts of demand, rests on similarly shaky ground. Under changing circumstances, especially rising costs of new supplies, demands are very likely to depart from patterns of the past.

Energy Used in Water Supply

Energy is used to move water, to treat water prior to use, and to treat wastewater prior to discharge. The energy requirements of these processes have been described previously.[12,13,14] Average energy requirements for California water supply systems are listed in Table 2. Here we briefly review salient results and then focus on implications for costs in particularly sensitive sectors.

Pumping energy is used in transporting surface water, and in lifting groundwater and pressurizing distribution systems. According to physical principles the minimum amount of work (energy) required to lift one acre-foot of water a height of one foot is 1.024 kwh. Actual requirements in practice are more like 1.7 to 2 kwh. Average pumping requirements, and expected costs, of various water projects are shown in Table 2. For surface water projects the anticipated costs of pumping energy alone exceed the price for water that is economical for forage crops, small grains, and irrigated pasture in 1980.[15] Declining-block pricing structures for electricity formerly created an incentive for groundwater overdrafting because it was then cheaper per unit to lift larger quantities of water. New inverted-block rate structures for electricity will remove that incentive and should help mitigate the problem of groundwater overdraft.

The importance of energy costs for the extent of groundwater overdraft has been emphasized recently by Noel and others,[16] who constructed an optimal control model of the allocation of groundwater and surface water among agricultural and urban uses. Applying their model to Yolo County, California, they show that:

> Energy costs can have an important influence on whether the model indicates a groundwater basin with an increasing or decreasing water table. For example, Upper Cache-Putah basin would be mined under a 2.6 cents [per kwh] energy cost assumption but would have a rising table under the 8 cents [per kwh] energy cost assumption. The

Table 2

Energy Requirements for California Water Supply

Estimated average energy requirements per acre-foot for California water supply in 1972, and anticipated costs under alternative energy cost projections (in 1981 dollars).

		$/Acre-Foot at	
	kwh/Acre-Foot	8¢/kwh	16¢/kwh
Pumping Energy			
Total water supply	270 (+)	$20 (+)	$40(+)
State Water Project	1600	128	256
Central Valley Project	350 (+)	28 (+)	56 (+)
Colorado River Aqueduct	2075	166	332
Groundwater	275	22	44
Water supply to farms			
State Water Project	625	50	100
Central Valley Project	340	27	54
Colorado River Aqueduct	2075	166	332
Groundwater	225	18	36
Municipal Water Treatment			
Prior to Use	30-135	2.40-11	5-22
Wastewater Treatment			
Municipal			
Primary and secondary	250 (+)	20	40
Tertiary	1000 (+)	80 (+)	160 (+)
Agricultural	various	?	?

remaining basins [in Yolo County] move in the same direction . . . at alternative energy cost assumptions. In those basins where groundwater use exceeds recharge under a 4.5 cents energy cost, the effect of higher energy costs is to slow down the rate of mining.

These results illustrate the possible role of energy costs in California's water situation.

Municipal water treatment uses energy in the course of aeration, flocculation-sedimentation, filtration, chlorination, and softening, and increasingly will use treatments by activated carbon. Wastewater treatments use energy for pumping and chemicals. Anticipated energy costs for tertiary treatment of municipal wastewater are comparable to the cost of supplying the water in the first place. Agricultural wastewater treatment projects for the San Joaquin Valley and the Imperial Valley will also use substantial quantities of energy.

In addition to energy used in operating water treatment processes, outlined above, energy is also embodied in the facilities for supplying and treating water. Rising costs of energy are a significant factor not only in operating water supply systems, but also in constructing new facilities. The costs for construction of facilities for storage, transport, and treatment are soaring. The rising energy costs of both construction and operations are changing the cost-effectiveness of conventional water-supply projects in comparison to alternative approaches to water use.

Rising costs of energy for water supply will fall most heavily on those sectors that have a high ratio of water used to value of product. The largest users of water are summarized in Tables 3 and 4. Comparison of Tables 2 and 4 reveals the vulnerability of some sectors to increasing costs of water. For example, the value of hay and pasture product in 1976 was $70 per acre-foot of water used (the reciprocal of "Direct Use"); for rice the value was $46 per acre-foot used. At 5¢/kwh (the average national price of electricity in 1981) the cost of energy alone in water supply to farms via the State Water Project would have been about $31 per acre-foot. At anticipated future prices for energy, the cost of transport alone will be $50 to $100 per acre-foot.[17] For those areas in which water for rice or hay and pasture uses State Water Project-average amounts of energy, rising costs of energy will force substantial increases in prices of crops or conversion to other crops, unless there is a massive subsidy to the sector.

Within the agricultural sector, vulnerability varies. Larger quantities of water per dollar of product are used in producing grain than in producing fruit and vegetables. Water-intensive crops that are especially vulnerable to rising costs of energy and water consume more than half of California's water. Hay and pasture, together with cotton and rice, consumed about 45 percent of the total developed freshwater supply for California in 1976[18] (see Table 3).

Table 3

Principal Water Using Sectors of the California Economy
Water Use (1976) in Million-Acre-Feet*

Agricultural Sector		Energy Sector	
Hay and pasture	11.3	Crude petroleum	0.2
Cotton	4.7	Petroleum refining	0.2
Rice	3.5	Electric companies and systems	0.04
Noncitrus fruit	3.5	Gas companies and systems	0.001
Vegetables	1.9	Natural gas and natural gas liquid	0.7
Corn	1.7		1.141
Wheat	1.4		
Sugarbeets	1.1		
Barley	1.1	Residential Sector	
Almonds	1.0	Owner-occupied real estate	3.7
Citrus fruits	0.8		
	32.0		4.841

*Total developed water supply is about 42 MAF.

Table 4

Direct and Embodied Water Use in Selected California Sectors

Use of water (in 1000 acre-feet) per million 1976 dollars output of sector shown.

ID	Sector	Direct	Embodied	Ratio
Agriculture				
1	Dairies	0.038	4.089	106.20
2	Broilers, chickens and eggs	0.005	1.401	269.42
3	Turkeys and other poultry	0.002	1.363	757.49
4	Cattle and calves	0.078	3.813	49.01
9	Cotton	5.618	6.067	1.08
10	Wheat	5.896	6.722	1.14
11	Rice	21.896	23.209	1.06
12	Barley	6.699	7.369	1.10
13	Corn	9.355	9.730	1.04
14	Hay and pasture	14.302	14.885	1.02
15	Oats	8.416	8.837	1.05
16	Sorghum grain	11.586	12.050	1.04
17	Grass seed	5.514	5.900	1.06
20	Walnuts	5.921	6.158	1.04
21	Almonds	5.173	5.431	1.05
22	Noncitrus fruits	2.567	2.901	1.13
23	Citrus fruits	1.908	2.251	1.18
25	Vegetables	1.421	1.719	1.21
28	Melons	1.728	2.039	1.18
29	Sugarbeets	5.777	5.950	1.03
Backward Linkages to Agriculture				
38	Agriculture and forestry services	0.037	1.578	43.12
44	Chemical and fertilizer mining	0.133	0.277	2.09
72	Agricultural chemicals	0.019	0.150	7.96
Forward Linkages to Agriculture				
52	Meat products	0.006	1.102	174.91
53	Dairy products	0.007	2.315	326.07
54	Canned and frozen foods	0.016	0.461	28.29
55	Grain mill products	0.003	2.768	865.17
56	Bakery products	0.003	0.503	186.29
57	Sugar	0.044	0.832	19.05
58	Confectionary products	0.050	0.406	8.05
59	Beverages and flavorings	0.014	0.425	30.15
60	Miscellaneous food processing	0.008	0.376	48.83
130	Water and sanitary services	0.0002	0.156	711.32
Energy				
41	Crude petroleum	0.063	0.154	2.44
42	Natural gas and natural gas liquids	0.182	0.278	1.53
78	Petroleum refining	0.013	0.126	9.73
128	Electric companies and systems	0.009	0.114	12.12
129	Gas companies and systems	0.0002	0.082	359.54

Source: California Department of Water Resources, Bulletin 210, p. 104-107.

The average costs listed in Table 2 obscure important differences between regions. In the South Coast area the energy requirements for transport of water via the State Water Project make such water prohibitively expensive for agriculture. In the Tulare Lake hydrologic basin, the average price of water supply to farms is about $13 per acre-foot, ranging from $7 to $51 per acre-foot.[19] The costs of SWP energy alone in that area, at 1981 average prices, is about equal to the average price of water supply to farms, indicating a subsidy implicit in those prices. At our anticipated prices for electricity (8 to 15¢/kwh) the energy costs alone of water supply to Kern County would be in the range of $25 to $35 per acre-foot—the price at which forage crops and small grains drop out (see reference 5). Such costs would have a large impact on agriculture and water use in that area: in 1975 about 1,400,000 acre-feet of water was used to irrigate forage crops and small grains in Kern County.[20]

Rising costs of energy (for pumping, treatment of water, construction of facilities) will make quite expensive any possible solution of the problem of build-up of salt in soils on the western side of the San Joaquin Valley and in the Imperial Valley. The full costs of water in those areas, if they are borne by the users of that water, will induce changes in agricultural practices and probably release substantial quantities of water for other purposes.

Water and Energy in California's Economy

While the foregoing analysis yields some important insights, it is too superficial to be useful for reaching conclusions on policy regarding either short-term contingency plans or long-range plans. A superficial policy, for example, might attempt to direct economic activity in California away from those sectors using relatively more water to those sectors using relatively less water (say, by various tax or pricing incentives). It is not valid, however, to assume that a ranking of sectors by their *direct* use of water will correspond to a ranking by their *total* use of water, including water used in various inputs to the sector in question. Moreover, there may be some sectors that are "critical" in the sense that their output in turn is required to produce the output of a whole range of industries. For example, the output of the energy sector may be needed as an input to every other producing sector of the economy. A cutback in energy output might therefore tend to reduce the output of every other sector. On the other hand, linkages of a sector such as owner-occupied real estate, or rice, with other sectors is much smaller. Linkages of this kind must be understood before any water policy, short-term or long-term, can be developed.

Table 3 indicates the sectors of the California economy that are the major *direct* users of water. Table 4 uses an *input-output (IO)* methodology[21] to calculate the direct and embodied use of water (measured in 1000 acre-feet) per million (1976) dollars of output in selected California sectors. The column labeled "ratio" is obtained by dividing the embodied use by the direct use for each sector shown. This ratio is a useful summary measure of the extent to which "appearances are deceiving" in the use of water by each sector. Consider dairies, for example. Direct use of water per unit output of dairies is miniscule, but when we allow for all of the water that indirectly went into producing that output (e.g., inputs of the hay and pasture sector), the accounting story is very different. The workings of an IO model can be illustrated by considering the effects of an increase in demand for the output of some sector. Consider in particular an increase in demand for dairy products. In order to satisfy it, additional output must be produced. This in turn requires that dairy input suppliers (as determined by fixed "recipe") increase *their* output—e.g., chemicals, electricity generation, business services, etc. To increase these outputs, their suppliers in turn must increase outputs. Typically, therefore, an increase in the final demand for one sector leads to increases in the output of many other sectors. Thus one dollar's worth of additional final demand for dairies may lead to considerably more than one dollar's worth of sales when aggregated over all sectors.

The simple message of the numbers presented in Table 4 is that the *embodied* use of water is much more evenly distributed across sectors than the *direct* use. The same message comes through with respect to energy use in California.[22] Use of water by dairies compared to rice changes from 1:576 (when measured as direct use) to 1:6 (when measured as embodied use). The various feed and seed crops obviously remain relatively heavy users of water however one does the accounting, but the great differences in direct use tend to disappear when an allowance for sectoral interdependence is made.

The quantitative results presented above are intended to be indicative of the analyses that could underlie the development of water policy to cope with shortages. Several remarks on the general policy relevance of IO analysis in this area are therefore in order.

There can be no presumption that any ranking of sectors by their direct water use (per dollar of output) will correspond to a ranking based on their total water use. Moreover, there are "critical" sectors whose output is required to produce the output of a wide range of industries. It may be necessary to ensure that water allocations for these key sectors are not reduced.

One should bear in mind that IO analysis assumes no substitutability among inputs. If, in fact, some inputs can be relatively easily replaced by others, their loss may not be critical. If, for example, cotton producers can more easily adjust their use of water (in combination with other factor inputs) than other sectors, a decrease in water supply available may not greatly affect related input or processing industries. These qualifications indicate the policy relevance of explicit general equilibrium numerical simulation techniques that explicitly allow for substitution possibilities.

It should also be clear that water is not the only scarce resource in California. A more complete analysis would have to consider a number of other factors as well—working capital, labor, and primary energy, among others. As long as these resources remain in scarce supply, the reorientation of economic activity to meet constraints on water supply must also take them into account. There is no value in a general policy recommendation for California to cut back its agriculture and emphasize manufacturing on the grounds that such action would minimize the state's water use, if there is not enough energy available at acceptable prices to produce the additional manufacturing output. Obvious though this seems, it may be difficult to remember in casual or intuitive policy discussions. The IO model can be used at least to define the quantitative dimensions of the trade-offs that a consistent and comprehensive water contingency plan must contain.[23]

Changing Circumstances

A broad array of changing circumstances will also shape future uses and supplies of energy and water. Among the many, we single out for attention rising marginal costs, externalities, and domestic and international contexts.

Rising Marginal Costs. Rising costs of new sources of water, energy, and other natural resources create new circumstances with profound social implications beyond those captured in direct economic calculations. Until recently the costs of water and energy were generally declining relative to other costs. Under such circumstances expansion of resource systems brought the benefits of lower prices to all users. Consensus on economic growth was easy to achieve, newcomers brought general benefits to old-timers, and the interests of consumers and of organizations dedicated to expanding supplies were consonant. When costs of new supplies of water (energy, etc.) start rising, however, expansion of the supply system brings higher prices to all users, enthusiasm for general growth wanes, and interests of consumers diverge from those of growth-oriented suppliers.

The politics of distributing increasing costs are very different from the politics of distributing increasing benefits. Fundamentally different economic and social circumstances create conditions for new coalitions and basic changes in public policy. For energy, California policy is now committed to restraining the growth of demand; private utilities are being molded into very new kinds of institutions under the suasion of both economic circumstance and new governmental policy. Most of the logic pointing to the benefits of more efficient use of energy applies as well to water; institutional changes leading to greater efficiency are suggested in several companion papers in this volume.

Public policies are not independent of private perceptions and expectations, behavior and lifestyles. Lifestyle even more than technological change can modify future uses of water. Different diets, for example, have very different requirements for embodied water (see Chapter VII).

The general point here is that rising marginal costs of water and energy have created fundamentally new circumstances, and fundamentally different expectations. Those changes are affecting both private behavior (demands, in ways not captured by conventional forecasting methods) and popular support for public policies and projects.

Externalities. Another major consideration in long-range planning is the future state of (1) the environmental systems that sustain economic production (for example, air, water, soil), and (2) environmental regulation. For some years environmental externalities have been central, not peripheral, to the determination of energy policies; they are now central to water planning as well, as illustrated by the dispute over the Peripheral Canal. The existence of large external costs or risks in the use of natural resources has broad implications for the economy: either society must learn to manage its use of environmental systems in a sustainable fashion or degradation of these systems will eventually constrain production.

While environmental regulation has worked to internalize some previously external costs of industrial activity, nevertheless large and real externalities remain. For energy, these include acid rains, carbon dioxide in the atmosphere, the destabilizing politics of world oil, nuclear proliferation, and possibilities for nuclear terror. For water supply, externalities include disruption of aquatic ecosystems to unknown effect, saltwater intrusions, physical degradation of aquifers and overdrafts of groundwater. For agriculture, externalities include depletion of soil fertility, soil erosion, and build-up of salts, pesticides, and fertilizer components in soil, in groundwater and surface runoff.

These externalities constitute real costs of production that are not being paid. Prices are therefore lower than they "should" be; demands are higher, and there is a strong tendency to over-consume and over-exploit resources. Exploitation means that soil depletion, groundwater overdrafts, salt build-ups, etc., will eventually force changes in the patterns of economic activity; many environmental constraints that once seemed distant now seem proximate. If demands are not constrained in the present by appropriate prices and/or policies, then they will be limited more painfully in the future by degradation of the resources on which production depends.

Substantial difficulties stand in the way of paying the full costs of supplying water and other resources, for many important externalities are resistant to quantification or monetization. Further, the costs and risks of many large-scale resource systems, including long-distance transport of water, are distributed differently from the benefits, with little prospect that the beneficiaries could compensate the losers even if they would. Where resources are brought from distant places, and where externalities are resistant to internalization, consumers can neither pay nor experience full costs.

The existence of large external costs that are not borne directly by the beneficiaries of the projects, therefore, yields both inequity and economic inefficiency. The general social values of equity and efficiency should lead to preference for technological developments that have the following characterizations: (1) external costs that are small in relation to internal costs, (2) external costs that are susceptible to internalization, and (3) intractable externalities (those that cannot be internalized) that coincide in space and time with the pattern of distribution of benefits of the technology.[24] It is not clear that long-distance transport of water can meet those criteria.

Consensus on this point of view does not exist, but problems of resistant externalities remain and will continue to plague development of systems for long-distance transport of water. Over the course of time the logic of events will likely crystallize and make vivid to a wider audience the force of the linkage among externalities, inequity and inefficiency. Circumstances may eventually produce an effective consensus on preference for technologies having the characteristics outlined above. Such a consensus would greatly restrain the further development of long-distance water transport systems.

Domestic and International Contexts. Long-range planning for water must take account of many other changing circumstances in addition to rising marginal costs and increasing environmental impacts: taxpayer rebellions, grassroots initiatives, costs of transport to distant markets, federal policies and subsidies for exports, and international economic instability, to name a few.

Changing national expectations and perceptions of problems and opportunities have impact on state priorities. New developments, even existing arrangements, are challenged by the tendency of parties, domestically and internationally, to see linkages and trade-offs among issues formerly considered separate and treated in isolation: e.g., Japan may link California's water subsidy for agriculture to negotiations with the United States on auto imports and access to Japanese markets, just as we link other nations' subsidies for steel to our policies on steel imports. In the 1960s, the decade of the California Water Project, well-informed people expected prices of energy to decline indefinitely and, generally, continued economic growth. Subsequent events (environmental problems, Vietnam, Iran,

Watergate, Three-Mile Island, stagflation) have done much to alter those expectations. There has been a fundamental refashioning of perceptions about both our economy and our ability to manipulate our environment.

In sum, analysis of quantifiable matters does much to illuminate our present problems and opportunities. The circumstances that surround planning for water in the 1980s, however, are so different from those of the 1960s that public attitudes toward economic development have changed qualitatively. A political consensus on water in the 1980s will not be based on the expectations and perceptions of the 1960s.

ALTERNATIVE FUTURES

In this section we examine three alternative futures for California water policy, described more fully in the introductory chapter of this volume: (1) the status quo prevails, and there are neither significant institutional changes nor significant new water supply projects; (2) institutional change allows the allocation, and continual reallocation, of water through a market (or marketlike) system with tradable property rights for water; and (3) additional supplies of water are developed by physical projects without any institutional change.

Scenarios 1 and 3 are both characterized by "segmented" markets, in which it is very difficult to transfer water from one sector to another, despite very different and/or changing benefits to society available in different sectors; existing institutional arrangements emphasize security of prior access or commitment. By "benefits" we mean aggregate economic product, measured in dollars, achieved through use of water in various productive processes. Scenario 2, in contrast, emphasizes flexibility in allocating water to the socially most valuable function—as measured by dollar value of product.

Scenario 1—Status Quo

Although it is difficult to transfer water in large quantities from agriculture to nonagricultural activities, farmers typically have considerable flexibility in adjusting cropping patterns; a shift by a farmer from one crop to another may amount to a reallocation of water among sectors *within* agriculture, say from lower-valued to higher-valued purposes. Economically, this means greater social benefit from the use of water. Since agriculture uses nearly 85 percent of California's developed water supplies, there is, consequently, substantial, though by no means complete, flexibility in reallocating total water supplies among alternative uses (though not among regions or contractors).

Responses within agriculture to changes in availability of hydrocarbons (as fuels and as fertilizer) have been modeled by Adams and others,[25] providing a rough caricature of the effect on cropping patterns (also total production and prices) of possible energy shortfalls. In general they found that alternative means of coping with energy shortfalls (e.g., restraint by allocation versus restraint by price increases) would have very different effects on both acreage and quantities of production of different crops. Simulations of their quadratic programming model indicate that acreage planted to field crops would increase in response to a large increase in energy costs, but decrease in response to an energy shortage handled by allocation (rationing) on either a statewide or subregional basis. In contrast, acreage in vegetable crops would decrease in both cases—but less than field crops in response to an allocation scheme. We do not here provide a critical assessment of the "realism" of their specific simulation,[26] but we point out the very fundamental implications of their work: energy supplies and costs will have great impacts on cropping patterns, hence on future demands for water. There are rich opportunities for further investigation of relationships among energy, cropping patterns, and forecasts of demands for water. Sensible water policies cannot be developed without better understanding of those linkages.

Scenario 2—Marketlike Allocation of Water

This scenario focuses on questions of water allocation rather than on augmenting water supplies. We assume a hypothetical economy in which water, like other factors of production (labor, capital, energy), can be bought and sold at will. Under pressure of the drought of 1976-77, marketlike transfers of water actually did occur. As described by the director of the Department of Water Resources:

> Another water management mechanism that has proven successful in spite of normal institutional constraints is the concept of water exchange. The Department of Water Resources has encouraged and developed water exchange contracts to voluntarily reallocate water from areas with sufficient supplies to water-short areas. Exchange agreements have been accomplished to transfer more than 430 cubic hectometers of water (355,000 acre-feet) to areas of need. (In allocating the exchange water, the state included a requirement that no exchange water be allocated to lands not irrigated last year.) Prior to the drought, who would have been so bold as to suggest that water from the State Water Project that had been allocated and contractually committed for delivery to Southern California would be voluntarily reallocated and by a rather complex physical and legal process delivered to a northern California county, which was not a State Water Project contractor nor within its service area? Nevertheless, it has happened.
>
> Not all of the exchange water has gone to municipalities. In fact, the lion's share, 370 cubic hectometers (approximately 300,000 acre-feet), has been reallocated from the highly industrialized and urbanized area of Los Angeles to the irrigated agriculture areas of the lower San Joaquin Valley. Some economists might argue that this seems inconsistent with economic theory, particularly in times of water shortage. However, it is sound if there is sufficient slack in the water demand schedule such that little is sacrificed by urban users in the way of productivity, profit, or even convenience compared with the very substantial gains (or the losses averted) by the irrigation farmers in the San Joaquin Valley.
>
> Perhaps most surprising is the evidence of such high payment capacity as demonstrated by the willingness of agriculture to pay the very high costs of exchange water. However, this willingness to pay is only for the short run and is the farmer's response to minimize losses or to avoid possible bankruptcy in a drought year and would not represent a long-term ability to pay for the water.[27]

For purposes of this scenario we assume the existence of tradable property rights for water in California. A general equilibrium numerical input-output (GENIO) model recently constructed for California[28] permits us to model explicitly how alternative sectors would compete water resources away from other sectors.

In the GENIO model, final demands, sectoral production and demands for factors of production are all related and determined through equilibrating movements in relative prices in the conventional neoclassical causal manner. Each sector produces its gross output using fixed quantities of intermediate inputs in the input-output manner, but it also employs variable quantities of primary factor inputs in an efficient (i.e., cost-minimizing) manner. In our model there are four general factors of production—working capital, labor, energy, and water. Each of these factors is assumed to be substitutable, with the exact ease of substitution varying from sector to sector. Our results here, focusing on the California economy as a whole, complement those of Chapter VIII on interregional water transfers.

Our model assumes that the available aggregate supplies of each factor in California are fixed. It therefore forces one to concentrate on the question of water and energy allocation, rather than on augmenting the available factor supply. One major difficulty with the use of standard input-output techniques, such as those adopted by the Department of Water resources[29] to study California water resources problems, is the implicit assumption that factors of production are available in unlimited quantities (as "required") at unchanging relative prices. Our GENIO approach relaxes both of these stringent, and all-too-often ignored, assumptions. We also assume that a severely distorted water pricing structure in favor of agriculture exists.

We have used the GENIO model to simulate changes in the direct water use of each sector in response to: 1) a statewide drought (25 percent shortfall in water supply) and 2) removal of the distortion in water pricing. The drought leads to a 33 percent increase in the price of water relative to prices of other factors. The removal of the subsidy to agricultural use of water (effectively an increased tax on water use by agriculture) leads to a 26.5 percent decline in the price of water relative to other factors.[30] The sectoral declines in water use in the drought simulation, shown in Table 5 in thousands of acre-feet, represent around 25 percent of 1976 usage. The removal of the subsidy causes a decline in water use of around 2.8 percent for each agricultural use, and increases averaging 70 percent for the nonagricultural sectors. This second result is not surprising—only small adjustments in agricultural use of water will be required in order to restore equilibrium to the whole California economy. This point is also emphasized in the simulations reported in Chapter VIII.

These results emphasize the substantial economic gains (i.e., greater production from existing resources) that could be realized by development of some form of tradable property rights to water, which would permit willing sellers to exchange water with willing buyers at prices beneficial to both. The GENIO model analyzes the specific effects in the California economy of an approach to water resources based on general economic reasoning. Clearly, substantial gains (to both existing and prospective water users and to the state as a whole) are available through development of institutional arrangements that emphasize tradability of water rights rather than security of tenure. In effect, the question before us is, given the circumstances that exist in 1981, "What restrictions on capitalist acts among consenting adults should we impose?" Given certain intractable externalities in the hydrologic environment (e.g., the common property problem in groundwater overdraft), we do not believe that the answer to the latter question will be "laissez-faire."

Table 5

Changes in Sectoral Water Use (in 1000 acre-feet)

ID	Sector	Drought	Subsidy
1	Livestock and livestock products	-27.2	-3.11
2	Cotton	-1169.3	-133.38
3	Wheat	-337.6	-38.51
4	Rice	-880.4	-100.43
5	Barley	-262.4	-29.93
6	Corn	-422.8	-48.23
7	Hay and pasture	-2837.5	-323.67
8	Oats	-28.9	-3.30
9	Sorghum grain	-126.5	-14.43
10	Other field and seed crops	-49.7	-5.66
11	Walnuts and almonds	-397.0	-45.28
12	Fruits	-1068.5	-121.88
13	Vegetables	-493.1	-56.25
14	Sugarbeets	-277.6	-31.66
15	Other vegetable crops	-208.3	-23.76
16	Miscellaneous agriculture and fishery products	-28.1	-3.21
17	Mining	-79.4	222.35
18	Construction	-3.9	10.95
19	Meat products	-4.3	12.18
20	Dairy products	-3.8	10.65
21	Canned and frozen foods	-28.3	79.25
22	Grain mill products	-1.1	3.17
23	Bakery products	-0.8	2.14
24	Sugar and confectionary	-14.2	39.69
25	Beverages and flavorings	-10.4	29.14
26	Miscellaneous food products	-7.5	21.02
27	Agricultural chemicals	-4.1	11.60
28	Petroleum refining	-35.5	99.38
29	Textile products	-2.6	7.38
30	Other non-durable manufacturing	-61.1	171.04
31	Durables manufacturing	-43.0	120.51
32	Transportation	-1.6	4.47
33	Electric companies and systems	-9.0	25.10
34	Gas companies and systems	-0.2	0.53
35	Water distribution services	-0.1	0.19
36	Wholesale and retail trade	-92.6	259.28
37	Finance and insurance	-2.0	5.71
38	Other services	-11.9	33.20
39	Government enterprises	-57.6	161.26
40	Miscellaneous industries	-22.06	61.79

Note: The change in water use for each simulation is against a 1976 benchmark general equilibrium solution for California.

Scenario 3 —Development of Further Water Supplies

The third scenario considered here assumes the physical development of new water supplies, by means of projects described in the introduction to this volume. Before the effects of such a scenario could be assessed, answers would have to be given to a series of questions, to some extent the same questions that would be raised in other political discussions. We believe the future of this scenario would in fact revolve around questions like the following, asked by all users of water, by taxpayer groups, municipalities, industry, and environmentalists as well as by agricultural interests:

(1) What are realistic, not optimistic, estimates of construction costs? How do these translate into costs per acre-foot? Using what kind of interest rate? What are the operating costs involved in transporting that water to various different sites of use?

(2) What are the environmental costs not captured in engineering-economic calculus? What are the long-term implications of those unintended side-effects? Who bears those unintended costs and risks?

(3) Where will that water go? To what users? At what prices? Who benefits from the projects?

(4) Where do existing supplies of water go? To what users? At what prices? What policies govern that allocation?

(5) The direct costs of new projects, not including externalities, are far above prices that agriculture can afford to pay (see Chapter VIII). Only by averaging new, expensive supplies with old, cheap supplies can prices be kept at "reasonable" levels. In time of scarce capital does it make sense to tie up large amounts of capital in massive, inefficient (i.e., not cost-effective) projects while more cost-effective means of water supply are available?

(6) Public discussion will highlight existing price differentials, or the subsidy to agriculture, under existing water projects. Urban users will become aware that they are paying much higher prices for new supplies than agriculture pays for old supplies from existing state and federal projects, and will also recognize that certain individuals stand to make profits from land speculation. It will become clearer to all that the cheapest future sources of water are the quantities now used in marginal agriculture, or excessive quantities used in those areas where water is cheapest.

(7) The changing rate structure for electricity might possibly solve the groundwater overdraft problem all by itself, by reducing or eliminating the previous incentive to over-produce. Further, the absence of cheap water, increasing costs of lifting groundwater, and of transportation to distant markets are likely to cause some marginal lands to go out of production and induce significant changes in cropping patterns, thereby reducing existing agricultural uses. Farmers having groundwater but only marginal land will see that they could make more money by selling the water than by using it to raise crops. Farmers' interests in tradable rights to water should increase and begin to merge with urban interests in the direction of institutional reform.

CONCLUSIONS

If the analyses in this and several companion papers in this volume are valid, then it follows that the preferred approach to long-range planning for water should have as its central focus the institutional changes aimed at more effective use of water, rather than physical development aimed at increasing supplies. It is also clear that this conclusion is in profound conflict with the preferred programs and policies of most current organized groups of water users and suppliers. Recognizing that political gulf, we review briefly the salient points of analysis which may suggest directions for future California water policy:

(1) Costs of existing supplies of water are rising in response to rising costs of energy and other operating expenses.

(2) Costs of new supplies will be much higher than those of existing supplies because a) the best sites were developed first, b) new supplies have to be moved relatively longer distances at higher operating costs, and c) capital costs of construction have escalated sharply.

(3) Environmental and social impacts of prospective new projects are substantial, though they are not specifically incorporated into the engineering-economic calculus of costs. Those costs, however, inevitably will be paid by someone at some time.

(4) Pricing structures for water result in very different rates to different classes of users. Rates have been low to promote extensive rather than efficient use. Especially low prices to agriculture represent a massive subsidy to that sector, much of which subsidy is capitalized in land values rather than passed through as savings to consumers.

(5) Higher prices for water clearly induce more efficient use and lower demands; users have very substantial capacity to use water more efficiently. Under present circumstances conservation of water is more cost-effective than are new supplies.

(6) The cheapest "new" sources of water are large, low-priced quantities used for purposes that provide only small value added in the course of production. About half of all California's developed water supplies are used for a few crops that have small value added. Much of current use, therefore, is vulnerable to rising costs of energy/water.

(7) Existing law emphasizes security of tenure of rights to water, virtually prohibiting even voluntary exchanges of water from lower-valued to higher-valued purposes. Some aspects of existing law encourage wasteful use as a means of establishing future "rights."

(8) Water-supply organizations, because they cannot bid for existing supplies of cheap and inefficiently used water, naturally turn to schemes for developing new supplies, regardless of costs—both direct and "external."

(9) General economic theory suggests that a system permitting some voluntary exchanges of existing water supplies would yield gains to both buyers and sellers, and substantial increase in net economic product from use of existing supplies of water, without new supply projects.

In sum, it is our contention that the legal and institutional arrangements for water supply in California are so structured as to encourage exploitation of the state's water resources, in development that is unnecessarily expensive and damaging for present and future generations. Long-range planning for water should focus on developing an institutional framework of law and organizations that can use California's water resources in a more efficient and environmentally sustainable fashion.

REFERENCES AND NOTES

1. Many sources, e.g., Robert H. Williams, "Industrial Cogeneration," *Annual Review of Energy*, 3(1978):316-318.
2. Many sources, some examples: Arthur H. Rosenfeld, D.B. Goldstein, A.J. Lichtenberg, and P.O. Craig, "Saving Half of California's Energy and Peak Power in Buildings and Appliances via Long-Range Standards and Other Legislation," Lawrence Berkeley Laboratory, LBL-6865, 1978; Gerald Leach, Christopher Lewis, Ariane van Buren, Frederic Romig, and Gerald Foley, *A Low Energy Strategy for the United Kingdom* (London: Science Reviews, Ltd., 1979); Robert Stobaugh and Daniel Yergin, editors, *Energy Future* (New York, N.Y.: Random House, 1979), especially Chapter 6; Roger W. Sant, *The Least-Cost Energy Strategy* (Arlington, Virginia: The Energy Productivity Center, 1980); Robert H. Williams, "A $2 Gallon Political Opportunity," Princeton University, Center for Environmental Studies, PU/CEES-102, 1980; Marc H. Ross and Robert H. Williams, *Our Energy: Regaining Control* (New York: McGraw-Hill Book Co., 1981); Solar Energy Research Institute, *A New Prosperity: Building A Sustainable Energy Future* (Andover, Massachusetts: Brick House Publishing, 1981).
3. G.W. Harrison and L.J. Kimbell, *The Impact of Petroleum Shortfalls on the U.S. and California Economy*, Report to the California Energy Commission, Sacramento, June 1981. See also E.N. Krapels, *Oil Crisis Management* (Baltimore: Johns Hopkins University Press, 1980).
4. Susan McGowan, *Potential Methods of Assessing Energy Requirements for California Agriculture*, Report prepared for the California Energy Commission, 1980, p. 15.
5. C.V. Moore, "Impact of Increasing Energy Costs on Pump-Irrigated Agriculture," *California Agriculture*, 35, January-February 1981.
6. California Department of Water Resources, *Measuring Economic Impacts*, Bulletin 210 (Sacramento: The Resources Agency, 1980). The numbers herein are not likely to be accurate in detail, but their utility for gross comparisons is not disputed.
7. *Electricity Tomorrow*, California Energy Commission, Preliminary Report, October 30, 1980. See especially p. 2 and pp. 216-227.
8. John Harte, "Water Resource Constraints on Energy Development" in Ernest A. Engelbert, ed., *California Water Planning and Policy: Selected Issues* (University of California, Davis: Water Resources Center, 1978), pp. 65-87.
9. J. Harte and M. El-Gasseir, "Energy and Water," *Science*, 199, (1978).
10. Note: Large uncertainties inhere in trying to quantify important aspects of this water use. For example, hydropower is conventionally regarded as *not* consuming water, although it is responsible for significant, uncounted, evaporative losses from reservoirs. Further, comparison of numbers between sources is commonly not feasible; for example, Harte distinguishes between water "withdrawn" (i.e., returned to stream or groundwater and potentially available for further use) and water "consumed" (i.e., not available for further use), whereas DWR Bulletin 210 makes no such distinction.
11. *Energy Tomorrow: Challenges and Opportunities for California*, California Energy Commission, 1981 Biennial Report to the Legislature.
12. Edwin B. Roberts and Robert M. Hagan, "Energy Requirements of Alternatives in Water Supply and Wastewater Treatment," *National Water Supply Improvement Association Journal*, January 1977, pp. 1-15.
13. Edwin B. Roberts, "Energy Requirements for Water Supply and Use in California," *California Water Planning and Policy*, op. cit.
14. Trac H. Pham, "Technical Documentation of the Agricultural and Water Pumping Sectors Forecasting Model: Electricity and Natural Gas," California Energy Commission, Staff Draft, 1979.
15. Moore, op. cit.
16. J.E. Noel, B.D. Gardner, and C.V. Moore, "Optimal Regional Conjunctive Water Management," *American Journal of Agricultural Economics*, August 1980.

17. DWR expects to have lower cost power available for the State Water Project. That lower cost stems from 1) ability to avoid high-cost, peak-load power and 2) access to particular low-cost hydropower, and facilities with lower costs than PG&E power, both because they are tax-free and because they are built with government-backed bonds that have low interest rates. The second category of economies are public subsidies to the use of water. See *The Peripheral Canal and Other SB 200 Facilities,* DWR booklet, July 1981.

18. See reference 6, p. 104.

19. See Chapter II of this volume.

20. W.D. Watson, C.D. Nuckton, and R.E. Howitt, *Crop Production and Water Supply Characteristics of Kern County,* Giannini Foundation Information Series No. 80-1, Division of Agricultural Sciences Bulletin No. 1895 (University of California: Giannini Foundation, April 1980). Figure calculated from data in Tables 3 and 5. Approximately 110,000 acres in alfalfa, using 4.5 acre-feet per acre; 100,000 acres in rice, using 7 feet; 80,000 acres in wheat and sorghum, using 2 feet; 60,000 acres in barley, using 1.5 feet.

21. Input-Output models represent economic activity in terms of transactions between industrial sectors. The basis interindustry accounting system identifies the dollar value of sales from each producing sector to other producing sectors (intermediate-use sales) and to final demand (end-use sales). Final demand includes all "disappearances" of gross output—purchases for consumption, investment, government use, and exports from the economy. For the sake of consistency, intermediate sales from industry to industry should be exhaustive, even if there are many zero elements. By dividing the intermediate-use purchases of each producing sector by the total outlay (valued at producer's prices) of that sector we obtain a simple linear "recipe" of inputs required to produce one unit of that sector's output. One key assumption of IO analysis is that this recipe does not vary with changes in relative-input prices (i.e., factors of production are not substitutable) or with the number of units of output produced (i.e., there are constant returns to scale).

If we remove the household sector from the valued-added and final demand categories and include it in the intermediate-use category, then there is an important second-round effect of some change in final demand. Not only does the primary-stimulus sector buy inputs from other industrial sectors, but it also purchases labor-power from households. Just as the secondary-impact sectors in turn need to purchase inputs from other sectors, so does the household sector purchase goods for consumption according to a fixed recipe. The additional output resulting from the inclusion of the household sector is referred to as *induced* output charges to distinguish it from the *indirect* charges discussed earlier.

The direct, indirect, and induced use of a resource (e.g., water, energy) taken together constitute the *embodied* resource.

22. An appendix, available from authors on request, presents similar numbers for the direct and embodied use of "primary energy," broadly defined, in the same California sectors.

23. It is possible to modify the IO model for a large economy to reflect certain features of subregions of the economy—see G.W. Harrison, L.R. Hoover, R.E. Montijo, and R.J. Pifer, *Economic and Social Assessment of the Central Valley Project,* Report to the U.S. Department of the Interior, Western Regional Office, Sacramento, June 1980, 2 volumes.

24. J.P. Holdren, G. Morris, and I. Mintzer, "Environmental Impacts of Renewable Energy Sources," *Annual Review of Energy,* (5)1980.

25. R.M. Adams, G.A. King, and W.E. Johnston, "Effects of Energy Cost Increases and Regional Allocation Policies on Agricultural Production," *American Journal of Agricultural Economics,* August 1977.

26. See L.J. Kimbell, and G.W. Harrison, "General Equilibrium Analysis of Regional Fiscal Incidence," invited paper, Applied General Equilibrium Conference, San Diego, August 1981; forthcoming in H. Scarf & J. Shoven, eds., *Applied General Equilibrium Analysis* (University of Chicago Press, 1982).

27. R.B. Robie, "Pressures Created by a Severe Drought on Water Institutions," *American Journal of Agricultural Economics,* December 1977, p. 938-942.

28. An appendix is available from authors on request.

29. See reference 6.

30. Strictly speaking there is just one (arbitrary) "numeraire" in terms of which the price of water is measured (and hence can be compared against). In our simulations the prices of all other (nonwater) factors did not change significantly relative to one another.

CHAPTER VI

ENVIRONMENTAL QUALITY AND RECREATION

by

Don C. Erman, Roger W. Clark, and Richard L. Perrine

ABSTRACT

Water supplies and uses in California form a closely connected system that reaches throughout the state. Changes in use or development of supply thus have implications for diverse sectors and sometimes in distant locations. The ways in which current and future needs for water have been met have certain similarities whether for energy, agriculture, domestic supply, industry or other uses. Traditionally, water has been impounded, diverted from stream channels and pumped from subsurface aquifers.

Insufficient regard has usually been paid to the effect of these activities on aquatic and related terrestrial organisms and habitats. Return flow following human use is often of much lower quality than the original water source, and the combination of lower quality and reduced quantity (especially in streams) has resulted in significant deterioration of aquatic habitat. Large reductions of naturally produced anadromous fish in some North Coast rivers, in the San Joaquin region and the Delta are symptomatic of the change. Much recreation in California focuses on water-related activities, and high quality water rates high in the desires of most recreationists. Preserving and enhancing environmental quality of water supplies normally will contribute to high quality recreation as well.

Future trends in water use can follow two broad directions. One is the development approach in which more water is provided by physical structures and diversions and used by other sectors at the expense of in-stream values and natural ecological communities. The other is a reallocation approach. This approach would make use of already existing methods for conservation and reduction of demand, and increase their emphasis. Greater attention would be paid to preserving in-stream resources and meeting ecological needs before committing water for other uses. Difficult problems will remain in restoring already degraded biological systems unless some water can be "bought back" and allocated to areas where sufficient quality and quantity of water no longer exist.

THE SIGNIFICANCE OF ENVIRONMENTAL

QUALITY AND RECREATION

Decisions about the future use, supply and distribution of water in California will have major implications for environmental quality and recreation. In periods of low precipitation, current use by other sectors in California already exceeds supply; groundwater pumping exceeds recharge in some basins, and many streams have greatly reduced or changed in-stream resources as a result of past water allocations and changes in quality. How California will meet its water needs while also providing for recreation and protecting environmental quality are major concerns. All sectors are connected by water and making adjustments in use or supply in one sector usually affects others. What may appear as relatively small adjustments in reservoir outflows can have major impacts on down-stream plants and animals as well as on domestic or irrigation uses. The scheduled reduction in the amount of Colorado River water available to southern California will have reverberations throughout the water-producing sections of the state as each segment of the system is pressed to adjust to a new equilibrium. The slack in the system is already nearly eliminated under current usage; hence, no part should be viewed in isolation.

"Environmental quality" may be assessed in numerous areas of human life, including all the varied uses of water. Recreation is one of these areas. It is perhaps misleading to combine environmental quality and recreation in one discussion, making the two topics seem homologous. Nevertheless, to focus on both quality and recreation draws attention to the close interconnectedness of all water uses in California.

Most people equate a healthy environment, containing a diversity of plants and animals, with an absence of chemical and microbiological contaminants in the water supply. They consider a high quality environment and abundant opportunities for outdoor recreation as essentials to the good life. For many, "pure water" symbolizes environmental quality. They seek unpolluted mountain lakes and streams for a host of activities for which few economic measures exist. "Environmental quality" also implies a sufficient *quantity* of water to retain in perpetuity a healthy ecosystem—stream, lake or interdependent terrestrial habitat. An ample supply of water also provides highly desirable opportunities for recreation.[1] Sufficient flows of water are essential for river rafting, kayaking, and canoeing, and reservoir levels must be high enough for water skiing. Thus maintenance of ecological systems and opportunities for recreation both depend upon water quantity as well as quality.

National perceptions of environmental quality have shifted in the last 20 years. In general people are more aware of the changing face of the landscape, the risks of hazardous wastes, and the losses of wildlife species. Endangered species have become special indicators of ecological change and symbols of degraded environmental quality. A rare small fish or a strange plant may halt or delay major water projects. But different definitions of environmental quality exist: for some it may mean employment in a healthy workplace and a quiet, safe neighborhood, while for others it may mean pure water and natural landscapes. Such differences of interpretation produce varying opinions about the scale of protection needed to ensure environmental quality. For this reason, debates about the meaning of environmental quality will probably persist, and conflicts will continue to arise concerning the appropriateness of alternative actions.

Ecologists believe that the designation of wilderness areas and wild and scenic rivers may help to preserve intact large areas of relatively unmodified natural systems in order to study the role of various species. Most of the country is not in wilderness, however, and the importance of maintaining a variety of plant and animal life outside designated areas still remains. From a strictly utilitarian view, many wild species are sources of new medicines, of genetic material needed in agronomy, forestry, and fisheries, of energy sources and of food supplies.[2] Less well understood are their roles in preventing accumulation of waste, in cleansing water and soil of pollutants, and in recycling vital chemicals such as fertilizers.[3,4,5]

Natural scientists do not know how far we can continue disturbing ecosystems and eliminating seemingly unimportant species before major, perhaps irreversible, changes occur in human-life-sustaining forces: "...the simple fact is that man is perturbing natural systems that once were assumed to have essentially infinite buffering capacity."[6] Scientists and many public interest groups believe that providing for environmental quality in the nation's water future means protecting natural ecosystems and enhancing those degraded through earlier actions.

Water-associated outdoor recreation provides other important values. Water is obviously essential for swimming, fishing, boating, waterfowl hunting and water skiing, and is desirable for picnicking, camping, hiking and hunting. Stream and lakeside sites are popular locales for outdoor activities of all kinds. In wild and scenic areas water also serves as an aesthetic inspiration for innumerable paintings, photographs, and feelings of grandeur and tranquillity.[7,8,9] Though these values cannot strictly be measured, others can be quantified. A significant fishing industry, for example, depends on high quality streams to provide stock. In 1974 commercial fishermen in California landed over 5.1 millions pounds of salmon from the northern region and 2.7 million pounds from the San Francisco region, worth over $8 million. The sport catch in the same year was approximately 1.2 million pounds (234,000 fish).

Demand for Environmental Quality: Guardians and Costs

Retaining and restoring environmental quality has become an objective of national and state law. Numerous statutes have been enacted to assure the quality of our water. Few projects of significant scale can now be planned without due regard for their impact on environmental quality. Public polls continue to show that citizens want environmental protection even if it means higher costs for other necessities.[10,11] Thus, institutions and public opinion support a continuing demand for environmental quality.

Water management for environmental quality (and hence the recreational opportunities dependent on it) has fallen historically on governmental agencies representing the public at large. Costs associated with polluted water or changes in natural aquatic communities were and are still not fully absorbed by those using the water. These costs are not firmly established like those associated with the buying and selling of goods; they emerge from the perceptions and values of our society, and are fraught with uncertainties and differences in evaluating pristine water bodies, natural communities, or unknown risks of subtle pollution. The problems of evaluation are sometimes seen as a choice of "people versus fish," but for many observers such evaluation represents recognition that the interconnected system of water in California affects all of us as members of larger natural systems.

KEY VARIABLES AFFECTING ENVIRONMENTAL
QUALITY AND RECREATION

Water Demand and Water Use

In a sense, all the major users—energy, agriculture, municipalities, industry—are the major variables affecting environmental quality and recreation. It is their combined demand for water (especially agriculture) and the changes in quality resulting from use which influence what remains for recreation and what the impact on the environment will be.

The Second National Water Assessment[12] has projected future water withdrawals and consumption to the year 2000 for regions of the U.S. For California this assessment projected an increase in withdrawals of about 4 percent more than in 1975, although consumption will actually increase 11 percent because more water will be reused. Reuse (e.g., recycling water for power plant cooling instead of once-through cooling; more efficient agricultural irrigation) may lead to higher rates of consumptive use in the future because water is lost to the atmosphere each time it is recycled. While recycling practices are often viewed as conservation measures, they may also lead to a loss in water quality and quantity downstream and, hence, to problems for in-stream uses.

To meet demand for water, the traditional approach in California and the arid West in general has been to store water in impoundments, increase groundwater pumping, and transfer water from areas of relative surplus to areas of relative deficit. The effects of these actions on environmental quality are already significant and if continued will make reconciliations with needs of a quality environment more difficult.

This traditional approach of planning for increased demand before considering environmental needs has created conflicts and crises over water. Projected demand becomes a self-fulfilling prophecy when cheap supplies and discount pricing lead to growth in water consumption. Meeting ever-increasing demands, however, need not be the basic assumption on which solutions to future conflicts are based. Common sense tells us that ultimately down the road comes a point where there is *no more water*. At that point no options are left. It seems wiser to limit demands now—especially when the pattern of environmental effects from current practices is already clear.

Growth of Population Centers

Human population growth is expected to increase in California and in the world. As long as this growth continues, solutions to water or other resource problems will be hard to come by. Adjustments in the way water is used (see Chapter III) can forestall shortages but not eliminate them if growth continues. In particular, expansion of urban areas will have significant impacts on the environment.

Urban expansion brings an increasing demand for high quality water for domestic purposes and at the same time may accelerate deterioration of local environmental quality. Wildland habitat is lost, species of plants and animals decrease or disappear, and surrounding agricultural land is gradually absorbed by housing or support services. Expanding urban areas also create more impervious surfaces, resulting in an increase in the magnitude of stream flooding.[13] Such flooding results in damage to homes and property on flood plains. As sediment loads increase in streams, aesthetic values may be lost due to widening and filling of the stream channel, and ecological values are diminished by habitat destruction and by declines in species diversity.[14] Careful zoning or land classification has sometimes proven successful in protecting lands around urban areas in California,[15] but new measures may be necessary in the future.

A river or stream may run for tens, hundreds, or thousands of miles, providing millions of people with opportunities for recreation, enjoyment of wildlife, and many intangible values—peacefulness, solitude, a chance to escape urban life.[16,17] The flood plain, a natural part of the river, is not suitable for human settlement; when built on, it often becomes a publicly subsidized problem area, necessitating extremely costly protective structures to save property from periodic natural flooding.

Studies conducted throughout the 1970s have indicated that demand for water recreation may never be totally satisfied, especially near major population centers. Rising energy costs mean that the distance traveled to reach recreation sites has substantially greater importance.[18] Many "river towns" have thus begun to realize the significant recreational value of open spaces, parks, and hiking trails along the river's edge, which provide urban dwellers with recreation close to home. Such areas also make people more aware of the quality of water in the river. Obvious examples are the City of Sacramento and many of the San Francisco Bay area communities. In these and other locations, water which has been developed for domestic use has the added benefits of providing recreation and environmental protection. Watershed lands of utility districts provide nearby open space and protection of semiwild habitats. Many domestic water storage reservoirs, even when restricted as swimming areas, are open to boating, fishing, and other outdoor activities. Full public access to such water resources, however, has been slow in coming. More cooperation with local communities is possible. At the same time better means for paying the costs of watershed control, safety, and public access must be found instead of relying primarily on those who pay their water bills.

Concentration of people in urban areas results in larger and more centralized sewage treatment facilities. California has been rated one of the worst regions in the U.S. for point source (sewage outfall) discharges which result in high biochemical oxygen demand (BOD) and total suspended solids (TSS). These measures are two conventional indicators of water quality and are considered inversely related to quality. Over 60 percent of the BOD and 50-60 percent of the TSS come from point sources in California; using the best practical technology for treatment could reduce BOD to 30-40 percent of the total from point sources.[19] However, some experts predict that with increasing size and centralization of sewage treatment facilities, pollution will continue because treatment is not complete (especially in systems that combine domestic and nondomestic wastes), and except under the strictest cases, does not remove nutrients and other chemicals.[20] The result over the next few decades may well be gradual worsening of surface water quality in urban areas and yet greater cost for water treatment facilities.

Concentrated urban areas are also major emitters of oxides of nitrogen and sulfur that eventually "fall out" as acid rain.[21] The effects of acid rain have been dramatic in the northeast of Canada and the U.S. and in Scandinavia.[22,23] Increasingly acid water in lakes has in some cases eliminated fish populations, and acid rain on soils may be causing important changes in chemical composition and fertility. Potential sites of greatest trouble are where geological rock formations provide little buffering for the increase in acidity. The granite regions of the Sierra, lying downwind from major source areas of acid rain and having rocks of characteristically poor buffering capacity, are highly susceptible to this pollution and may deteriorate rapidly. Elsewhere the effects of acid rain have been recognized more slowly because the areas affected were far removed from the cause and the changes were gradual.

Impoundments

Probably no single form of water development has as much impact on environme.ital quality and recreation as dams. Dams eliminate productive bottom lands which are essential to wildlife (and in many areas essential to farmers as well). Loss of winter range for big game has been a major problem of impoundments throughout the West.[24] In the filling of Trinity and Lewiston Reservoirs the area population of black-tailed deer was reduced an estimated 4,000 to 7,500 animals.[25] Extensive attempts to mitigate these losses by habitat improvement have been only partially successful, and even potential conversion of timber-producing lands to deer habitat would not restore the area's deer producing potential.[26] This example illustrates the irreplaceability of certain wildlife habitats; many other organisms also depend on the vegetation and related features along water courses.

For migratory fish such as steelhead trout and salmon, dams are formidable barriers to up-stream spawning migrations. Even where fish ladders allow some passage, they present obstacles to later down-stream escape of young on their seaward journey. The Trinity River, for example, has been a major spawning ground for fish in the Klamath River system. Completion in 1963 of dams, impoundments, and hydroelectric power facilities on the Trinity River Division of the Central Valley Project destroyed an unknown amount of coho salmon habitat, 59 miles of chinook salmon spawning and nursery habitat, and 109 miles of similar habitat for steelhead trout.[27] Major losses of chinook salmon and steelhead trout (80 percent and 60 percent reductions respectively, compared to pre-project populations) have occurred on the river in part as a consequence of impoundments.

In addition, conditions below an impoundment change as a result of new temperature and flow regimes. These changes are often deleterious to native plants and animals in the streams; as a result less desirable exotic species, particularly fish, may come to predominate.[28] In California's inland waters 50 of the 133 fish species are now exotic. This shift has resulted from extensive changes in natural waterways which favor exotics over native species as well as from the deliberate or accidental introduction of exotic species.[29] (Not all exotics, of course, are problem species. A few, e.g., striped bass, various trout, and some sunfishes, are highly prized sport fish adapted to their new surroundings.)

While impoundments change and destroy many stream-dependent communities, they provide lake-dependent organisms new habitat. In 1980 the State Water Project provided 5.7 million days of recreation activity around reservoirs and aqueducts.[30] Water supply reservoirs near population centers are another source of water-based recreation. Management of these reservoirs for recreational boating, fishing and other uses is an enormous task. Sport fishing, for example, is often dependent on the release of hatchery-grown fish of various sizes. In theory, multipurpose reservoirs can be managed to provide many environmental objectives. In practice, however, most have a dominant use which supersedes other uses.[31] Fluctuating water levels in some reservoirs reduce the productivity of shallow zones and make recreation difficult. Yet down-stream demands often make such shoreline fluctuations common. Increasing future demands on stored water will likely increase the frequency and magnitude of water level fluctuations. Thus in the future reservoirs may provide less useful recreation. Reservoirs also substitute one kind of recreation for another—lake for stream. In some cases existing impoundments may provide a means of rehabilitating degraded down-stream areas by water exchanges or modification of project operation[32] and may thus enhance environmental quality and recreation.

Diversion

Removal of water from in-stream flows may also affect environmental quality. Intensive studies of the flow requirements of stream biota are now defining the quantitative relationships between stream hydrologic variables (depth, current, etc.) and survival of organisms.[33,34] Such research may lead to a more definite answer to the question of how much water is needed in streams to sustain aquatic communities.

Once again, an example from the Trinity River is illustrative of the effects of diversion. Salmon and trout habitat in the Trinity River is currently severely limited because of the amount of water diverted up-stream. Current project releases from the Trinity River Division of the Central Valley Project amount to 120,500 acre-feet per year for down-stream needs. By way of contrast, to restore fish populations to pre-project levels an estimated 340,000 acre-feet per year would have to be released. This requirement is in addition to watershed rehabilitation, streambed management and need for regulation of fish harvest, and does not fully address the need for large peak flows to flush out sediments.[35]

These estimates are not, however, universally accepted, and other investigators using different methods have proposed different flows. The case illustrates two important facets of in-stream flow evaluation. First, different methodologies for determining flow needed to sustain a fishery or a stream ecosystem (at various levels) may produce different results.[36] Second, the entire field of research and analysis of in-stream flow is relatively new. Refinement of techniques is to be expected as the science matures. In the meantime, best estimates will continue to be provided; with follow-up, monitoring recommendations can be judged and, if necessary, readjusted.[37]

The Secretary of the Interior is authorized to regulate flow from the Trinity River Division to preserve fish and wildlife. Additional releases (above 120,500 acre-feet) will subtract from the Central Valley Project. The Trinity Division currently makes up 14 percent of the Project's "firm yield".[38] In addition to supplying water for irrigation, the Trinity provides 20 percent of the 5.5 billion kwh of hydroelectric generation for the entire Project.

Declines of salmon on the Merced River similar to those on the Trinity followed impoundment and diversion of water for irrigation. Increased flows on the Merced River were eventually negotiated for salmon spawning when Exchequer Dam was enlarged. From a low of 100 spawners a year in the early 1960s, as many as 1000 fish now use the spawning channels made possible by increased flows.[39]

Diversion is also a major constraint on the environment of the Sacramento-San Joaquin Delta. Large pumps in the south Delta remove freshwater for the federal Central Valley Project and California's State Water Project. These projects divert 30 to 40 percent of the inflow to the Delta; when local consumption is included, up to 80 percent of inflow is diverted.[40] These diversions cause flow reversals in some channels, and up-stream intrusions of saline water. Complex changes in the hydrology of the Delta have resulted in losses of many aquatic organisms which use the area extensively as a nursery ground. A major loss of fish (e.g., striped bass) occurs by direct transport of eggs and young out of the Delta by pumps.[41] Expensive screen devices at intakes are marginally successful, but salvaged organisms must be hauled by truck back to a "safe" location. The landward flow of seawater as a result of diversion of freshwater also threatens to increase the salinity for part of the Contra Costa County domestic water supply. The proposed Peripheral Canal would divert water from the Sacramento River above the Delta and, if a large fish screen is successful, solve many of the problems associated with the large pumps. However, without firm regulations for flow standards and water quality, the solution may be only transitory.

Another example of great current interest is Mono Lake. This naturally saline lake, which receives the freshwater runoff from a portion of the eastern Sierra, has had most of its surface inflow siphoned off for many years.[42] As a result, the lake has been receding. The benefit has been a cheap, energy-efficient source of supply for about one-sixth of the eastern Sierra fraction of Los Angeles' water supply. An indigenous brine shrimp *(Artemia monica)* and brine flies *(Ephydra hians)* provide a food source for a host of nesting and migratory birds at Mono Lake. In turn, the shrimp and flies are supported by a food-chain of microorganisms which have adapted to the salty lake waters. One result of the lowered lake level is that nesting colonies of California gulls *(Larus californicus)* originally sited on protective islands have become attached to the mainland, exposing them to predation. Interest groups have become incensed by this potential sacrifice of a unique significant wildlife species to obtain a modest added source of cheap water.

Although return of diverted water after use to natural channels makes a significant contribution to annual flows, greater reuse and hence consumption may lead to further reductions in in-stream flows, unless more releases are made to compensate. Returned water, especially from irrigated agriculture, is greatly lowered in quality. Streams in the Central Valley become loaded with nitrogen and phosphorus and contain the residues of pesticides. Many of the streams (42 percent) now have medium or high (51 percent) levels of nitrogen, and 57 percent have very high concentrations of phosphorus. Similarly, high concentrations of nutrients are found in other agricultural areas of the state.[43] These nutrients contribute excessive fertility to streams and lakes into which they flow.

Groundwater

Concern over quality and excessive use of groundwater in California is a historical problem. As recently as January 1980, the California Department of Health Services closed 37 public wells supplying water to more than 400,000 people in the San Gabriel Valley, because of contamination with hazardous trichlorethylene.[44] Concern for potential health risk has strongly inhibited the development of reuse of treated wastewater through groundwater injection in southern California.[45] Overuse and the consequent lowering of groundwater quality are major problems in the San Joaquin Basin where 40 percent of the water for irrigation comes from within the basin, mostly from groundwater. Overdrafting has resulted in massive land subsidence and reduction of underground water storage capacity. This basin has been identified as one of the few national regions suffering from all major forces of desertification: poor drainage of agricultural lands, overgrazing, cultivation of highly erodible soils, overdraft of groundwater, and damage from off-road vehicles.[46]

In other regions, contamination of groundwater has occurred through historical land practices and waste disposal. Septic tanks have proven to be effective waste treatment systems, yet where septic tank waste disposal systems are concentrated, contamination of groundwater has resulted.[47] Surveys of wells in the Los Angeles area found widespread instances of nitrate concentrations exceeding the Public Health Service drinking water standard of 24 mg/liter.[48] Sources probably included fertilizer applications made years earlier, septic tank leach fields, and natural causes. Elsewhere in southern California high nitrate concentrations are suspected to result from land fills and land disposal of waste.[49]

The general problem of land disposal of wastes with subsequent contamination of ground and surface water supplies is of potentially enormous significance. Several factors contribute to this problem. First is an increasing level of activities which produce wastewater—salt from irrigation return, mining (as demand for metals increases) and petroleum production.[50] Second, as environmental standards are applied more stringently to air and water quality, industry and municipalities produce and retain more wastes in the process of meeting standards; these wastes are disposed on land. Third, alternatives to land disposal are currently limited. The Marine Protection, Research and Sanctuaries Act of 1972, for example, limits ocean dumping of hazardous wastes. As a result the Environmental Protection Agency is limiting dumping: 10.8 million tons in 1973 down to 8.7 million tons in 1979, with ocean disposal of municipal sewage sludge and harmful industrial wastes to end in 1981.[51] Land disposal of wastes will continue to increase until alternative effective reuse and recovery systems are developed and implemented.

A proposed major solution for the problem of San Joaquin soil and groundwater salinity is construction of a drain facility. The drain would ultimately transport saline water to the middle of the Delta. Disposal into the delta region, however, may become another example of transfer of an environmental concern to downstream users.[52]

Land Use in Undeveloped Areas

Most water in California originates in wildlands where timber production and grazing are predominant activities. Environmental quality is intimately linked with these and other land-use practices, for food, fiber and energy production all have impacts on terrestrial and aquatic systems. Improperly conducted, these activities can lead to accelerated rates of erosion and subsequent stream sedimentation. Careful conversion of some brushlands by controlled burning has been suggested as a means of increasing water flow from these watersheds. Often brushland manipulation can provide benefits to game animals and reduce the threat of wildfire. In order to minimize risks of erosion, however, converted areas must be small in size and carefully selected by slope and soil type.[53,54]

In some areas of the north coast where natural rates of erosion are among the highest in the world, human disturbance from logging has resulted in 2 to 20 times the natural erosion rate.[55] Loss of salmon spawning and rearing areas on the Trinity River have been linked to watershed deterioration which increased sedimentation, especially without flood flows to flush out sediments.[56] Road systems are often the primary source of erosion and sedimentation through improper water drainage, bank failure, and inadequate stream crossings. Logging also is a major source of "slump."[57] Special methods for estimating erosion hazards and for modifying logging and road construction are needed.[58,59]

Once sediment reaches a stream, its impact is felt at all levels of the food web.[60,61] If the natural drainage pattern of the watershed is substantially altered—such as by extensive road networks or surface mining—sediment loss to streams may become a persistent problem, collecting in down-stream impoundments and causing reduced storage capacity in reservoirs.

After the 1976 National Forest Management Act called for improved practices, the Secretary of Agriculture issued specific directions in 1979 for land management planning for all national forests, aimed at achieving a balance between goals of economic efficiency and environmental quality. Timber harvest was to be limited to a level that can be sustained in perpetuity ("even flow" of timber). Short term departures from "even flow" nevertheless are allowed—for example, President Carter requested such a departure in 1979 with an aim toward lowering housing costs and inflation. Thus federal forest practices may again contribute to degradation of watersheds in California if proper precautions are not taken during accelerated harvests.

Preventing stream sedimentation and maintaining diversity of plants and animals are expressed goals in forest management. The California Forest Practices Act (Z'berg-Nejedly) requires private timber operators to prevent water quality degradation. For example, clearcutting large areas or other extensive timber harvesting activities adjacent to rivers have impacts beyond stream sedimentation. Both federal and state actions have drawn attention to the need to protect zones of vegetation adjacent to water bodies, which may act as buffers to climatic conditions (insulating water from temperature extremes) and reduce the impact of land use.[62] Although particularly important as wildlife habitat, few such undisturbed zones remain along many streams in the agricultural valleys or in heavy timber-producing areas. Rapid change in vegetation has led to the loss or threatened loss of many terrestrial and aquatic organisms. Even if small areas of habitat remain, they seem to be insufficient to protect dwindling populations.[63]

A number of California's rivers have been accorded wild and scenic status—a tribute to their immense natural beauty and their opportunities for recreational activities. They are not yet, however, fully protected.[64] Efforts toward developing wild river management plans continue. Regulation of land use practices along major and tributary waterways has been slow in coming, and it may take years before environmental benefits are achieved.

ALTERNATIVE FUTURES FOR ENVIRONMENTAL
QUALITY AND RECREATION

Current Status

Without significant change in the current supply, use, or allocation of water, environmental quality will continue to decline and recreational opportunities will be diminished throughout the state. Insufficient in-stream flows from existing projects will persist, and reductions in native aquatic populations will continue. Water quality problems, especially those associated with agricultural return flows, will be improved only where water use is voluntarily reduced and more efficient technology is adopted. Overdrafting of groundwater in the San Joaquin Basin, land subsidence, and desertification will expand in severity, with some areas becoming irreversibly damaged due to diminished recharge capacity and accelerated soil loss.

Under these conditions, significant natural resources such as Mono Lake would in the future be permanently lost, as would possibly unique genetic strains of salmon which barely persist in tributaries of the San Joaquin and elsewhere. Pressures to expand existing systems such as San Francisco's Hetch Hetchy Project, and to build new systems such as Southern California Edison's Upper San

Joaquin Project, would continue. Thus, additional aquatic systems would be altered, natural landscapes deluged, and riparian habitats lost.

Environmental quality would continue to be a secondary consideration in decisions to supply water demanded by other sectors. Incomplete mitigation of losses in environmental quality would persist, and recreational opportunities such as stream fishing for native species would diminish. Increasing concerns for environmental quality by the general public and by organized groups would perpetuate and exacerbate existing political and legal conflicts throughout California. During "crisis" periods of below average water yield, pressure would build to lift protective regulations. Stressed systems with suboptimal instream flows or poor water quality may be unable to absorb further stress and could be forever lost. Thus, the future for environmental quality and recreation under current conditions would be a gradual decline, with rapid deterioration occurring during droughts and periods when environmental safeguards are suspended.

Reallocation

Environmental quality and recreation could potentially improve under a state-sponsored system for reallocating existing water supplies. Under this system, marketlike mechanisms for redistributing surface water and for the sale or rental of water would reduce inefficiencies in the current system of allocation. But like other market systems, there remains an unresolved problem in giving full consideration to nonmarket values such as scenery, clean water, in-stream flows and the freedom to recreate in a natural setting. A fuller application of the Public Trust Doctrine may be the best basis for establishing and protecting such uses.[65]

If environmental quality is to benefit from this alternative, it must be treated as coequal with other allocation objectives. For example, as water rights are transferred to new users, regulatory agencies such as the State Water Resources Control Board should review and revise in-stream flow requirements. Specific legislation and implementation measures may also be required to protect special ecosystems such as Mono Lake and the Delta.

Other improvements in environmental quality may come about through an emphasis on maximizing water conservation. Agencies which formerly concentrated on developing new water supplies could shift their efforts toward improving efficiency of use and assisting water users in learning how to conserve existing supplies. Funds committed to construction could be used for improving wastewater treatment, for research and development of efficient irrigation systems, and for providing loans, grants, and other incentives to individuals and industries who need capital for improving operations.

Although such measures may halt declines in environmental quality, emphasis must still be placed on restoring degraded systems. Reallocation must include water for improving in-stream flows, for restoring riparian habitats, for recharging groundwater supplies, and for providing a full range of water-based recreation opportunities. Recent changes in the Water Resources Control Board Administrative Code procedures may improve the ability of the Board to implement measures to protect in-stream flows and recreational uses,[66] but these new procedures already are under legal challenge.

Within the marketlike structure envisioned for reallocating water, ways should be developed for water users to assume the full costs of their use. Some private groups would purchase conservation rights just as municipal and agricultural users would purchase reallocation rights. However, state agencies would continue to play a key role in protecting in-stream flows and riparian habitats and in restoring degraded watercourses.

This alternative holds the greatest potential for improving environmental quality and recreation. As methods improve for estimating the amount of water needed to protect environmental quality, there must be provisions for readjusting allocations. All sectors should assume a greater responsibility in assuring that non-market values become fully integrated into the reallocation structure.

Development

This alternative would perpetuate the traditional approach to water problems in California, i.e., creation of new supplies by physical development. Environmental costs would be high; negative effects of new development would spread over even a greater area and affect a larger population of people, plants, and animals. Violent conflicts between development interests and environmental groups would increase, and costly delays in development could be expected. There would be additional costs associated with law enforcement and with the legal actions which inevitably would follow.

If future development departed from the large capital-intensive projects of the past, modest improvements in environmental quality could occur. Modifications such as enclosing transfer canals could reduce evaporation and potentially reduce the need for new reservoirs. But unless such developments are combined with a statewide effort to improve efficiency and to reduce consumption, environmental quality would continue to decline.

Reservoir-based recreation would benefit from development. There would be more opportunities for water skiing (assuming economic conditions allow people to purchase boats and equipment), and operators of lakeside resorts would proliferate. (But new sites would likely be far from cities and masses of people, necessarily limiting their benefits.) River and stream-based recreation would decline, and conflicts between recreationists would become more common. Opportunities to participate in a spectrum of water-based recreation activities would also decline, as would opportunities to enjoy the wild and scenic remnants of California's landscape.

Perhaps the greatest cost associated with the development alternative is that it reduces options for the future. A major drought would be catastrophic in an economy based on inflated levels of consumption and waste fostered by continued development. A foreign pathogen could eliminate domestic strains of sport fishes common to the homogeneous habitat of reservoirs. Finally, development would merely delay the time when Californians *must* confront the question of how to live with a limited supply of water.

Preferred Alternative

Our preferred alternative would emphasize reallocation and conservation of California's water to achieve modest increases in the supply, while improving degraded watercourses and protecting existing opportunities for water-based recreation. Reallocation should be accompanied by programs and incentives to promote conservation and to restore damaged watercourses and to fully support nonmarket values such as wetlands. Reallocation would be a positive step toward a more efficient system of water distribution and use. It responds to short-term needs and may delay additional losses in environmental quality and recreation. But fundamental shifts are needed in our willingness to accept ultimate limits in the supply of water. Development of new water supplies would be only a short-term solution to a long-term problem. The viability of obscure fish and aquatic populations is merely an index of the viability of entire ecosystems. Unless measures are implemented to restore and protect the productivity of these systems, our quality of life and potential for the future will be sacrificed.

Environmental quality and recreation are easily ignored in responding to the needs of a growing economy. It is convenient to discount the costs borne by future generations when the present benefits of more water appear so essential. We do not advocate environmental quality at the expense of farming, logging, construction, or any of the many livelihoods which depend upon water and watershed lands. Rather, we support a creative search for means to enhance our many "ways of life" within limited supplies of water and other resources.

REFERENCES AND NOTES

1. Valerius Geist, "Wildlife and People in an Urban Environment—the Biology of Cohabitation," undated manuscript (University of Calgary, Alberta, Canada: Faculty of Environmental Design).
2. Council on Environmental Quality, *Environmental Quality—1980: The Eleventh Annual Report of the Council on Environmental Quality.* (Washington D.C.: U.S. Government Printing Office, 1980).
3. W.E. Westman, "How Much are Nature's Services Worth?", *Science* 197(1977):960-964.
4. B. Schlesinger, "Natural Removal Mechanisms for Chemical Pollutants in the Environment," *BioScience* 29(1979):2, 95-101.
5. D. Pimentel et al., "Environmental Quality and Natural Biota," *BioScience* 30(1980):750-755.
6. W.S. Fyfe, "The Environmental Crisis: Quantifying Geosphere Interactions," *Science* 213(1981):105-110.
7. William Dritschilo et al., *California's North Coast Wild and Scenic Rivers: Analysis of Inter-Agency Planning and Technical Issues,* Report No. 80-35 (University of California, Los Angeles: Environmental Science and Engineering, 1980).
8. Janet Baas, F. Dane Westerdahl and Richard L. Perrine, eds., *Non-Point Source Water Quality Monitoring, Inyo National Forest, 1975,* Water Resources Center Contribution No. 156 (University of California, Davis: Water Resources Center, March 1976).
9. Valerius Geist, "A Philosophical Look at Recreational Impact on Wildlands," unpublished manuscript (University of Calgary, Alberta, Canada: Faculty of Environmental Design, 1978).
10. Council on Environmental Quality, *Public Opinion on Environmental Issues.* (Washington D.C.: U.S. Government Printing Office, 1980).
11. "National Affairs," *Newsweek,* June 29, 1981, p. 29.
12. U.S. Water Resources Council, *The Nation's Water Resources 1975—2000.* Vol. 2, *Water Quality, Quantity and Related Land Considerations. Second National Water Assessment.* (Washington D.C.: U.S. Government Printing Office, December 1978).
13. T. Dunne, and L.B. Leopold, *Water in Environmental Planning* (San Francisco: W.H. Freeman and Company, 1978).
14. R.M. Ragan, A.J. Dietemann, and R.A. Moore., *Effects of Urbanization on the Hydrological Regime and on Water Quality* In Proceedings, Amsterdam Symposium (International Association of Hydrological Sciences and UNESCO, 1977), pp. 324-333.
15. R.L. Wall, "California's Agricultural Land Preservation Programs," *Land Use: Tough Choices in Today's World* (Ankeny, Iowa: Soil Conservation Society of America, 1977), pp. 131-134.
16. Robert K. Kawaratani and Richard L. Perrine, eds., *Wilderness Water Quality: Bishop Creek Baseline Study, 1974,* Water Resources Center Contribution No. 150 (University of California, Davis: Water Resources Center, June 1975).
17. Geist, "Wildlife and People in an Urban Environment—the Biology of Cohabitation."

18. Ibid.

19. U.S. Water Resources Council, *The Nation's Water Resources 1975—2000.*

20. M.L. L'Vovich, *World Water Resources and Their Future,* translation edited by R.L. Nace (New York: American Geophysical Union, 1979).

21. J.G. McColl, *A Survey of Acid Precipitation in Northern California,* Final Report, Project CA-B-SPN-3664-H, University of California, Berkeley, 1980.

22. "How Many More Lakes Have to Die?" *Canada Today* 12(1981):2, 1-11.

23. J.P. Nilssen, "Acidification of a Small Watershed in Southern Norway and Some Characteristics of Acidic Aquatic Environments" *Int. Rev. Geo. Hydrobiol.* 65(1981):177-207.

24. T.W. Box, "Some Environmental Effects of Water Use in Western Energy Development," in *Energy, Water and the West,* ed. E.R. Gillette (Washington D.C.: American Association for the Advancement of Science, 1976), pp. 37-40.

25. J.G. Kie et al., "Mitigating the Effects of Reservoir Development on Black-tailed Deer in Trinity County, California." *Cal-Neva Wildlife Trans.* (1980), pp. 27-40.

26. Box, in *Energy, Water and the West,* ed. E.R. Gillette.

27. U.S. Fish and Wildlife Service, *Management of River Flows to Mitigate the Loss of the Anadromous Fishery of the Trinity River, California,* Final Environmental Impact Statement, Vol. 1 (Sacramento, California: 1980).

28. P.B. Moyle and R.D. Nichols, "Decline of the Native Fish Fauna of the Sierra Nevada Foothills, Central California," *American Midland Naturalist* 92(1974):72-83.

29. P.B. Moyle, "Fish Introductions in California: History and Impact on Native Fishes," *Biological Conservation* 9(1976):101-118.

30. A.C. Gooch, California Department of Water Resources, personal communication, June 1981.

31. J.S. Bain, "Water Resource Development in California: The Comparative Efficiency of Local, State, and Federal Agencies," in T.H. Campbell and R.O. Sylvester, eds., *Water Resource Management and Public Policy* (Seattle: University of Washington Press, 1969), pp. 12-29.

32. Governor's Commission to Review California Water Rights Law, *Final Report,* Sacramento, California, December 1978.

33. J.S. Gore, "A Technique for Predicting In-stream Flow Requirements of Benthic Macroinvertebrates," *Freshwater Biology* 8(1978):141-151.

34. K. Bayha, *Instream Flow Methodologies for Regional and National Assessment.* Instream Flow Information Paper No. 7 (Washington D.C.: U.S. Fish and Wildlife Service, 1978).

35. U.S. Fish and Wildlife Service, *Management of River Flows to Mitigate the Loss of the Anadromous Fishery of the Trinity River, California.*

36. Bayha, *Instream Flow Methodologies for Regional and National Assessments.*

37. Governor's Commission to Review California Water Rights Law, *Final Report.*

38. U.S. Fish and Wildlife Service, *Management of River Flows to Mitigate the Loss of the Anadromous Fishery of the Trinity River, California.*

39. L. Feinberg and T. Morgan, *California's Salmon Resource: Its Biology, Use and Management.* Sea Grant Report Series 3, California Sea Grant College Program No. 72 (University of California, La Jolla: Institute of Marine Resources).

40. D.E. Stevens and H.K. Chadwick, "Sacramento-San Joaquin Estuary—Biology and Hydrology," *Fisheries* 4(1979):2-6.

41. Jack J. Coe, et al., "Report of Interagency Task Force on Mono Lake." (Sacramento: California Department of Water Resources, December 1979).

42. Thomas R. Vale, "Mono Lake, California: Saving a Lake or Serving a City?", *Environmental Conservation* 7(1980):190-192.

43. E.G. Farnworth et al., *Impacts of Sediment and Nutrients on Biota in Surface Waters of the United States* (Athens, Georgia: Environmental Research Laboratory, Office of Research and Development, United States Environmental Protection Agency, 1979).

44. Council on Environmental Quality, *Environmental Quality—1980.*

45. Ernest A. Englebert and Richard L. Perrine, eds., *Institutional Barriers to Waste Water Reuse in Southern California,* Report OWRT/RU-79/4, (U.S. Department of the Interior, Office of Water Research and Technology, 1979).

46. Council on Environmental Quality, *Environmental Quality—1980.*

47. U.S. Environmental Protection Agency, *The Report to Congress: Waste Disposal Practices and Their Effects on Groundwater,* Executive Summary (Washington D.C.: U.S. Government Printing Office, 1977).

48. California Department of Water Resources, *Nitrates in Ground Water in the Los Angeles Drainage Province* (Department of Water Resources, Southern District, 1977).
49. D.K. Fuhriman and J.R. Barton, *Ground Water Pollution in Arizona, California, Nevada and Utah,* Water Pollution Control Research Series (Washington D.C.: U.S. Environmental Protection Agency, 1971).
50. U.S. Water Resources Council, *The Nation's Water Resources 1975—2000.*
51. Council on Environmental Quality, *Environmental Quality—1980.*
52. U.S. Water Resources Council, *The Nation's Water Resources 1975—2000.*
53. California Department of Forestry, Chaparral Management Program, *Final Environmental Impact Report* (Sacramento: 1981).
54. U.S. Forest Service, Brushland Management, *The Grindstone Way* (Mendocino National Forest, U.S. Forest Service, Pacific Southwest Region, 1981).
55. R.N. Coats, "The Road to Erosion," *Environment* 20:16-39 (1978).
56. U.S. Fish and Wildlife Service, *Management of River Flows to Mitigate the Loss of the Anadromous Fishery of the Trinity River, California.*
57. S. Gresswell, D. Heller, and D.N. Swanston, "Mass Movement Response to Forest Management in the Central Oregon Coast Ranges," USDA Forest Service Resource Bulletin PNW-84 (Portland, Oregon: Pacific Northwest Forest and Range Experiment Station, 1979).
58. D.A. Falletti, "Sediment Prediction in Wildland Environments: A Review," *Soil Erosion: Prediction and Control,* Proceedings of a National Conference on Soil Erosion (Ankeny, Iowa: Soil Conservation Society of America, 1976), pp. 183-192.
59. R.M. Rice and S.A. Sherbin, *Estimating Sedimentation From an Erosion—Hazard Rating,* USDA Forest Service Research Note PSW-323 (Berkeley, California: Pacific Southwest Forest and Range Experiment Station, 1977).
60. Farnworth, et al., *Impacts of Sediment and Nutrients on Biota in Surface Waters of the United States.*
61. D.C. Erman, J.D. Newbold and K.B. Roby, *Evaluation of Streamside Bufferstrips for Protecting Aquatic Organisms,* Water Resources Center Contribution No. 165 (University of California, Davis: Water Resources Center, 1977).
62. J.R. Karr and I.J. Schlosser, *Impact of Nearstream Vegetation and Stream Morphology on Water Quality and Stream Biota,* Ecological Research Series EPA-600/3-77-097 (Athens, Georgia: U.S. Environmental Protection Agency, 1977).
63. Council on Environmental Quality, *Environmental Quality—1980.*
64. Dritschilo et al., *California's North Coast Wild and Scenic Rivers: Analysis of Inter-Agency Planning and Technical Issues.*
65. F.E. Smith, *The Public Trust Doctrine, Instream Flows and Resources,* discussion paper prepared by The California Water Policy Center (Sacramento: U.S. Fish and Wildlife Service, 1980).
66. California Administrative Code, Title 23, Sec. 1050-1060, *Procedures for Protecting Instream Beneficial Uses* (Sacramento: State Water Resources Control Board, 1980).

CHAPTER VII

LIFESTYLES

by

Ted K. Bradshaw, Edward Vine, and Gunther Barth

ABSTRACT

As competition for water increases in California in the coming years, potential resolution of the water imbalance will be focused not only on technical "fixes" but also on changes in lifestyles which affect the patterns of consumption and development of water. Different patterns of water use are evident in California's culture and tradition. Through the evaluation of water-intensive and water-conserving modes of behavior, lifestyles can be assessed for their adaptability to future change.

In examining the relationship between lifestyles and water, a typology was constructed on the basis of two variables: (1) consumption of water versus activities in or on the water which allow multiple uses, and (2) direct use of water versus indirect (embodied) use of water. This typology resulted in four different categories: (1) direct residential consumption of water for gardening, bathing, cooking, and drinking; (2) indirect consumption of water embodied in food and manufactured goods; (3) direct "experience" of water as in sports and recreation; and (4) indirect "experience" of water as part of tourist sites and ecological settings. Examination of these categories reveals that certain lifestyles use or depend on large quantities of water, and that some of these lifestyles are associated with demographic features (e.g., income and education) which are projected to increase in California in the next twenty years.

Nevertheless, in contrast to a likely increase in water-intensive lifestyles, water-conserving lifestyles are expected to increase also. In an era of increasing energy prices, water costs, sewage treatment and septic tank overloads, capital constraints, and environmental degradation, supply options appear to be less favorable than conservation as remedies to the water problem. Demographic trends, positively correlated with income and education, also favor water conservation. The drought experience in California during the mid-1970s demonstrated that water conservation by individuals and municipalities was an effective and practical approach for meeting regional water needs.

If opposition to large-scale construction of water projects continues, as expected by many observers of California water politics, encouragement of water-conserving lifestyles may be one of the few legitimate policies government will be able to pursue without resorting to overt force. Future scenarios for California suggest that conflict between water-intensive and water-conserving lifestyles will continue to exist; however, cooperative arrangements will be developed more easily if water conservation is an acknowledged policy.

LIFESTYLES AND THE COMPETITION FOR WATER

The resolution of present struggles for increased allocations of water among agricultural, industrial, and residential interests in California will be strongly shaped by alterations in people's lifestyles—their values, aspirations, and beliefs about how water contributes to a high quality of life. For some, increasing amounts of water are needed to ensure the types of gardens, domestic appliances, recreational pursuits, and industry which they believe necessary to their quality of living. For others, conservation and moderate consumption provide a safeguard rather than a sacrifice for their styles of life, and the appreciation of water in its natural state is valued as part of a complex and natural ecosystem essential to a high quality of life for present and future generations.

The interests of the various sectors involved in the water debates are often evaluated in purely organizational, economic, and political terms, while the role of lifestyles is minimized. The outcome of the competition for scarce water, however, will in fact largely be determined by the ability of the public and policymakers to allocate available supplies between competing uses of water in modern life for recreation, residential gardens, diet, and environmental preservation. Changes in lifestyles, rather than technical "fixes," may provide the key to meaningful solutions for the water problem. Policymakers and social researchers have increasingly become convinced that wasteful lifestyles contribute to the energy crisis, that good health and fewer heart attacks may be more easily achieved by sensible exercise and the avoidance of smoking than by more hospital facilities, that the educational problems of many school children may be traced to homes where a learning environment is lacking, and that some welfare problems stem from apathy bred by a "culture of poverty" mentality.[1]

This paper seeks to explore the various ways in which lifestyles affect patterns of consumption of water, and to suggest the potential that changing beliefs and habits have for easing future problems. California's rapidly changing and diverse lifestyles have been somewhat ignored by policymakers and resource managers, while sociologists, journalists, and novelists have treated them as peculiar, wacky manifestations of the "westward tilt"—the notion that the continent tilted towards the Pacific during the great westward migration, and that anything loose or unconnected elsewhere gathered in California. Yet today, more than at any other time, it is necessary to understand the ways in which California's highly educated and affluent, but especially diverse, innovative, and obsessively dynamic population[2] makes choices about the uses of water.

Lifestyles Defined. For the purposes of this paper, it is most meaningful to define lifestyles broadly. They are patterns of social behavior shared by groups of people with a sense of distinct experience and an awareness of a common culture. Lifestyles reflect the yearnings and opportunities of social groups, and include patterns of belief, modes of participation and production, and habits of consumption. Thus lifestyles are a set of interdependent forms of behavior including consumption, leisure, and work. In California, lifestyles do not merge into one standard of behavior, but express themselves in many forms, using different amounts of water, and in different ways. Consequently, no single California lifestyle is representative of water use,[3] but the many variations contribute to the need to balance alternative patterns of water consumption.

This examination of lifestyles and patterns of water use focuses directly on those aspects of lifestyles that are water-intensive and water-conserving, rather than on all lifestyles. It would not be very informative to consider lifestyles linked to the performing arts, spectator sports, or mass media, where water is more or less irrelevant. On the other hand, gardening, swimming, and tourism have significant water use implications which need to be evaluated. It is also important to note that water-intensive and water-conserving behavior is fundamentally concerned with issues of water *quality* as well as *quantity*. The purity of water is critical to its fullest use in various lifestyles, and quantity may be irrelevant if water, though abundant, is salty, dirty, and unhealthy.

This paper is divided into two broad sections. In the first, we consider the role of water in various water-intensive lifestyle patterns and develop a typology of four different types of water use. Each has its own constituencies, trade-offs between quantity and quality, and socioeconomic bases. Taken together, they provide a means by which policymakers can understand the several competing forces shaping patterns of private water use. In the second section we consider the water-conserving lifestyle. Cutting across each of the four types of water use, conservation may be both a means to make available supplies go further and a lifestyle in itself. In conclusion, we suggest policy options for managing lifestyle decisions.

WATER-INTENSIVE LIFESTYLES

The purpose of this section is to explore the various ways that water fits into modern Californian lifestyles. Whole civilizations have been shaped by the natural abundance or lack of water, but in California carefully engineered canals and pipelines have supplied practically unlimited water to the state's urban areas, and lakes, streams, and rivers have been managed so that water is available for multiple uses in all parts of the state. Thus, California's lifestyles have up to now not been shaped by limited water, but by abundant water. How has this affected today's Californians, and how will past strategies figure in the future?

The relation between lifestyles and water use may be examined by constructing a typology of four distinct patterns. The typology involves the intersection of two primary characteristics of water use—*how* the water is used and the *form* in which it is used. In the first case, we distinguish between water that is *consumed* so that it cannot be easily used again, and water that is *not consumed* but used for sports, observed, aesthetically appreciated, or otherwise valued without rendering it unavailable for other uses. Second, we distinguish between different forms in which the water is used—if it is consumed *directly* by individuals or if it is used *indirectly,* being embodied in materials and food which are consumed, or serving latent functions for some social groups (see Table 1). This typology of four features has shaped the following discussion.

Some General Definitions

(1) Residential. Most of the water consumed directly in the private sector is residential—water for gardening, bathing, cooking, and drinking. A special category of this form of consumption is the collective use of water for public lawns, parks, and commercial and business establishments.

(2) Consumer goods. Water which is consumed indirectly is embodied in purchased items such as food. Agriculture absorbs over 85 percent of the state's water. Ultimately agricultural products are consumed by people in their diet or clothing; manufactured items embody about 5 percent of the state's water.

Table 1

Types of Water Use in Modern Lifestyles

How Water is Used	Form in Which Water is Used	
	Direct	Indirect or Embodied
Consumed	(1) Residential	(2) Consumer goods: food, fiber, and manufactured products
Available for additional uses	(3) Sports and recreation	(4) Tourism

(3) Sports and recreation. This includes activities such as swimming, boating, fishing, and other water contact sports. In these cases virtually none of the water is consumed, although some degradation of quality may occur.

(4) Tourism. Water "experienced" in scenic vistas and tourist attractions is neither consumed nor contacted. Tourism is one of California's largest industries today, often focusing on unique water resources in national parks and forests, at the seashore, and at resorts. Proximity to bodies of water often has impact on land and housing values, and of course water is important for environmental quality.

These four patterns of water use will be considered in more detail.

Residential Water Use

In California, only about 10 percent of total available water is used for residential purposes, the remainder going to agriculture (85 percent) and industry (5 percent).[4] Approximately one-half of residential water is consumed inside the home and one-half outside the home.[5] This apportionment varies widely from region to region in the state: for example, exterior water use constitutes a small percentage in the wetter areas of the North Coast, whereas it is much larger in the drier areas of Southern California. About three-quarters of interior water consumption is in the bathroom—toilets using 45 percent, bathing and personal use 30 percent. Laundry and dishwashing account for 20 percent, and drinking and cooking 5 percent. Irrigation of lawns, shrubs, and home vegetable gardens accounts for 90 percent of exterior water use, while car washing, swimming pools, and the cleaning of driveways, sidewalks, and streets account for the remaining 10 percent.[7]

The largest concentration of people in California is in the semiarid south, a fact which by itself is no longer particularly striking, although it once reversed the traditional settlement pattern of the American westward migration that followed rivers and streams and sought out areas of rainfall sufficient for conventional agriculture. When climate, space, and industry attracted steadily growing numbers of people to Southern California, the newcomers faced the task of making over a desert in the image of their more watered homelands. As a result, the California residential and landscape tradition has never been natural, but an attempt to cultivate verdant English garden lushness adapted to a Mediterranean scene. Green lawns, expansive flower gardens, and integration of the house with the outdoors all reflect a water-intensive adjustment to the dry California climate.

The Spanish novelist García Ordoñoz de Montalvo wrote in 1510 about an island called California "very near to the Terrestrial Paradise," which established the first link between the Garden of Eden and that part of the west coast of North America that came to carry his place name.[8] In subsequent centuries races and ethnic groups in California used gardens to tighten the knot between their barren land and the blissful places they imagined. Although gardening took many forms, they all depended on water. When an irrigation technology came into existence, it merely updated usage such as the practice of the Klamath River Shasta,[9] who in dry weather watered their tobacco gardens by hand with baskets.

The proliferation of attempts to fuse house and garden as a distinct element in the California way of life dates from the beginning of the twentieth century, although some Spanish and Mexican settlers had located gardens in the central court of their adobes. In the 1920s William E. Smythe[10] stressed the importance of the concept of home-in-a-garden, conceived by his fellow Californian Franklin K. Lane, who as Secretary of the Interior proposed it to President Woodrow Wilson in 1919. It envisioned relocating city workers in a series of "garden homes," a kind of rustic suburbia with enough arable land for each family's garden.

The home-in-a-garden idea did not take hold in its visionary form, but some of its notions became part of the garden-home perspective in the following decades. Recently, Sally B. Woodbridge has shown the significance of the emerging ideal of landscape gardening and outdoor living as the central feature of the California residence, with the garden and patio framed by a house that is more a temporary shelter than a primary residence:

> In many ways the ideal California house has become a gimmick to express perpetual vacation time. Its leisure laden components...the outdoor living room, the landscaped setting with patios, terraces, decks, pools, and bar-b-q's represent the eternal varieties of California living. . .[11]

The fusing of the outdoors and its lush gardens with a dwelling is deeply rooted in California architectural history. Its clearest statement is by a group of Berkeley residents whose Hillside Club wrote, "Hillside architecture is landscape gardening around a few rooms for use in case of rain."[12]

As time has passed, concern for ecologically grown produce and rising costs of food have made gardening a kind of last frontier of freedom.[13] These considerations continue to link diverse groups of people together in their "rurban" (neither urban nor rural) settings[14] and make gardening the most common western U.S. leisure activity with 40.5 percent of adults participating.[15] Gardening activities touch on many layers of concern and the literature on therapeutic horticulture attests to it.[16] Gardening also continues to be a special source of satisfaction providing evidence that the task of supporting people with the labor of one's hands can still be accomplished in one's garden in California—if the water continues to flow that keeps sprinklers going and watering cans filled.

The residential consumption of water largely depends on the number, composition, and location of household units. Three trends are particularly notable in terms of household composition. First, the average size of households has been decreasing rather drastically, while the number of households and the total count of California residents has grown markedly. In 1970 the average household had 2.95 persons; by 1980 this figure had dropped to 2.68, and it is projected to continue to decline to 2.53 by 2000.[17] This trend reflects the movement of the baby boom population into their 20s and early 30s, the age when most households are formed. It also results from changing family lifestyles: people marry later, postpone child bearing, have fewer children, divorce more often, and when elderly, longer maintain independent households. As a consequence, between 1970-80 the number of households increased by 2,059,000 (31 percent) while the population increased by 2,633,000 (13 percent).[18]

Second, the average house has been getting smaller, with more units per acre, more condominiums, and very much higher prices. For example, from 1970-1972 average square footage of newly constructed single homes declined slightly and the average lot size declined 8 percent.[19] Equally significant is the rise in the number of multiple family dwellings such as apartment houses. By 1970 California had 30.2 percent multi-unit residences, up from 23.5 percent in 1960. Over 40 percent of new construction was multi- units.[20] Permits were issued for over 50,000 units to be converted to condominiums between January 1977 and September 1979.[21] These trends all point in the same direction: a reduction in size and private ownership of outdoor yard areas per household, implying a reduced outdoor water use.

Third, for the first time this century, more people are locating in nonmetropolitan and rural areas than in urban centers and their suburbs. Since 1970 non-metropolitan areas of California have grown more than twice as fast as metropolitan ones, constituting a major reversal of population trends. Many of the new residents have moved into small towns which have inadequate water systems and waste treatment facilities. Most of the new migrants desire better lifestyles by moving away from cities, yet major problems are developing for providing adequate water to them.[22]

Unquestionably, outdoor lifestyles are highly desirable for many California residents. As incomes go up, people want more yard and lawn areas and gardens. However, to the extent that home and property costs increase even faster than income, many people will be forced reluctantly into smaller residences with less yard area.

Water and Consumer Goods

The second way in which water fits into the modern California lifestyle is through the water consumed on farms and in factories to produce the consumer items which Californians purchase. These items embody water, though most of that water is not seen as part of the product because the water was necessary for production. It is not generally recognized that indirect consumption accounts for most of the agricultural and industrial water used or exported by California.

In a statewide survey, Californians believed that residential use was much higher than it actually is—the median estimate for residential water consumption was 30 percent opposed to its actual 10 percent; agriculture was estimated at 40 percent versus its actual 85 percent; and commercial/industrial was estimated at 30 percent versus its actual 5 percent.[23] Thus, the bulk of water Californians use is indirectly consumed through food and fiber and, at a much lower rate, through industrial goods.

The water consequences of different diets are considerable. Herbert Schulbach and Thomas Aldrich have estimated that a typical daily diet requires 4,530 gallons of embodied water, or on a yearly basis, about 5 acre-feet of water.[24] From their figures huge variations in the amount of water represented in different diet configurations may be calculated. Beef requires the most water—according to their calculations, over 2,600 gallons per 8-ounce serving. Pork is considerably more water-efficient, at about 800 gallons for an 8-ounce serving; chicken is the most efficient, at only 400 gallons per 8-ounce serving. If it takes three cups of milk to make each serving of cheese, 200 gallons of water are required per serving. Eggs require about 68 gallons each. Consequently, a vegetarian diet substituting eggs and cheese along with beans, nuts, and whole grains would take just under 1,000 gallons a day, while a low-meat diet would register just over 1,300. The low-meat diet is 3.5 times less water-intensive than the typical beef diet (see Table 2).

The total impact of these figures on water use is very difficult to determine, since many different patterns of land use and sources of supply are included. Beef is largely raised on rangeland which is not irrigated and generally not suitable for other commercial purposes. California's rangeland is estimated at 35,968,000 acres; it produces about 60 percent of the feed required for the meat animals produced on Californian farms and ranches.[25] California imports about 47 percent of the beef, 98 percent of the pork, and 70 percent of the broiler chickens consumed in the state, while it exports some turkeys.[26] Alfalfa is the major feed for California's dairy industry with 878,000 cows, and these dairy animals use about 70 percent of all hay consumed in the state.[27] Cattle and calves on feed (rather than on rangeland) in 1980 totaled about 764,000, while other cattle and calves total nearly 2.9 million. California produces between 6 and 8 million tons of alfalfa each year for animal feed.[28] The local production of meat and dairy products includes some reliance on the importation of many of the grains and forage on which they are fed. For example, about 250,000 tons of alfalfa hay is trucked into the state from neighboring states, and much of the feed for chickens is imported as well.[29] In total, King et al. estimate that about 80 percent of the feed grain supply is produced in state, with the rest being imported.[30]

It is clear from these estimates that a reduction of beef consumption in California would have a smaller impact on irrigation water consumption than if all beef were raised in-state on irrigated pasture. Since half the beef eaten here is imported, and only 40 percent of the remaining animals' feed is irrigated forage and grains, the elimination of beef from the Californian diet would save the state only about 20 percent of the 3,910 gallons (782 gallons) charged to beef in the average diet. Even so, this is almost as much as included in the entire vegetarian diet. Eliminating pork would have virtually no local impact since virtually none is raised here (although many indirect changes would surely occur because of food price changes).

These considerations are balanced by the realization that meat consumption as a part of the American diet has probably doubled since World War II.[31] This is partly a response to affluence and partly a misinformed attempt to eat better. Other trends contribute as well. Nearly one-third of all meals in California are

Table 2

Water Embodied in Alternative Diets
(gallons per daily serving)

	Beef	Low-Meat	Vegetarian
Rice cereal	18	--	--
Milk	65	--	--
2 Toast	15	15	15
2 Eggs	--	136	136
Grapefruit	26	26	26
Margarine	92	92	92
	216	269	269
1/4 lb Hamburger	1,303	--	--
Bun	16	--	--
French fries	6	--	--
Coke (1 oz. sugar)	10	--	--
Cheese sandwich	--	200	200
2 Bread—wheat	--	15	15
Margarine	92	92	92
Apple	--	16	16
Walnuts	--	20	20
	1,427	343	343
Steak, 8 oz.	2,607	--	--
Potato	9	--	--
Green beans	18	--	--
Chicken, 8 oz.	--	408	--
Beans (dry)	--	--	40
Rice	--	36	36
Tomatoes	--	3	3
Carrots	--	8	8
Lettuce	6	6	6
Watermelon	100	100	100
Margarine	92	92	92
Milk	65	65	65
	2,897	718	350
	4,540	1,336	962

Source: Schulbach and Aldrich, 1978

now consumed in restaurants or fast-food places; most of these meals are high in meat content. More home meals are frozen or prepared in part outside the home, offering few nonmeat options. Thus, current lifestyles seem to have less opportunity for meals embodying minimal water.

Nevertheless, a recent cultural phenomenon is the rise of many groups advocating a low-meat, fresh vegetable diet for better personal health and the ensuring of a more adequate world food supply. During the last few years a major trend has been proliferation of health food stores, vegetarian restaurants, low-meat cookbooks, and related dietary changes. Physical exercise has also increased, with jogging and hiking gaining popularity; for example, 16 percent of westerners jog (compared to 12 percent in the rest of the U.S.). In terms of diet, the western lifestyle is also becoming healthier.[32]

It is harder to estimate amounts of water consumed in the manufacturing of goods. A cotton shirt requires a substantial amount of water—each half pound of cotton lint requires 427 gallons.[33] An automobile needs about 10,000 gallons of water for its steel, plastic, fabric and assembly.[34] In general, most manufactured goods represent significant amounts of embodied water, although the total amount per year is probably small compared to other water uses. Furthermore, many of the most water-intensive manufactured consumer products are imported from out of state, meaning lower local impacts on water supply.

Sports and Recreation

The third type of relation between water and lifestyles involves direct contact with water, but not its actual consumption. Recreational sports such as swimming, fishing, and boating presuppose contact with water, but allow the water to be used for other purposes. Hence, the wise multiple-purpose management of water resources often increases the amount of pleasure available in freshwater. Sportsmen, however, are sometimes the most vocal critics of water projects (e.g., the construction of reservoirs) which divert and transform the flow of rivers.

The best data on California recreation and water sports have recently been collected for the State Department of Parks and Recreation by the Center for the Continuing Study of the California Economy.[35] These figures, collected from four surveys of about 1,000 persons during each season of 1978-1980, detail participation in 118 different recreational activities. The samples were randomly drawn, and accurate projections from them may be made to the entire California population. The data describe the extent to which Californians use park and recreational facilities involving water, and data on the demographic characteristics of users are available for understanding trends.

Swimming and beach-related activities are by far the most common form of recreational activity for Californians. Table 3 shows that over a quarter of all participation days (i.e., the total of all days all participants engaged in these activities) were spent in swimming or beach-related activities. Fishing and boating had much lower participation rates, although the same actual number of days (well over one day per person) were spent in each during the summer of 1978.

Participation in recreation and leisure activities of all types is strongly related to personal income and desired lifestyle. These factors are different in individuals of different ages. Consequently, it is important to evaluate the association of water-related sports and recreational activities with income and age. Table 4 shows the participation rates of different income groups in California. In all but one category, the higher income groups participate more than lower income groups in water-related recreational activities. Additionally, the data show that more affluent people participate more frequently, thereby amassing more total participant days of recreation. (The exception is fishing, where the highest income group does not as actively engage in fishing as other income groups, although the relation holds for low and medium income groups.) These data suggest that on average the lowest income group is significantly excluded from participating in water-related sports and recreational activities, as in general they are from most forms of sport and recreation.[36]

Table 3

Total Participation Days in Recreational
Activities, Summer 1978

Activity	Participation Days Actual (Millions)	Percent
Swimming and beach	142	25.6
Sports	77	13.9
Jogging	47	8.5
Visiting places	42	7.6
Partying	39	7.0
Picknicking	31	5.7
Camping	26	4.6
Bicycling	24	4.4
Fishing	21	3.8
Boating	21	3.8
Nature appreciation	18	3.3
Games	15	2.6
Hiking and backpacking	14	2.6
Crafts and hobbies	14	2.5
Attending sports	6	1.2
Off-road vehicles	5	0.9
Horseback riding	5	0.8
Hunting and target shooting	4	0.7
Rock climbing	3	0.5

Source: Arnold et al., Center for the Continuing Study
of the California Economy, Tables 3.1 and 3.3.
Based on estimates of California population 12
years or older.

Water-oriented recreation is also strongly related to age, with the younger population participating much more frequently than older individuals (see Table 5). As an illustration, in the 12-17 age group, the average youth spends almost 19 days at the beach or swimming pool. In contrast, members of the 35-44 and 45-54 age groups devote 40 percent and 25 percent as much time respectively to beaching or swimming. Old people average only one day each during the summer. In sum, these data clearly show that persons of all ages enjoy water-related sports and recreation activities, but that the younger participants are the strongest enthusiasts.

A growing ethnic population also affects water sports participation. Hispanics participate in water sports somewhat less than nonhispanic whites, with blacks much less than either. For example, nonhispanic whites participated an average of 8.8 days per capita in swimming and beach-related sports, while hispanics averaged 6.2 days and blacks averaged 2.5 days.[37]

Table 4

**Percent of Population Participating in Recreational
Activities by Income Groups, Summer 1978**

Activity	Income				
	Less than $7,000	$7,000-$14,999	$15,000-$24,999	$25,000-$34,999	$35,000 & Over
Swimming and beach	21.9	39.9	46.7	40.1	65.0
Visiting scenic areas	33.0	37.7	45.1	49.9	46.4
Fishing	11.2	15.3	25.1	26.9	16.7
Boating	6.1	16.0	15.8	22.8	41.2
Nature appreciation	10.9	16.4	17.0	22.1	22.6

Source: Arnold et al., Table 5.5

Table 5

**Participation Days Per Capita in Recreational
Activities by Age Groups, Summer 1978**

Activity	Age Groups						
	12-17	18-24	25-34	35-44	45-54	55-64	65 +
Swimming and beach	18.7	11.1	7.9	7.2	4.5	1.4	0.8
Visiting scenic areas	1.9	3.0	3.3	5.2	1.7	0.9	1.2
Fishing	1.2	0.6	1.5	1.5	2.2	0.7	0.3
Boating	1.2	1.2	2.3	1.4	0.9	0.3	0.0
Nature appreciation	0.8	1.8	0.8	1.1	0.6	1.0	0.7

Source: Arnold et al., Table 6.6.

Other factors affect water-based recreation patterns. Data have consistently shown a marked decline in the average work week. In 1947 the work week averaged 40.3 hours; by 1980 it fell to 35.3 hours, largely because of increased productivity, the desire to take leisure time instead of income, the growth of service jobs, the inclusion of more women and teenagers in the changing labor force, and the availability of more flexible scheduling with flex-time and job sharing.[38] It is hard, however, to know how to interpret these figures because they so much reflect changing industrial structure.

Desire for water activities creates a need for the provision of water-based facilities. For all water-related activities, over half take place within governmental jurisdictions such as parks, reserves, or wilderness areas. This confirms the observation that there is a strong need for public involvement in the provision of facilities for water sports.[39]

The issue of water for recreation versus consumption is brought into sharp focus in the development of new water projects. Nowhere was this more poignantly illustrated than in the case of the Friends of the River's effort to stop the filling of the New Melones Dam. The Friends of the River and other environmental organizations stressed that the New Melones Reservoir, if filled, would completely flood the only remaining free-flowing section of a wild and scenic river east of the Central Valley.[40] Having made a detailed study of the Stanislaus River as well as protests at the endangered river itself, the Friends of the River advocated not filling the New Melones Reservoir above a level which would protect the controversial sections of the Stanislaus and yet still achieve many goals of the dam's construction.

A dramatic action made this issue public. By chaining himself to a rock near the water line in May 1979, Mark DuBois, former president of this environmental organization (but not acting on their behalf), called national and international attention to the conflict between development and resource preservation for recreational use. DuBois was effective within a week in bringing many issues to a head. Governor Jerry Brown, in response to DuBois' efforts, sent a telegram to President Carter urging that part of the river scheduled for flooding be included in the wild river system as part of the federal Wild and Scenic Rivers Act. In addition, the Army Corps of Engineers, who were constructing the dam, announced that they would not fill the reservoir above the level where DuBois was chained, although they denied that his presence had anything to do with the announcement of their plans. As of June 1981, the reservoir had not been filled, although with the wet winter in 1980 it rose above the level where DuBois had been chained.

Judicial and legislative actions continue to keep the future of the Stanislaus in doubt. This controversy, however, placed in public view the sharp debate over California lifestyles between those who desire waterways for sports and recreation and those who want water development pursued.

Tourism and Aesthetic Factors

The fourth and final classification of water related to lifestyles includes tourist and other "uses" of water neither directed toward consumption nor experienced in direct contact.

Tourism is a relatively "remote" use of water in that it characteristically provides visual experiences, where water may be the focal point in particular aesthetically pleasing settings. Tourism is wedded to water in a fundamental way. The relationship goes far beyond a refreshing drink to quench the thirst or an invigorating shower to wash off the dust of a long day's drive. Since the beginning of the twentieth century growing numbers of Americans have embraced the pleasures of tourism, setting out to discover and appreciate their country's areas of undefiled nature. For many of them the pursuit became a quest for creeks, rivers, streams and waterfalls, as well as gorges, ponds, and lakes. A burgeoning industry has established itself to cater to the desires of Californians to view water in its natural bodies, and even as winter snow and ice. Today tourism is one of

California's largest industries. Data from the U.S. Travel Data Center estimate that United States travelers spent over $19.1 billion in California during 1979,[41] while foreign travelers spent another $2 billion or more. Most indicators suggest that this makes tourism the state's largest industry, although such claims are also disputed. The amount of economic activity generated by tourism accounts for approximately seven percent of the gross state product. About half this amount is for transportation, the remainder for lodging, food, entertainment, and recreation. No estimate is available on expenditures specifically near waterways, although they are probably substantial. One indicator of the impact on areas near water comes from data on the use of parks and recreation areas. Since 1945 the population of the state doubled, but park use increased fourteenfold, as shown in Figure 1.[42]

Figure 1

**Increase in Use of the California State Park System
Compared with California's Population**

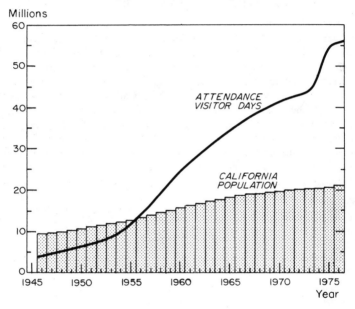

Notes: Based in part on California, the Resources Agency, Department of Parks and Recreation, *California Outdoor Recreation Resources Plan* (Sacramento: February 1974), p. 1. Additional 1974-1976 park use data from the department's *Statistical Report, 1974-75* and *Statistical Report, 1976-77* (Preliminary); population data from California Department of Finance, *California Statistical Abstract*, 1976, p. 6.

Proximity to water is a significant factor in determining property values, and in some cases provides the opportunity for unique lifestyles. We have not been able to find good data on the contribution made by proximity to bodies of water on land and housing values, although several references suggest it is a positive determinant.[43]

At a more aesthetic level, water is of vital importance to California spirit and culture. Novels set in California have frequently used the "drama of reclamation" as their theme, setting development against the beauty of an unspoiled sector of the state. For example, May Austin's novel, *The Ford*,[44] merges her anguish about the fate of Owens Valley, which she saw sacrificed to Los Angeles water interests, with her memories of the southern San Joaquin Valley; the result is a compelling description of drought and a vivid account of relief through irrigation.

In sum, Californians have in water, as in other natural resources, a bountiful and valuable asset. As Kevin Starr points out in *Californians and the American Dream*,[45] this abundance has influenced people in two ways. On the one hand, natural resources inspire awe, even worship, and elicit the desire to preserve them. On the other hand they challenge the best of men to exploit their richness. This tension between desires to conserve and to exploit is inherent in the lifestyles of many Californians.

WATER-CONSERVING LIFESTYLES

This second major section of our paper explores water conservation rather than use. Traditionally, water has been considered virtually a "free good," unlimited in quantity and thus commanding no price except for what it costs to deliver it. As a result, Lyon notes, "water intensive processes have been favored where there has been adequate supply,"[46] and efforts to conserve have only been favored during times of drought. The recent 1976-78 California drought brought into focus, however, the range of conservation activities available in California as well as the interconnection between water conservation and other resource conservation activities, what Elgin and Mitchell call "voluntary simplicity."[47] Water conservation is thus both a means to secure available supply at economical rates and a growing, popular, and politically influential lifestyle itself.

In recent years, water-conserving processes have been encouraged partly in response to some of the following trends:

(1) *Increasing water costs as new supplies are more costly to develop.*

(2) *Growing consumer resistance to increased water rates.*

(3) *Rising energy prices (reflected in higher water bills).* It takes energy to pump, treat, and heat water.

(4) *Problems with sewage treatment and septic systems.* Overloads in these systems occur as demand from population growth exceeds capacity.

(5) *Lack of capital* for constructing large sewage treatment plants and water projects.

(6) *Increasing failure of bond issues* for financing further expansion of water and wastewater projects.

(7) *Further environmental degradation* as a result of the construction of large water systems.

(8) *Pressure from water management agencies* (Public Utilities Commission, state and federal water agencies) to conserve water.

Water conservation is presently being viewed as a "management tool applicable at all times and in all areas of the country...To associate water conservation too closely with drought is a mistake."[48]

Determinants of Residential Water Conservation

Methods of encouraging water conservation vary, but they can be categorized as (1) mandatory (e.g., regulations, standards, and restrictions) or (2) voluntary (via economic incentives and disincentives or public information/education programs). Selection of these methods is based on those determinants of residential consumption presumed to be significant in reducing water use: the price of water and the prices of other goods, consumer wealth, the availability of technology, consumer habits, values, attitudes, and beliefs. A brief discussion of these determinants will provide context for the examination of the potential for water conservation in California.

Price of water. Water until relatively recently has been priced only for delivery cost and has commonly been regarded as a "free good." Nevertheless, according to economic theory, the price of water can be set at a sufficiently high level to act as a disincentive for high levels of water use. Studies of the "price elasticity" of water (the percentage change in water consumed associated with a percentage change in price) have indicated that the impact of variations in price has not been very dramatic.[49] Specifically, the domestic ("in-house") use of water has been found to be relatively "price-inelastic": an increase in price does not result in a corresponding reduction in demand.[50] For outside uses of water (e.g., lawn sprinkling and car washing), demand is more sensitive to price increases.[51]

The use of price as a mechanism for reducing water consumption is constrained by at least five factors:

(1) The cost of water has historically been very low and constitutes only a small portion of the household budget. Thus, it appears that, to be effective, the price of water would have to be raised very significantly above current levels to stimulate the reduction of water consumption.[52] However, consumer resistance to such rate increases and the inequalities they produce may constrain the use of this mechanism.

(2) There is no practical substitute for water: a certain amount of water is necessary to sustain life and to promote hygiene and health. It is true that consumers could use bottled water, public gardens, and communal swimming pools as substitutes for some present residential uses.

(3) Price-induced savings may only be temporary. In many cases, residential reductions can be attributed to the repair of leaky plumbing fixtures in the home.[53]

(4) Pricing will have minimal or no impact on certain types of water users: self-supplied or unmetered users, consumers who rely on lawn or yard irrigation as a form of recreation and relaxation, and people who live in areas where precipitation frequently meets their minimal outdoor water demands.[54]

(5) The absence of an understandable feedback mechanism makes it very difficult for consumers to monitor their consumption in order to know which household activity they should reduce to save water.[55] In addition, feedback is delayed because bills are received long after consumption has occurred. Despite these constraints, it is still possible that the increased price of water will be an effective mechanism in reducing use, particularly when one recognizes that price elasticities increase with time because consumers have more time to experiment and adjust to changes in price.[56]

Consumer wealth. A statistically significant association between per capita municipal water use and per capita income levels has been reported in several studies.[57] This relationship is also stable over time. No other demographic variables (e.g., sex, education, age, and race) display this type of relationship. When income is taken as a measure of lifestyle, the relationship between water use and income is not surprising: higher per capita income often permits the purchase of water-using devices (e.g., garbage disposals, clothes washers and swimming pools), larger houses on larger lots, and more landscaping.[58] However, the relationship between income and price of water is uncertain: it is assumed that as incomes rise, the cost of water becomes a smaller proportion of household expenditures so that water consumption becomes less responsive to price.[59]

Technology. Until recently, most household technology associated with residential water use was not influenced by the amount or cost of water. In response to some of the trends mentioned previously, water-efficient technologies are gradually being incorporated into both new and existing housing for interior and exterior needs. These technologies are often inexpensive, cost-effective, acceptable to consumers because they demand few behavioral changes, and highly effective in reducing water demands.[60] An array of possible technological devices can reduce water use in new homes by 20 to 55 percent and in existing homes by 19 to 43 percent: the installation of low-flush toilets, low-flow showerheads and kitchen and lavatory faucets, pressure-reducing valves, low-water clothes washers and dishwashers, and insulation of hot water lines.[61] Further reductions are possible with more expensive, aesthetically unattractive, or less convenient devices which may not be acceptable to the consumer.[62] Constraints to the adoption of these technologies are: (1) absence of verifiable data on effectiveness and performance, and (2) the lack of water-conserving devices in the customary plumbing fixture outlets, such as hardware stores and plumbing supply outlets.[63]

Consumer habits, values, attitudes, and beliefs. Water has generally been regarded as a "basic necessity, even a right, not an economic good."[64] Certain household items which require large amounts of water, formerly regarded as conveniences, are now perceived as necessities: clothes washers, dishwashers, indoor showers and toilets, and garbage disposals. Similarly, more people are using more water outside the home: extensive flower gardens with water thirsty plants, swimming pools, and frequent car washes. Many of these activities are so ingrained in the household ethos that any proposed change in the valuation of water or in the limitation of its use would be met with extreme resistance by many consumers. Hence, it is clear that customs, values, attitudes, and beliefs have an important interactive effect with the price of water, consumer income, and the technology itself in determining the amount of water used in the household. Some even urge a stronger case: "...the way a nation uses water is less affected by technological forces than by the taboos and traditions of its people."[65]

A greater awareness of the relative scarcity of water will doubtless lead more people to embrace the "conservation ethic." It will be adopted by more people in regard to water, as with energy. Water conservation will be enhanced not only by some of the trends mentioned earlier but also by some of the following beliefs:[66]

(1) a belief that a resource shortage exists and constitutes a problem for a group with which an individual identifies;

(2) a moral commitment to a "fair" contribution to group welfare;

(3) a belief in the efficacy of personal efforts to achieve a collective solution;

(4) a belief that the personal cost of inconvenience resulting from conservation efforts will not be great;

(5) a conviction that others in the relevant group will also conserve.

These beliefs extend beyond the sphere of personal action so that the consumer's sociocultural perspective becomes very important. For example, a person's knowledge of water conservation efforts made by a municipality (such as turning off water fountains or allowing fairways on public golf courses to dry out) or by a public institution of which he or she is a member (such as the installation of low-flow shower heads in university gymnasiums) or by a recreational group of which he or she is a participant (such as talks on drought-tolerant plants given by a horticultural association) will undoubtedly have a positive and direct effect on the individual's own efforts to conserve water. Conservation efforts by others in the community demonstrate that there is a consensus that a resource shortage exists and that action is necessary to resolve the problem. The reverse is also true: the sight of careless frequent watering with excess water flowing onto pavement would have the effect of telling others that there is no water supply problem. This interaction between individual behavior and community goals has been evident in the related field of energy conservation: people are more likely to conserve if they feel others are doing the same.[67]

Water Conservation in California

In the winters of 1976-77 most regions in California experienced a second consecutive dry winter; many water districts were prompted to adopt emergency conservation and rationing programs involving their residential users. Program goals in the San Francisco Bay area, for example, varied from 10 to 57 percent reduction of water consumed residentially.[68] Conservation methods practiced by some communities ranged from educational campaigns urging voluntary conservation to bans on certain usages, service shutoffs, and moratoriums on new connections. Other communities changed plumbing codes to require low-usage fixtures in new construction; distributed retrofit kits for toilet and bathroom fixtures; recycled wastewater; established water rate surcharges; expanded water metering; and gave out warnings and fines to violators.[69] Many of these conservation programs were effective. Participating communities reported water savings generally above 10 percent, commonly at least 20 percent, and at times ranging to over 50 percent.

Water conservation measures are typically promoted when a service area faces a shortage of supplies or when an overloaded waste treatment system requires reduced waste flows. Some communities and individuals in California have nevertheless continued to promote water conservation during times of relatively abundant water supplies.[70] For example, in a survey of a random sample of residents of the City of Davis during the summer of 1980, 47 percent of the respondents reported that they were currently taking special steps to save water (90 percent reported that they had taken similar steps during the drought of 1977).[71] Most actions were first directed to limiting exterior water use prior to reducing the amount of water used inside the dwelling. Other findings also show that exterior water use is more "elastic" than interior water use. Differences in elasticity are most evident during the summertime between residential samples of metered and unmetered homes.[72]

These data suggest that people are willing to reduce water use even during times when water crises or shortages are not imminent. If individuals and communities were to continue voluntary conservation in the residential sector, significant savings could be achieved. By the year 2000, over 1.2 million acre-feet of water could be conserved simply by adopting various cost-effective technological devices. Similarly, if major urban areas in California were to reduce water use in their jurisdictions by 30 percent, approximately 1.2 million acre-feet would be saved.[73]

The important question is, however, if a conserving lifestyle would be acceptable to California's population. Data from the Stanford Research Institute and from other researchers suggest that "voluntary simplicity," meaning the conservation and efficient use of resources such as energy and water, is currently being practiced by large numbers of Californians and other citizens—and may attract more adherents in the years to come.[74] Recent statewide evidence supports the view that Californians favor water conservation: 95 percent of the public believes that it is important to conserve the state's water (69 percent say it is *very* important). Moreover, 56 percent of the public believes that residential consumers can conserve the most water without creating real hardship, compared to 27 percent who believe the commercial/industrial sector can conserve the most.[75] This survey supports the view that residential consumers are willing to conserve water.

A significant anomaly, however, appears upon examination of our current data. Conservation activities are strongly associated with higher levels of income and education, and thus the "voluntary simplicity" movement represents people who pursue conservation largely because of values and beliefs, rather than because of economic necessity.[76] Yet this more affluent group also represents those for whom water use is greatest, because of swimming pools, large yards, convenience appliances, and rich diets. On the other hand, poorer persons and ethnic groups seem much less willing to embrace conservation. In fact, there may be a tendency for those social groups who have done without water-related amenities to be much less willing to forego their aspirations for them.

Lifestyles and Politics: The Case of Mono Lake[77]

Lifestyles become particularly significant in the political sphere when certain groups actively support or oppose water development projects. One recent representative illustration of the interaction between lifestyles and politics is the controversy surrounding the City of Los Angeles' diversion of about 100,000 acre-feet of water from tributaries that flow into Mono Lake, a spectacular site with unique geological formations located east of Yosemite National Park. Since 1970, the Owens Valley-Mono Lake watersheds have furnished approximately 80 percent of the water for the City of Los Angeles. The present conflict concerns changes caused by the recent drop in lake level of about two feet per year; thousands of acres of dry lake bed have been exposed, creating a land bridge to the lake islands, which endangers the population of 50,000 California gulls that nest and breed there.

The conflict over the diversion of water from Mono Lake centers on ecological preservation versus water districts' interests in meeting projected demand for water. The Mono Lake controversy has become a highly political issue, cutting across a number of policy areas. A key group is the Mono Lake Committee, founded in February 1978 to protect the ecosystem of the lake. Unlike many water conflicts, the focal point of this one has been water conservation as a means to ensure environmental protection. The Mono Lake Committee and its supporters have repeatedly asserted that statewide water conservation (not just by the City of Los Angeles) could reduce demand for water sufficiently so that diversions from the Mono Lake area would be unnecessary. They claim that lifestyle changes due to conservation would be minor compared to the benefit of saving a unique natural resource. The California Department of Water Resources has meanwhile recommended that the City of Los Angeles reduce its water consumption by 15 percent and expand its use of reclaimed wastewater. Nevertheless, the advocates of continued water diversion cite the health problems associated with reclaimed wastewater, the loss of energy from hydroelectric facilities, and the pressing needs of a growing population.

The political battles are being fought on a number of different fronts. The Mono Lake Committee is active in traditional advocacy organization activities: public education, fund raising, litigation, and lobbying local, state, and federal legislators and other public officials. In addition, a lawsuit has been filed against the Los Angeles Department of Water and Power. State and federal legislation was introduced, but subsequently voted down or approved with a weakly amended version. A state task force has investigated the problem and published a report. The water district has responded with its own publicity and litigation. The significance of the issue is seen in the fact that the national media have given extensive coverage to the controversy, making it well known outside the local area.

The case of Mono Lake is the most current symbol of California's water deficit.[78] Future water proposals affecting the distribution of California's water will undoubtedly also be hotly debated as the issue of water-conserving versus water-intensive lifestyles becomes a focal point in the resolution of competing demands over water.

CONCLUSIONS

Many of the conflicts between organizations advocating water for particular uses may hinge on the issue of lifestyles. As shown above, a number of trends are presently developing which may lead to new and more varied patterns of water use. Because lifestyles are strongly rooted in tradition and culture, they may not be easily abandoned or altered. But our contention is that lifestyles reflect individual differences of opinion on what constitutes a high quality of living—and that more varieties of that definition are being generated as society becomes more affluent, educated, cosmopolitan, and complex.[79]

Lifestyles are not directly manipulable or regulatable by public policy in the same way as legal or economic structures. We have learned a number of things, however, about how public policy can better use lifestyles to advance one or another policy alternative.

• Lifestyles are somewhat flexible, especially in cases of broadly shared public goals and in times of crisis. Educational campaigns, public leadership, and grass roots organizations continue to produce significant behavior changes. Many of the benefits of such efforts remain after the crisis is over, as, for example, after the drought of the 1970s.

- Lifestyle changes need to be demonstrated at a public level if they are to achieve collective goals. For example, public agencies should take the lead in water conservation by planting native drought-tolerant species and monitoring water usage. Small, well-publicized efforts of this sort are effective.

- Lifestyles in California have tended to become organized in interest groups and advocacy organizations. Many groups, though competitive with each other, represent a substantial resource to build cooperation and to monitor changes among the wider population. The inclusion of these groups in the policy-making process is critical, although selection of groups may be difficult.

- Many lifestyles are deeply rooted in culture and tradition, and the aspirations of whole classes of people are tied to their definitions of quality of life. As the social and economic circumstances of groups change, their consumption patterns may alter, changing even broader social patterns. Understanding of such social evolution is necessary to avoid conflict.

- Finally, there is broad agreement in California that the unique environmental resources of the state enhance the citizens' overall quality of life. Balance is needed between development and wilderness, between man's efforts to redesign his environment and to preserve the natural ecology.

REFERENCES AND NOTES

1. Ted K. Bradshaw and Edward J. Blakely, *Policy Implications of Changing Life Styles* (University of California, Berkeley: Institute of Governmental Studies, 1978).
2. Ted K. Bradshaw, "Trying Out the Future," *Wilson Quarterly* (Summer 1980), pp. 66-82.
3. Ted K. Bradshaw, "California As A Post-Industrial Society: Assessing Theories of Future Social Development," paper presented to the meetings of the American Association for the Advancement of Science, San Francisco, January 7, 1980.
4. California Department of Water Resources, *Water Conservation in California,* Bulletin No. 198 (Sacramento, 1976), p. 11.
5. Murray A. Milne, *Residential Water Conservation,* Water Resources Center Contribution No. 35 (University of California, Davis: Water Resources Center, 1976), p. 16.
6. Ibid.
7. Department of Water Resources, *Water Conservation in California,* 1976, p. 22.
8. García Ordoñez de Montalvo, *Las Sergas de Esplandian* (Toledo, Spain, 1510).
9. Shirley Silver, "Shastan Peoples," in Robert F. Heizer, ed., *Handbook of North American Indians, Vol. VIII: California* (Washington, D.C.: Government Printing Office, 1978).
10. William Ellsworth Smythe, *City Homes on Country Lanes: Philosophy and Practice of the Home-in-a-Garden,* 1921.
11. Sally B. Woodridge, "The Ideal California House: Domestic Implications of Eden," paper presented at the AAAS Meetings, San Francisco, January 1980, pp. 21-22. (See also, "The California House," *Wilson Quarterly* IV (Summer 1980), pp. 83-91.)
12. Woodbridge, 1980, p. 10.
13. Bruce Butterfield, "The Impact of Home and Community Food Gardening on America" (Burlington, Vermont: Gardens For All, 1981).
14. Edward Duensing and Christopher Brune, "Urban Community Gardens," Vance Bibliographies, Public Administration Series, November 1979, pp. 3-4.
15. *Sunset Newsletter,* Western Market Report, June/July 1980, No. 3 (Palo Alto, Calif.: Lane Publishing Company).
16. Charles A. Lewis, "Comment: Healing in the Urban Environment," *APA Journal,* July 1979, pp. 330-338.

17. Isabel Hambright, Population Research Unit, California Department of Finance, personal communication. She cautions that in the case of increasing housing shortages, the size of households might not decline to this level.

18. U.S. Department of the Census, 1980.

19. California Housing and Community Development Department, *California Statewide Housing Element, Phase II* (Sacramento, November 1973), p. 180.

20. California Housing and Community Development Department, *California Statewide Housing Plan, 1977* (Sacramento, 1977), p. C-15 and C-42.

21. "Condominiums and Cooperatives—A Statewide Survey on Conversions," *Western City,* Vol. LVI, No. 8, August 1980, p. 5.

22. Ted Bradshaw and Edward Blakely, *Rural Communities in Advanced Industrial Society* (New York: Praeger, 1979), and Bradshaw and Blakely, *Resources of Recent Migrants to Rural Areas for Economic Development: Policy Implications* (University of California, Davis: Cooperative Extension, 1981).

23. The Field Institute, "The Peripheral Canal and Related Water Issues," *California Opinion Index,* Volume 5, August 1980.

24. Herbert Schulbach and Thomas Aldrich, "Water Requirements for Food Production," *Soils and Water* 38(Fall 1978):13-17 (University of California: Berkeley, Cooperative Extension).

25. James H. Cothern, "The Economics of Livestock Production on the Central Coast," paper presented at the Alameda County Planning Meeting, Hayward, Calif., February 5, 1980, p. 2.

26. Gordon A. King, Harold O. Carter, and Daniel J. Dudek, *Projections of California Crop and Livestock Production to 1985,* University of California Cooperative Extension Information Series in Agricultural Economics, No. 77-3, May 1977, p. 27.

27. James H. Cothern, *Processing, Transporting and Pricing California Alfalfa Hay,* Leaflet 2890, Division of Agricultural Sciences, University of California, Berkeley, June 1977, p. 3.

28. James H. Cothern, "The 1980-81 Alfalfa Situation," paper presented at the Alfalfa Hay Growers' Meetings, Paso Robles, October 29, 1980.

29. Cothern, 1977, p. 4.

30. King et al., 1977.

31. Annual per capita beef consumption increased from 64 to 95 pounds from 1960-1976. Chicken increased in the same period from 28 to 43 pounds.

32. Data from a survey of health habits of adults indicate that residents of western states are more likely than those in the remainder of the U.S. to take vitamins (55% in west vs. 43% in rest of the U.S.), eat yogurt (37% vs. 25%), eat wheat bread (57% vs. 36%), or jog (16% vs. 12%). See *Sunset Newsletter,* Western Market Report, February/March and April, 1981, Nos. 1 and 2.

33. Schulbach and Aldrich, 1978.

34. Fritz van der Leeden, *Water Resources of the World* (Syosset, New York: Water Information Center, Inc., 1975), p. 521.

35. Robert K. Arnold, Steven Lecy, Theresa Wilkinson Carey, and Steven Olsen, "Summer Recreation in California, 1978," report prepared for Planning Division, California Department of Parks and Recreation (Palo Alto: Center for the Continuing Study of the California Economy, July 1980).

36. Leisure and recreation for lower income groups is much more home- and family-centered, according to other studies. See Neil H. Cheek, Jr. and William R. Burch, Jr., *The Social Organization of Leisure in Human Society* (New York: Harper and Row, 1976); and Sebastian De Grazia, *Of Time, Work, and Leisure* (New York: Doubleday, 1964).

37. Arnold et al., 1980, Table 7.6.

38. Security Pacific Bank, *Economic Report* (Los Angeles, March 1981), p. 7.

39. Managing water resources for recreational use involves both improved management and new opportunities. For example, the use of reservoirs near urban areas for recreation presents a number of opportunities, according to Alex Calhoun, John Heslep, and Henry Hjersman, "The Recreational Potential of Closed Water Supply Reservoirs in California," Task Force Report to California Resources Agency and Human Relations Agency (Sacramento, September 1969).

40. Friends of the River, personal communication, Fort Mason, San Francisco.

41. California Office of Visitor Services, *The Economic Impact of Travel in California, 1979* (Sacramento, 1980).

42. Bradshaw and Blakely, 1978, p. 6.

43. Timothy D. Schroeder, "Local Parks and Recreation Services and Property Values: A Review and Bibliography," Vance Bibliographies, Public Administration Series, January 1981, p. 640.
44. Mary Austin, *The Ford* (Boston: Houghton, 1917).
45. Kevin Starr, *Americans and the California Dream, 1850-1915* (New York: Oxford University Press, 1973), p. 418.
46. Donna K. Lyon, *Water Conservation in the Las Vegas Valley: Pricing and Alternative Measures*, Water Resources Center Contribution No. 41056 (University of Nevada, Reno: Desert Research Institute, 1978).
47. Duane Elgin and Arnold Mitchell, "Voluntary Simplicity," *Co-Evolution Quarterly* 14(1977):4-19.
48. William E. Sharpe, "Municipal Water Conservation Alternatives," *Water Resources Bulletin* 14(1978):5, 1080-1087.
49. For a review of studies of price elasticities see Steve H. Hanke, "A Method for Integrating Engineering and Economic Planning," *Journal of American Water Works Association* 70(1978):9, 487-491; Rodney L. Clouser and William L. Miller, *Household Demand For Water and Policies to Encourage Conservation*, Water Resources Center Technical Report No. 124 (Purdue University, West Lafayette, Indiana: 1979); and Williams-Kuebelbeck and Associates Inc., "The Feasibility of Achieving Water Conservation in the State of California Through Water Pricing," prepared for the California Department of Water Resources, 1977.
50. Ernest J. Flack, Samuel G. Bryson, and Robert C. McWhinnie, "Urban Water Conservation: A Case Study of Denver, Colorado," unpublished manuscript, 1974, p. 5; Lyon, 1978, p. 4; Sharpe, 1978, p. 1082.
51. Lyon, 1978, p. 4; Sharpe, 1978, p. 1082; Hanke, 1978.
52. Sharpe, 1978, p. 1083.
53. Sharpe, 1978, p. 1082; Flack et al., 1974, p. 5.
54. Steve H. Hanke, "Some Behavioral Characteristics Associated with Residential Water Price Changes," *Water Resources Research* 6(1970):1385; Sharpe, 1978, p. 1082.
55. Richard A. Berk, Thomas F. Cooley, C.J. LaCivita, Stanley Parker, Kathy Stredl, and Marilyn Brewer, "Reducing Consumption in Periods of Acute Scarcity: The Case of Water," *Social Science Research* 9(1980):2, 104.
56. Hanke, 1970, p. 1385.
57. Dale W. Berry and Gilbert W. Brown, "Predicting the Municipal Demand for Water," *Water Resources Research* 10(1974):6, 1239; Clouser and Miller, 1979.
58. Flack et al., 1974; California Department of Water Resources, "A Technique for Estimating the Effect of Water Conservation on Urban Per Capita Water Use," unpublished manuscript, December 1978; Berry and Brown, 1974, p. 1240.
59. Robert A. Young, "Price Elasticity of Demand for Municipal Water: A Case Study of Tucson, Arizona," *Water Resources Research* 9(1973):4, 1072.
60. Sharpe, 1978, p. 1083.
61. California Department of Water Resources, Bulletin 198, p. 1.
62. Milne, 1976.
63. Sharpe, 1978, p. 1084.
64. Berk et al., 1980, p. 102.
65. Milne, 1976, p. 9.
66. Berk et al., 1980, p. 101.
67. Raymond J. Burby and Mary E. Marsden, *Energy and Housing: Consumer and Builder Perspectives* (Cambridge, Mass: Oelgeschlager, Gunn, and Hain Publishers, 1980), p. 46.
68. William H. Bruvold, "Residential Water Conservation: Policy Lessons from the California Drought," *Public Affairs Report* 19(1978):6, 3.
69. California Department of Water Resources, *The California Drought—1977* (Sacramento, 1977), p. 24.
70. Ann L. Riley, "Community Involvement Promotes Water Conservation Projects," *Western City* June 1979, p. 24.
71. The Davis data were collected by the Davis Energy Research Group composed of researchers at the University of California, Davis and Berkeley campuses, and the Lawrence Berkeley Laboratory. The water use questions were part of an investigation examining the relationship between energy consumption and attitudes and behaviors.
72. Telephone conversation with Dan Heath, Urban Water Conservation Unit, California Department of Water Resources, May 18, 1981.

73. Figures estimated in California Department of Water Resources, 1977, p. 78, Table 10. It is important to note that these figures are based on 1972 data so that the possible savings are underestimated if a 1981 data base is used.

74. Dorothy Leonard-Barton and Everett Rogers, "Voluntary Simplicity: Precursor or Fad?", paper presented at meetings of American Association for the Advancement of Science, San Francisco, January 1980; and Elgin and Mitchell, 1977.

75. The Field Institute, 1980.

76. Leonard-Barton and Rogers, 1980.

77. Information for this section was taken primarily from the newsletter of the Mono Lake Committee; the issues reviewed were from Vol. 1, No. 1 (Spring 1978) to Vol. 4, No. 1 (Summer 1981).

78. *San Francisco Chronicle and Examiner,* March 11, 1979.

79. Bradshaw and Blakely, 1978.

CHAPTER VIII

THE ECONOMICS OF WATER ALLOCATION

by

Richard E. Howitt, Dean E. Mann, and H.J. Vaux, Jr.

ABSTRACT

Historically, Californians have accommodated to scarce water through a series of strategies that focused on the development and augmentation of new supplies. The institutions that evolved for managing scarce water included a system of water rights that emphasized security of tenure as well as a commitment to the construction of massive storage and conveyance facilities. The attitudes embodied in this system of institutions viewed water scarcity as something to be conquered physically. Water unused in economically productive endeavors was assumed to be wasted.

This historical tradition has probably served Californians well over the last century but it does not seem suitably adapted to meet the intensifying competition for water supplies over the next 40 years. Increasing demands for the public dollar coupled with increasing public resistance to part with that dollar suggest that public funding for development of new water supplies is not likely to be available on a scale remotely comparable to the past. Additionally, the recent emergence of strong preferences for the environmental amenities associated with free-flowing water suggests that proposals for future development will be bathed in intense political controversy.

Over the next 40 years, it appears that the institutional means for dealing with water scarcity must evolve in a fashion better accommodated to the notion of limited supplies. Such an institutional evolution will not be simply achieved, since it will pose perceived threats to many principal beneficiaries of current water institutions. In our judgment, a limited marketlike system for allocating relatively fixed supplies of water among competing demands holds some promise, although it, too, will entail substantial institutional change.

An interregional programming model is utilized to examine the implications of a market in which water can be transferred between geographical regions as well as between agricultural and urban sectors. The model reflects the fact that trade will occur when a potential user is willing to pay the prevailing market price for the water plus the costs of transporting it. Linear demand and supply functions are estimated for three agricultural sectors (north, south, and the Imperial Valley) and two municipal and industrial sectors (north and south). Interregional (sectoral) transfer prices are also estimated. Temporal changes in supply, demand and transfer prices are also estimated beginning with a base year (1980) and thereafter for 1995 and 2020. Water demands are assumed to grow over time in response to increases in population. Supply functions and transfer prices shift over time in response to changes in the cost of energy required to pump and convey water.

Three scenarios are examined with the aid of the interregional programming model. In the first, it is assumed that current institutions are maintained and no new supplies of water are made available. In the second, current institutions are maintained and new supplies are made available when users are willing to defray their costs. Urban sectors are the beneficiaries of these new supplies, experiencing substantial reductions in the price of water and modest increases in the quantities available. The third scenario assumes that institutions will evolve so as to permit regional and sectoral markets in which water can be traded. New supplies can be developed in response to consumer demand. In this scenario the price of northern agricultural water increases modestly while the price of Imperial Valley water increases fivefold. These price changes are the consequence of interregional trading wherein northern agriculture sells some water to the northern urban sector and the Imperial Valley sells to the southern urban sector. As a consequence, the urban sectors enjoy prices substantially lower than those that would obtain in the absence of trade. The fact that trade occurs voluntarily deserves emphasis.

The limited marketlike system posited for scenario three would result in savings of up to 2 MAF of water annually and would benefit buyers and sellers of water in an amount of over $70 million in 1980, increasing to $83 million annually by 2020. The benefits would be reduced if California's position as a supplier of food and fiber to the nation and the world becomes substantially more important. In the absence of institutional change, these benefits are unrealized and thus should be counted as costs. A comparative analysis of the three scenarios suggests that changes in institutional arrangements are likely to be the most economical means of resolving water scarcity.

I. INTRODUCTION

Historically, the resolution of the physical fact of water scarcity in California has focused almost exclusively on the development and augmentation of water supplies. In the best tradition of the old West, water scarcity was viewed as something to be conquered rather than managed. Substantial amounts of public resources were invested in the construction and operation of vast storage and conveyance facilities. Property rights to water were conceived in a fashion that would ensure security of tenure. Plentiful, low-cost water supplies were widely promoted as the key to economic development and growth. All of these actions were guided by a set of institutional arrangements and policies premised on the notion that water need not be limiting if only enough ingenuity and funds were devoted to wresting it from the few places where it was plentiful in a predominantly arid landscape.

These institutions and policies have governed the development and allocation of water in California during the first 130 years of its growth as a modern, industrialized state. On balance, it is difficult to argue that California and its citizens have not been well served by them. Circumstances are changing, however. California is no longer the virgin land of 1848. Population and the demands of modern industry press inexorably upon the resource base. The nearly universal satisfaction of basic demands for food, shelter, and clothing has generated new tastes and preferences for goods and amenities that were previously enjoyed only by the very few who were very rich. Demands for continued expansion of water supplies must now compete with a host of other demands for the public dollar—a dollar which the citizenry seems increasingly less willing to part with.

We suggest that the water institutions that have served California well in the past are not well suited to either current conditions or the conditions that are expected to evolve over the next 40 years. Water management institutions must evolve in a way that recognizes more realistically the fact that water supplies ultimately have economic if not physical limits. They must also evolve in a fashion that allows more flexibility in the management of our water resources, to adjust the allocation of relatively limited supplies of water among a host of competing and nearly insatiable demands.

Markets are an almost classic economic institution for allocating scarce resources flexibly. Given certain reasonable preconditions, markets operate, often almost invisibly, to satisfy the wants and demands of diverse producers and consumers with diverse desires and wants. Even where some of the preconditions cannot be fulfilled, marketlike institutional arrangements emulate the operation of actual markets in a wholly satisfactory way. In this paper, we argue that development of a limited marketlike institution to aid in managing and allocating scarce water supplies would serve Californians better in the coming decades than the institutional arrangements that have characterized the past.

In Section II, we review briefly the institutional history of California water development, suggest reasons for suspecting that its traditions are no longer appropriate, and discuss some basic institutional modifications that are required if marketlike institutions are to be successfully adopted. Section III describes our formal analytical framework. In Section IV three scenarios are described and analyzed. Some concluding remarks are contained in Section V.

II. THE INSTITUTIONAL SETTING

Some Institutional History

In the developmental period of the West, public policy at the federal level facilitated growth through various forms of subsidies. Grants of rights of way to the railroads were perhaps the most notable example, but land grants to settlers and water development projects to supply water to at least a portion of the predominantly arid lands were also of importance. These water development projects were often heavily subsidized through interest-free construction money, formulas for repayment based on the ability to pay, use of revenues from hydropower to repay irrigation costs, and basinwide accounting to allow construction of noneconomic projects. Moreover, federal pricing policy emphasized recovery of costs only—and this only partially—rather than charging for water at its true economic value.

Public water policy clearly has focused on the supply side of the production process. With enormous acreages of arable land that could be made productive by the application of water and with large numbers of people who were disposed to make their livelihoods in farming, this may have been an efficient approach to development. However, the determination of appropriate water policy and decisions on specific projects were made in the terms of projected "needs." These needs were not expressed in terms of demands in the economic sense, but rather as estimates of the quantity of water required to supply a given tract of land at a price that would induce people to settle on the land.

This developmental thrust coincided with the early conservation movement and its emphasis on wise use. In terms of water policy, this meant that available water should be put to use; water that flowed to the sea was regarded as wasted. The construction of storage reservoirs made it possible to regulate the annual flows of rivers and to ensure a supply of water at the times required for irrigation. For the most part, there was little competition for these water supplies and relatively little concern for aesthetics or in-stream values. The development of water supplies for agriculture was viewed as compatible with the development of supplies for municipal, industrial, and hydroelectrical generation purposes. At least one controversy demonstrated the dominance of this ideology and a portent of the future—the vigorous battle over Hetch Hetchy Dam on the Tuolumne River in which John Muir pitted his influence against the City of San Francisco and the forces of development and lost.[1]

Low resource prices buttressed the dominant popular and political imagery of a virtually unlimited resource base. The principal task of both the public and private sectors was the discovery and development of those resources. Public development of water resources involved political justifications that often had little to do with concepts of economic efficiency. This, in turn, meant that water was usually underpriced relative to its scarcity value or true worth to society. This resulted in both over-investment in and over-utilization of the resource. Increased demand for water was reflected not in higher prices but in demands for additional water development projects that were often more costly than those that preceded.

Thus decisionmakers as well as local interests tended to ignore the opportunity costs of development.[2] When benefits exceeded costs, little attention was paid to the possibility that other forms of public investment or private investment encouraged with public funds might prove more beneficial. Benefit-cost ratios were often contrived owing to the utilization of unrealistic interests rates and the tendency to exaggerate benefits and minimize costs. Many reimbursable costs in large-scale multipurpose projects were included in nonreimbursable categories. The appropriate rate of interest remained a matter of controversy throughout this developmental period; most observers concluded that the discount rates actually used by political decisionmakers, purportedly to meet long-term social needs, were far below what was appropriate.[3]

The argument in favor of subsidized water development in the West was bolstered by the region's sense of injustice over federal policies that seemed to favor other economic sectors. High freight rates and protective tariffs brought higher costs to westerners and they felt justified in seeking subsidies of their own to compensate. Federal decisionmakers, on the other hand, wanting to encourage regional development, were prepared to use federal taxes to build a long-term physical infrastructure, particularly when it could be combined with encouragement of small-scale agriculture and the family farm. The 160-acre limitation on those receiving federally developed water was the most notable feature of this social policy.

Water policy was formulated nationally through a political process that has been aptly described as "distributive" politics.[4] Its principal characteristics were the following: (1) local sponsorship of water development projects with the support of state agencies that often mediated disputes among parties; (2) technical and political support in design of projects by federal agencies such as the Bureau of Reclamation and the U.S. Army Corps of Engineers; (3) the formulation of acceptable political packages by committees of both houses of Congress; (4) the absence of clear standards for judging the desirability of the project on the basis of costs and benefits to the nation; (5) the reliance upon the federal Treasury for the major share of the funds necessary to construct the project with a relatively modest return of these funds to the federal Treasury; and (6) a configuration of private interests, including land developers and a construction industry, that benefited from development of civil works. The incentives for the principal actors were the apparently cost-free benefits to local communities, political credit for politicians, and continued work for federal agencies and their contractors. In the absence of perceived alternative uses of the water or tax money, the narrow focus on water development avoided major conflicts over policy issues or specific projects.

Changing Conditions for Water Policy Making

The conditions that led to "distributive" politics with respect to water policy have changed. Seckler and Hartman argue that the principal conditions that have changed are two: first, the transformation from an economy that placed primary emphasis on the production of economic goods to an economy that now places greater emphasis on nonmaterial goods and amenities; and second, the traditional mode of evaluation of water projects—benefit-cost analysis (even as contrived and obscurantist as it often was)—has lost its dominant position in a world in which major value shifts have occurred.[5]

The transformation in the economy is reflected best in the rise of the environmental movement. Water is no longer considered "wasted" if it flows to the sea. It is valued as the medium for propagation of fish, wildlife, plants and other living creatures in ecological communities that clearly have less direct economic value than products that might be fashioned with additional inputs of water. It is valued for recreation pursued in and on it. It is valued simply because of the contributions it makes to our aesthetic sense, to our appreciation of natural beauty.

The value shift is also a reconceptualization of resources, in which free-flowing water, to use one example, is considered a unique resource that should be protected because there is so little of it left. While of greater value in storage when measured in terms of contribution to gross national product, it may have a higher societal value (as measured by political preferences expressed in polls and at the ballot box) when left in a natural watercourse. Moreover, water is a crucial element in ecological systems. Significant alterations in the natural state of water may disturb other elements in ecological communities, thus depriving society of important, if not crucial, organic structures of the biosphere.

The conflict over values is reflected in the competition for water as a scarce commodity. Municipalities and industry are capable of paying significantly higher prices for water because of its higher value in those uses and thus can compete more successfully for scarce supplies. Equally as important is the capacity of urban industrial centers to compete successfully at the ballot box. Eighty-five percent of the water in California may be used in agriculture, but ninety percent of the users are found in nonagricultural places and occupations.

There is no shortage of water in an absolute sense in California—there is a shortage of cheap water. Given the fact that new water is developed by public entities—the State of California, the federal government—costly proposals for water development are likely to compete with other contestants for scarce public fiscal resources. The passage of Proposition 13 in California appears to be only the most notable event of a period reaching back well into the decade of the 1970s in which the voters have been rejecting local bond issues for such vital services as education. The Reagan Administration now emphasizes cutting budgets and taxes and the state administration in California demonstrates a lively sense of voter preferences for lower public spending. The federal government has moved strongly in the direction of increased cost-sharing, requiring the states to provide a significant share of total cost of development projects at the beginning of a project. Voters are less prepared to mortgage the future through such financing arrangements, making the public financial support that was characteristic of the first phase of the State Water Project less likely in the future.

Combined with this disposition is a realization that the demand for water is in fact not inelastic. Evidence from both the agricultural and urban sectors of the economy has revealed that individuals and firms do tend to reduce their consumption of water in response to increases in its price.[6] Thus, there are no absolute "needs" for additional water in Southern California or in the San Joaquin Valley—rather, there are demands for given quantities of water at given prices. Increasingly, public decisionmakers are inclined to examine proposals for water development in the framework of sound economic reasoning. This does not necessarily mean that decisionmakers will make decisions based on noneconomic grounds such as support for a given kind of farming, protection of environmental values, or protection of communities against economic decline, but their rationale will be more clearly related to standards for measuring value.

Following this rationale, we assume in our subsequent examination that economic analysis is pertinent. The evaluation of our three scenarios is explicitly an economic evaluation. The institutional underpinnings are crucial, however, and we do not underestimate the difficulties associated with changing entrenched institutions in which influential members of the body politic perceive a personal stake. In order to alter existing institutional arrangements to permit the use of even a very modest market-type system for allocating scarce water supplies, a number of fundamental changes will have to be made.

Changes in the Institutional Structure

It is at least arguable that a trend toward the creation of markets exists and that the increasing price of water will tend to facilitate that trend. It may be expected that such changes will occur piecemeal as the institutional structure is modified, as expensive options seem less feasible, and as individuals and groups find it to their advantage to enter into transfer arrangements. Indeed, the State of California has already engaged in some effort to evaluate the feasibility of such transfers.[7]

The extent to which a market for water presently exists in California is not entirely clear. Lee notes that there has been little empirical work in this area but cites several examples of transfers that have occurred or have been attempted unsuccessfully. Lee and Phelps et al. refer to transfers that occur within districts and in fully adjudicated basins in Southern California. During the 1976-1977 drought there were a number of significant transfers involving water under contract with the Bureau of Reclamation and the State Water Project.[8]

Marketlike institutions for transferring water rights exist in other western states, notably Colorado and New Mexico. Hartman and Seastone have examined the legal and administrative arrangements that exist in those states and the extent to which they facilitate or impede transfers and increase efficiency of use.[9] A recent study of that region concluded, ". . .there is strong evidence to support the conclusion that the more proficient water rights markets will be found in those precise locations where the increasing demand for water is greater relative to the available supply." At least in the basins studied in four states (including Utah and Arizona also) the market appears to be performing the function of allocating and reallocating to its highest economic use.[10]

The changes that might be made to facilitate transfers may be classified along the following lines: water law and water rights; public attitudes; water administration; information and uncertainty; and financial arrangements.

Water Law and Water Rights. Water rights are of three kinds: riparian and appropriative rights to surface water flows and groundwater rights. Surface water rights are either rights to use direct streamflows or rights to water stored in reservoirs. Groundwater rights are associated with overlying land ownership, constrained only by the doctrine of correlative rights which establishes an obligation to share water from a common groundwater basin. The use of surface water is constrained by the doctrine of beneficial use which prohibits waste and limits water rights to reasonable beneficial use. Except for riparian rights, surface water is not attached to land but is governed by priority of application of water. It may be transferred, subject to state approval.[11]

Hartman and Seastone argue that the problems associated with transfers are less the result of existing laws than the consequence of uncertainties with respect to the physical hydrologic system and the effects of the transfers themselves. This is largely a question of information regarding the quantities that are available for transfer, the effects on third parties, and the impact the transfers will make on the hydrologic system as a whole. They argue that the New Mexico system is preferable to the Colorado system because of the ability of the State Engineer to ascertain the condition of hydrologic systems and to maintain records on appropriations and water rights. The Colorado system relies on the courts, which, it is argued, are less effective in developing the necessary systematic information to reduce these uncertainties.[12]

One of the greatest sources of uncertainty concerns the nature of the water rights held by individuals. Lee notes that riparian rights are the most uncertain in California since they are subject "to substantial variation in quantity."[13] Appropriative rights are more definable, but pre-1914 appropriative rights were not required to be recorded and post-1914 rights were, until 1969, recorded only as to flow rate and seasonal restrictions but not total quantities. Lee finds other uncertainties associated with municipal and state claims to rights.

The impacts of these uncertainties are reduced incentives to engage in purchases of water rights. With reason, purchasers need to have confidence that they will obtain full title to water and not be subject to claims that others might bring against purchased rights.

The cost of defining and quantifying water rights may be high and the process may require considerable time. Some of these rights are recorded and defined and therefore meet the test of property rights that can be sold, purchased, rented or leased. Other rights, such as most riparian and some appropriative rights, are not recorded and defined. For those rights to be made part of a transfer market they would have to be defined.

Public Attitudes. To a considerable extent, the failure to adopt a system for transferring water rights is the result of public, and particularly farmer, resistance to the concept. Ronald Robie, Director of the California Department of Water Resources, reported that the opposition was particularly pronounced in the water-rich northern parts of the state where there was a fear of the impacts of such transfers on local economies. He identified several instances where the Department of Water Resources had proposed transfers, only to be defeated by local opposition.[14] In a DWR study, it was reported that "the willingness of farmers to participate will depend that (sic) assurances can be made that the decision by growers to sell their water will be voluntary and they will not thereby impair their water rights."[15]

It is clear that the specter of a repetition of the experience of the water transfers out of the Owens Valley looms large in the minds of many observers. As Robie notes, dissension over that transfer continues after 50 years and it is still in litigation.[16] Brown et al., after looking at water transfers in four western states, conclude "that the pressures associated with water reallocation are creating considerable social tension, leading to extensive litigation, and demanding increasing political attention in the West."[17] Similar opposition was registered among farmers who were questioned about potential transfer systems in connection with a study of conservation in the Tulare Basin.[18]

Third-Party Effects. Perhaps the most perplexing of all issues relates to the methods for dealing with third-party effects. These commonly result from changes in the time and place of water diversion. Such changes may harm those who depend upon return flows for their supplies. A different type of third-party effect stems from the decline in economic activity in a community from which water may be transferred. The latter effects are particularly difficult to deal with because the parties at interest may be extensive and far removed from transactions leading to the market exchange.

The protection of the interests of those parties who depend on return flows is the responsibility of the State Water Resources Control Board in California. A seller of post-1914 appropriative rights must obtain approval of a transfer from the SWRCB where the transfer might change the point of diversion, place of use, or purpose of use. Where injury may occur to a downstream diverter, the Board must disapprove of the sale.[19] Phelps et al. conclude that under current law, "it appears that the mere presence of users down-stream of an appropriator's discharge may be sufficient to disallow a sale of the appropriation."[20]

The State Legislature facilitated transfers by passing legislation in 1980 which authorized the State Water Resources Control Board to approve trial transfers on a temporary basis (one year) where possible detrimental effects are difficult to determine. The Board is also authorized to approve long-term transfers (greater than one year) when no substantial injury would occur.[21]

Again, the problem appears to be one of uncertainty. There is general agreement that an appropriator should be able to sell only the amount equal to his consumptive use. Additionally, a down-stream user's right may be protected only in the amount of return flow to which he may lay claim. Each of these quantities must be determined in proceedings before administrative agencies such as the SWRCB.[22] For new appropriations, the National Water Commission recommended that the appropriator be granted a property right in the return flow, thus clarifying the nature of the transaction required in the event of a subsequent transfer.

Another alternative, of course, is that compensation be paid by the purchaser of water rights to those whose interests may be affected by such a purchase.

The question of the community's interest in water transfers is debatable. The assertion that secondary interests such as farm implement companies or banks should be represented in the transactions flies in the face of the fact that private transactions in other property encounter no such obstacle. Indeed, the decline of industries and communities that are no longer competitive is one means through which our economic system ensures continuing growth and prosperity. It is clear, however, that the opposition of these secondary interests to transfers is an important obstacle to market transactions.

In-Stream Uses. Those who have a stake in in-stream water uses may also constitute third parties to water transfers. To some extent, these interests are highly specific in the form of fishermen and recreationists, while in other instances, they are more general, as with community interests in maintaining free-flowing streams, water quality, the aesthetic qualities of riverine environments, and desirable ecological communities.[23]

These values are not usually protected by water rights, however. They depend largely on administrative determinations of the requirements for minimum and average flows, releases from reservoirs, and the installation of devices in dams to ensure protection of fish and wildlife. Protection of these values in California is largely the responsibility of the State Water Resources Control Board which is charged with the obligation of protecting such values when applications for appropriation for other purposes are being considered. In addition, there has been statutory protection of some streams against development, particularly through the California Wild and Scenic Rivers Act. Recently, these streams have achieved additional protection through their incorporation in the National Wild and Scenic Rivers System.

This administrative process has probably not provided adequate protection of such values. This process has been appropriately characterized as "reactive" since in-stream requirements are usually determined only in response to license applications for water rights or hydroelectric plants and not on the basis of independent and previously established in-stream standards.[24] In cases of conflict, negotiated settlements have often resulted in long-term declines in in-stream values. This is partly due to the lack of adequate information, the piecemeal process by which such matters are decided, and the frequent absence of effective intervenors on the side of in-stream values.

Various approaches to the protection of in-stream values include the granting of rights to individuals and groups to appropriate water for in-stream uses; the extension of the reasonable beneficial use doctrine to include protection of in-stream values; the purchase of water rights by the State to ensure protection of in-stream values; and the enforcement of county-of-origin statutes to protect these values. The Governor's Commission to Review California Water Rights Law urged reliance on administrative measures by the State Water Resources Control Board to set and gain compliance with comprehensive in-stream flow standards on a stream-by-stream basis. It also recommended that the Resources Agency be given authority to purchase water for in-stream uses. It specifically recommended against allowing the appropriation of water for such uses.

The protection of such values may therefore become an important constraint on the extent of proposed transfers. But the mechanism for protection may not necessarily be limited to administrative fiat. Present California law prohibits the acquisition of water rights for in-stream purposes but other states, such as Colorado, permit appropriations of water for those purposes. It is at least arguable that permitting appropriations for in-stream uses is a desirable step. This type of appropriation would place in-stream uses on the same footing as appropriations for consumptive uses and would permit society to measure the opportunity costs of protecting such uses. With the adoption of a marketlike system, the state could purchase the rights necessary for the protection of values in excess of those to which it is already presumptively entitled through the existence of in-stream standards. The extent of the cost of such purchases is unclear, but they would probably not increase substantially the budgets of purchasing agencies such as the State Department of Fish and Game.[25]

The Role of Water Districts. One of the impediments to water transfers is the existing organization of the water economy. Water districts perform several crucial roles for individuals who have entitlements to water including water development, management, distribution, and protection. They are authorized to exercise an array of powers, including the powers to tax, issue bonds, receive financing, and contract with federal and state agencies, but they are not allowed to make a profit. The districts vary, however, in the extent of their powers, the exercise of those they have, the system of voting rights that govern their decisionmaking, and the sophistication with which they pursue their objectives.[26] They vary substantially in the manner in which they impose charges or taxes on their membership or on land within their jurisdictions. They manage water from a variety of sources: locally developed surface and groundwater and water under contract from state and federal agencies.

To make water transfers, the districts and their members must have some incentives to engage in sales. Since most do not have excess water to sell, sales must be premised on the assumption that there will be a reduction of consumption within district boundaries. There are often restrictions contained in both general district law and specific district acts with respect to sales of water outside individual districts. In most cases, these restrictions limit sales to "surplus water" and require approval from the State Treasurer.[27]

Based on experience with water transfers during the 1976-1977 drought and the analysis of incentives that presently operate, Phelps et al. argue that each water district should issue to farmers clear title to use of the water it delivers. The title to the water must be separable from the land, thus permitting individuals to transfer the water to others outside the district. All limitations on out-of-district transfers would have to be eliminated. Any transfers under such an arrangement would still have to receive the approval of the State Water Resources Control Board because of the changes in point and time of diversion.

In keeping with this recommendation, it would be important that the Bureau of Reclamation and the California Department of Water Resources allow the districts receiving water from the Central Valley Project and the State Water Project to trade their water shares freely. The prices at which those shares were traded would have to be sufficient to guarantee the repayment of the contracts by the water districts.

Limitations on Who May Transfer Water. Transfers of groundwater or groundwater rights would have to be subject to some limitations, lest overlying landowners with no history of groundwater use were to drill wells in order to enter the market for the first time. It has been suggested that participation in the market could be limited to those with a ten-year history of pumping groundwater for irrigation purposes. Similar problems might arise with respect to surface water rights in those cases where individuals had an entitlement to water by virtue of their lands being located within a district even though they might never have used their allotment.

Transfer Facilities. For a transfer system to be effective, there must exist a physical facility for making the transfers—the canals through which the water would flow. The most likely transfers would be from Northern California to the San Joaquin Valley or Southern California. Phelps et al. make the point that some exchanges can be made without actual physical transfers of water to the purchasing area. Third parties might transfer the water to the purchaser, with the third party actually receiving the newly purchased water.[28] Robie nevertheless suggests that the existing "plumbing system" is presently being used nearly to capacity and that new facilities would be required to make a market transfer system feasible, with all of the complex questions of financing and environmental impacts to be resolved.[29] However, it may be sufficient to improve present transportation facilities for certain kinds of transfers, particularly from Northern California to the San Joaquin Valley and Southern California. The Peripheral Canal or some other transfer facility for the Delta may be necessary to ensure protection of ecological and water quality values.

Financial Obligations of Those Who Sell Water. Individuals who might wish to sell or otherwise transfer water rights face resistance from water districts because of the implications of such sales for the financial structure of the districts. Districts often have bonded indebtedness and contractual obligations to federal and state water supply agencies. Water right sales would have to incorporate arrangements by which the district would receive sufficient payment to offset the loss of revenue from tolls and property taxes arising from reductions in water use within the district as a consequence of transfers.

Brokering Institutions. It is difficult to discern, as yet, the character of the market as it might develop. Given the central role of the State of California in managing water, it is possible that the Department of Water Resources would perform the function of brokering water. Its capacity to deliver water over long distances, its ability to make exchanges that might avoid large transportation charges, and its concern for the protection of water quality would all tend to justify a central role for some state institution. The Department has so far declined to advance itself as a potential participant in such a market system.

On the other hand, a private institution or a number of private individuals and/or institutions might develop to negotiate such trades, exchanges, and sales. These could take the form of private companies whose business it would be to bring parties together. One would expect entrepreneurs to perceive the opportunity for profit-making and to seek out parties on both sides of the exchange.[30]

The principal sources of market imperfection might be in the role of the middleman and the possibility of an oligopolistic pattern of water rights ownership. The brokering institution, especially a single institution like a government bureau or a central private marketing institution, might tend to monopolize information and thus control access to the market. A central institution could engage in discriminatory practices with respect to pricing, quality of water, favoritism to a particular region or to a given industry or municipality. A government bureau might tend to do so for reasons that it deemed socially beneficial or even politically advantageous. A private firm might be tempted to accept under-the-table payment for preferential treatment. The potential for oligopoly is illustrated in the Gila River Basin in New Mexico where a few large corporate enterprises—particularly mining companies—dominate the market and could influence water prices significantly.[31]

There is no reason to assume that these market imperfections are inevitable. The free flow of information, the watchfulness of interest groups, access to the legislature and the courts to correct abuses, and, ultimately, the right of a group to recapture its water if provisions for doing so are written into the contracts, would appear sufficient to remedy abuses that might arise from market imperfections.

III. AN ANALYTICAL FRAMEWORK

We envision three basic scenarios that could depict the future of water management in California. The first two scenarios characterize a situation in which historical trends of water management in California will continue into the indefinite future and the only means of alleviating the increasing scarcity will be through the construction of more water supply facilities. The allocative implications of such a situation will be analyzed both in the absence (Scenario 1) and presence (Scenario 2) of such new supplies. The third scenario presumes that certain basic changes are made in legal and governmental institutions that will permit the transfer of water between sectors and regions. These transfers will be governed by region-specific and sector-specific water prices. The prices are established jointly by the interaction of regional supplies and demands and by the costs of transferring water between regions and sectors. Development of new supplies occurs only when the economic demand or willingness to pay justifies it.

The scenarios are characterized by (1) a general set of assumptions relative to the institutional setting and some physical parameters and (2) a set of regional supply and demand conditions which capture the costs of supply and the willingness of users to pay for water for the years 1980, 1995, and 2020. Basic institutional and physical assumptions describe those factors whose influence on water use will remain essentially unchanged with time. These assumptions are discussed in the next section where the scenarios are described. The supply and demand relationships capture the factors which, in our opinion, are most likely to affect change in water use over time. In this section a basic analytical model is presented and the time-dependent variables likely to affect water use are identified.

For purposes of analysis, we divide the state into three water use regions. The northern region includes the area north of the 36th parallel (which bisects the state approximately 30 miles south of Fresno). The southern region includes the area south of the 36th parallel with the exception of the Imperial Valley, which constitutes the third water use region. Water use in the northern and southern regions is divided between an agricultural sector and an urban (municipal and industrial) sector, each characterized by a different set of supply and demand relationships. Water use in the Imperial Valley is assumed to be entirely agricultural.

The basic analytical model used to assess the economic implications of interregional trade in water follows a form initially suggested by Enke and Samuelson.[32] A simple graphical illustration of the model for two regions is presented in Figure 1. The graph on the right hand side of the figure depicts an excess supply region with demand D_1D_1 and supply S_1S_1. Such a region would be characterized as one with abundant, relatively cheap supplies of water. The graph on the left hand side depicts an excess demand region with demand D_2D_2 and supply S_2S_2. An excess demand region would be characterized by relatively scarce and expensive water supplies. It follows that the price of the commodity (water) in region 1 (P_1) would be less than the price of the commodity in region 2 (P_2). If transportation costs are less than the difference between P_1 and P_2 gains can be realized from trade.

Figure 1

Interregional Equilibrium Prices and Flows

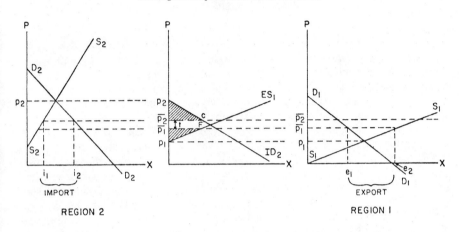

ES_1 on the middle graph represents the cost to region 1 of supplying excess water for export. ID_2 represents the demand curve for water imported by region 2. A rightward movement along this curve occasioned by the availability of cheaper imported supplies represents the marginal benefit to region 2 of being able to obtain its water more cheaply through imports than if it had to rely on its own supplies. Transportation costs are defined in this instance as t. The net social payoff from trade is the sum of the payoff or benefit to each region net of the transportation costs. The benefit to region 1, the exporting region, is equal to $P_1\bar{P}_1F$. This is the net revenue received by the region from the sale of a portion of its excess supply that would otherwise remain unused. The benefit to region 2, the importing region, is equal to $P_2\bar{P}_2c$ and accrues because that region is able to obtain cheaper water supplies via importation. The total social payoff is the sum of the benefits to the two regions.

In the context of the California water situation, it is important to recognize that institutions which impede or inhibit transfers may impose economic losses by preventing regions or individuals from realizing potential gains from trade. Of course, if there are not significant differences in the conditions of supply and demand between regions or if the costs of transportation are high enough to offset the gains from trade, then no such social losses will be imposed. Subsequently, it will be shown that gains from interregional water trade in California do exist.

The interregional programming model that is used to analyze water transfer possibilities in California incorporates five sectors. In effect, the agricultural and urban (municipal and industrial) sectors of the northern and southern regions are treated as though they were distinct regions. Any sector can purchase water from any other sector provided it pays the going price plus the costs of transportation. Linear supply and demand functions for the five sectors have been estimated for 1980, 1995 and 2020. These functions are based upon data from a variety of sources and were linearized where necessary to facilitate the computation of solutions.[33]

The urban demand functions, which are relatively inelastic, shift over time (for 1995 and 2020) solely in response to population growth projected by the California Department of Finance.[34] The agricultural demand functions, which are relatively more elastic, are of two types: (1) nominal agricultural demands which grow at one percent per year, and (2) high agricultural demands based on the premise that demand for California produce will increase sufficiently above nominal levels to justify bringing into production between 1990 and 2020 all of the potentially irrigable acreage in the Central Valley plus an additional one million acres south of the Tehachapis.

The supply functions were estimated from existing data and were assumed to change over time in response to changes in the real cost of energy which increases from \$0.025/kwh in 1980 to \$0.08/kwh in 1995 and 2020 (see Chapter V). Adjustments were made to reflect the differing energy intensity of surface and groundwater supplies. Groundwater supplies were constrained to approximately the quantities currently pumped. The functions for new water supplies and the prices of transporting water between regions were estimated from data compiled by the Department of Water Resources and respond over time to changes in real energy costs.

The solution of the five sector interregional trade problem which emerges is moderately complex. However, the linear form of the supply and demand functions permits solution of the problem with a quadratic programming formulation originally suggested by Takayama and Judge.[35] The programming formulation equilibrates the equations appropriate for each scenario and each time period, and yields the equilibrium water prices and quantities used. The equilibrium conditions are characterized by: (1) the net price of water in each region; (2) the quantity of exports or imports for each region; (3) an identification of the exporting and importing regions; and (4) an estimate of the volume and direction of trade.

In the next section, the basic institutional and physical parameters of each scenario are characterized and the water allocation implications of each scenario generated with the aid of the interregional programming model are reported.

IV. THREE SCENARIOS: AN ANALYSIS

Scenario 1

This scenario envisions that existing water institutions remain largely unchanged over the next forty years. Its most prominent characteristics can be described as follows:

(1) The definition of water rights remains essentially unchanged. A complex mixture of surface water direct flow rights (both appropriative and riparian), rights to stored water, and groundwater rights remain essentially unchanged and are defined administratively by the State Water Resources Control Board and

judicially through the courts. Constraints on water use such as the doctrine of reasonable beneficial use and correlative rights continue to apply to surface and groundwater respectively. They continue to be relatively ineffective instruments for achieving increased efficiencies in the absence of other incentives.

(2) Water rights are not subject to transfer from one place to another, one use to another, or one river to another, except under limited local circumstances and under conditions of emergency. There is no "market" for water rights. Lack of significant financial incentives to conserve and sell or rent water in excess of wants causes individual farmers and irrigation districts with low-cost water to retain existing water rights with very little in the way of reallocations to higher economic uses.

(3) Farmers and districts that might otherwise buy supplemental water from lower valued uses continue to seek water from new sources in the Sacramento River system and on the North Coast of California. Major controversies with local interests in areas of origin and with environmentalist organizations continue unabated.

(4) The cost of water to farmers who are supplied by federal reservoirs increases significantly as water supply contracts with federal agencies are renewed, reflecting higher energy costs. The cost of water from the State Water Project also escalates because of rapid increases in the cost of pumping, and the costs of groundwater rise.

(5) Groundwater levels of the southern San Joaquin Valley continue to decline as pumping at rates in excess of recharge continues. Significantly increased costs to farmers lead to shifts in cropping patterns and ultimately to the withdrawal of some lands from production.

(6) The threat to the agricultural industry in the southern San Joaquin leads to increased pressure for a scheme of groundwater management along the lines recommended in the report of the Governor's Commission. In the absence of supplemental water, there is great resistance to such management approaches.

The economic picture that characterizes this scenario is presented in Table 1. For 1980, the prices and quantities are generally reflective of current prices paid and quantities used. Between 1980 and 1995 with nominal agricultural demands, prices increase rather sharply and there is a modest reduction in the quantities used by all sectors (except the Imperial Valley where there is no quantity adjustment since the supply is inelastic) in response to the anticipated increase in energy costs. The absolute price increases are nearly identical for the northern and southern urban sectors. The price of water for northern agriculture increases proportionately more than the counterpart price for southern agriculture primarily because groundwater, which remains cheaper than most surface supplies despite lower water tables and increased energy costs, accounts for a greater percentage of total southern supplies. The sharp price increase in water in the Imperial Valley is totally reflective of increases in the demand for that water and should, therefore, be viewed as an opportunity cost.

The total quantities used statewide decline by 2.9 MAF About two-thirds of this reduction occurs in the agricultural sectors and one-third in the urban sectors. Proportionately, urban sectors reduce consumption more than the agricultural sectors, largely because the demands for urban water are more elastic or price-responsive than those for agricultural water in the prevailing price ranges. The 2.9

Table 1

Scenario 1: Water Prices and Quantities

Region and Sector 1980	Nominal Agricultural Demands		High Agricultural Demands	
	Price (1980 Dollars)	Quantity (in MAF)	Price (1980 Dollars)	Quantity (in MAF)
Northern agriculture	$ 20.95	13.78	20.95	13.78
Southern agriculture	30.46	11.64	30.46	11.64
Imperial Valley	6.45	2.905	6.45	2.905
Northern municipal and industrial	139.47	1.26	139.47	1.26
Southern municipal and industrial	172.71	2.90	172.71	2.90
Total		32.485		32.485
1995				
Northern agriculture	$ 34.35	12.826	51.81	14.14
Southern agriculture	42.53	10.63	53.49	11.06
Imperial Valley	15.35	2.905	15.35	2.905
Northern municipal and industrial	250.51	1.06	250.51	1.06
Southern municipal and industrial	288.43	2.13	288.43	2.13
Total		29.551		31.295
2020				
Northern agriculture	$ 44.10	13.367	66.17	14.89
Southern agriculture	51.48	10.82	65.17	11.30
Imperial Valley	27.69	2.905	27.69	2.905
Northern municipal and industrial	268.07	1.14	268.07	1.14
Southern municipal and industrial	295.42	2.21	295.42	2.21
Total		30.442		32.445

MAF of surplus water would presumptively be available for storage as protection against drought. It should be emphasized that this water is surplus in the economic sense and not surplus to "needs" as historically defined.

The price increases in the period between 1995 and 2020 are not as sharp. For urban sectors, these increases are induced solely by a growth in demand; the price increases for agricultural water, assuming nominal demands, are reflective both of increased demand for agricultural products and increases in supply costs attributable to continued lowering of groundwater tables. The quantities consumed by all sectors increase modestly, though not back to the 1980 levels.

If high agricultural demands prevail, the same general patterns are observed with two exceptions. The price of agricultural water in the northern and southern sectors increases between $10 and $18 per acre-foot for both 1995 and 2020. Under high agricultural demands, the northern agricultural sector would experience continued growth in water use through both 1995 and 2020. In the southern sector, water use declines but is about 400,000 to 500,000 acre-feet more than it would be under nominal agricultural demands. High agricultural demands would cause water use statewide to increase by about 1.7 MAF in 1995 and 2.0 MAF in 2020 over what it would be in those years with nominal agricultural demands. The urban sectors would be unaffected.

Scenario 2

Scenario 2 is identical to Scenario 1 except for the availability of new supplies. For Scenario 2, it is assumed that construction of storage facilities in the Sacramento River system is possible if demand (price) warrants. Proposals for projects on the North Coast rivers remain in abeyance and continue to be the focus of intense controversy. Groundwater management regimes fail to materialize largely because the recipients of new supplies are urban users and agricultural users continue to resist such regimes. The results for this scenario are summarized in Table 2.

For the base year, 1980, the prices and quantities prevailing in the agricultural sector are identical to those in Scenario 1. This reflects the fact that only urban sectors are willing to defray the relatively high costs of new supplies. The urban sectors, then, are the principal beneficiaries of the new surface supplies. The quantities of water used by the urban sectors increase by roughly 20 percent over levels in Scenario 1. Urban water prices are significantly reduced with the northern sector experiencing a larger price decline than the southern sector primarily because of the lower costs of transportation. New supplies of 420,000 acre-feet are developed. About 40 percent of this goes to northern urban use, with 60 percent devoted to southern urban use.

The patterns of prices and use over time (for 1995 and 2020) under both nominal and high agricultural demands are generally consistent with the patterns in Scenario 1. For 1995, the availability of new supplies buffers the decline in total use by about 500,000 acre-feet since new supplies are also subject to the anticipated increases in energy cost. The additional 500,000 acre-feet flow to urban areas. The availability of new supplies saves northern urban users approximately $66.25 per acre-foot while southern urban users save about half that. The agricultural sectors are unaffected by new supplies irrespective of whether nominal or high demands prevail.

For 2020, changes are due mainly to the impact of growing demands. The quantities of water allocated to the urban sectors return to quite near their original 1980 levels and urban users also reap substantial benefits in the form of lower prices. This scenario suggests that the primary beneficiaries of new supplies will be urban water users as long as current institutions are not modified. It is, of course, true that more new supplies could be made available and agricultural sectors could benefit from them if a decision were made to subsidize some of the costs of these supplies publicly. The precise quantities and the allocation of those quantities between sectors would depend upon the extent of public willingness to defray costs and upon allocative decisions arrived at largely in response to political considerations.

Table 2

Scenario 2: Water Prices and Quantities

Region and Sector 1980	Nominal Agricultural Demands		High Agricultural Demands	
	Price (1980 Dollars)	Quantity (in MAF)	Price (1980 Dollars)	Quantity (in MAF)
Northern agriculture	$ 20.95	13.78	20.95	13.78
Southern agriculture	30.46	11.64	30.46	11.64
Imperial Valley	6.45	2.905	6.45	2.905
Northern municipal and industrial	94.68	1.42	94.68	1.42
Southern municipal and industrial	146.92	3.16	146.92	3.16
Total		32.905		32.905
1995				
Northern agriculture	$ 34.35	12.83	51.81	14.14
Southern agriculture	42.53	10.63	53.49	11.06
Imperial Valley	15.35	2.905	15.35	2.905
Northern municipal and industrial	184.26	1.28	184.26	1.28
Southern municipal and industrial	254.92	2.47	254.92	2.47
Total		30.115		31.855
2020				
Northern agriculture	$ 44.10	13.367	66.17	14.89
Southern agriculture	51.48	10.82	65.71	11.30
Imperial Valley	27.69	2.905	27.69	2.905
Northern municipal and industrial	199.64	1.40	199.64	1.40
Southern municipal and industrial	267.98	2.64	267.98	2.64
Total		31.132		33.135

Scenario 3

This scenario assumes that substantial changes in water institutions and policies occur that permit the use of a limited market system for transferring water between sectors. The prominent features of this scenario are:

(1) The current limitations on voluntary transfers of water rights are removed, allowing water rights and water to be transferred permanently through sales, or on a temporary basis through leases and rental agreements. These arrangements are consummated by willing buyers and sellers at prices mutually agreed upon.

(2) The marketing arrangements require the determination of any effects on third parties associated with transfers. Legislative standards are required but specific conclusions with respect to time, place, quantities of water and the level of compensation will require administrative arrangements and decisions, subject ultimately to judicial appeals.

(3) Special institutions, presumably with a regional orientation, are developed to facilitate the exchange of water. These institutions locate willing buyers in other regions and willing sellers within their own region and negotiate acceptable terms between the parties directly involved. They also make suitable arrangements with third parties.

(4) Given the fact that water might have to be conveyed for long distances, arrangements will be required for transporting water in canals owned and operated by the federal and state governments. Marketing agreements would be subject to allocation of canal capacities and to pumpage and wheeling charges imposed by two levels of government.

(5) Given the complexity of the water rights available for marketing in a given region, the interdependencies of those using the same aquifer, and the financial obligations of landowners in districts, it is inevitable that water districts organized under state law would be the principal agents of marketing arrangements or at least be major participants in any transfer agreements. Such involvement may require alterations in the legal authorities under which various districts presently operate. Groundwater management districts of the sort recommended by the Governor's Commission would undoubtedly play an important role in the export of groundwater in order to protect the interests of the various parties who are dependent on aquifers.

(6) Some individuals who would be willing to sell water through their districts might be subject to contractual obligations with federal and state governments. These sellers would have to make appropriate arrangements for purchasers to continue payment on those obligations to the district and through the district to the water delivery agency.

(7) Federal and state agencies sell their water at the cost of producing and delivering the water, usually with some form of subsidy. Even with subsidy elimination, prices pegged to costs of water production and delivery would still not reflect the scarcity value of the water in a relatively free market. Such agencies might appropriately charge for water at its scarcity value and thereby contribute to the allocation of water to its highest valued use. The issue of who should reap the windfall revenues from such a policy would have to be resolved.

(8) While the basis for legal title to water would not be changed, the existence of a market would tend to have all water—whether surface or groundwater—treated in a like fashion. Sellers would seek to sell that water from which they would achieve maximum profits; they would manage their surface and groundwater supplies in such a way as to gain maximum benefit while examining the possibilities of achieving additional profits from sales of water that could not be economically put to use.

(9) The pricing scheme that emerges is a marginal-cost pricing scheme. Average cost pricing or "melded" prices are not used. While a few purveyors may have trouble covering costs in the long run, the consequence of marginal-cost pricing is to shift water to its highest valued uses.

(10) The consequence of marketing arrangements is likely to be a reduction in the pressure for achieving water supply solutions through the construction of additional storage projects. There would be a modest reduction of agricultural acreage. The losses associated with the elimination of low efficiency uses and low value crops would be compensated for by shifts of water to more productive uses in agriculture and municipal and industrial uses.

(11) Marketing arrangements could facilitate the purchase of water rights by those who are concerned with the protection of values associated with in-stream flows.

(12) The most important effect of such an arrangement would be to impose on all water users the opportunity cost of using the water in the region and activity in which its value is highest. Thus, each user would be constantly faced with the decision of whether to continue current uses of water or to sell the water to some other region or sector where its value (less the costs of transport) is higher.

The results for this scenario under nominal agriculture demands are presented in Table 3.

Table 3

Scenario 3: Water Prices and Quantities With
Nominal Agricultural Demands

Region and Sector	Price (1980 Dollars)	Quantity (in MAF)
1980		
Northern agriculture	$ 22.90	13.38
Southern agriculture	32.45	11.21
Imperial Valley	32.45	1.737
Northern municipal and industrial	55.90	1.55
Southern municipal and industrial	102.46	3.645
Total		31.522
1995		
Northern agriculture	$ 36.63	12.28
Southern agriculture	42.52	10.63
Imperial Valley	37.78	1.74
Northern municipal and industrial	119.63	1.50
Southern municipal and industrial	206.79	2.95
Total		29.10
2020		
Northern agriculture	$ 45.25	12.705
Southern agriculture	51.49	10.82
Imperial Valley	49.81	1.423
Northern municipal and industrial	127.25	1.665
Southern municipal and industrial	218.81	3.44
Total		30.053

For 1980, the most striking difference between this scenario and the others is the change in prices. With nominal demands, prices of northern and southern agricultural water increase very modestly while the price for Imperial Valley has increased almost fivefold. At the same time, the price of municipal and industrial water for both the northern and southern urban sectors has declined quite substantially. The price changes are a consequence of interregional trade in which water is sold to urban sectors by agricultural sectors. It is instructive to notice that the difference in price between the northern agricultural sector and the northern urban sector is exactly equal to the cost of transporting the water from the former to the latter ($33.00/acre-foot). A similar relationship can be observed between the Imperial Valley and the southern urban sector (transport cost = $70.00/acre-foot), and between the southern agricultural and urban sectors (transport cost = $70.00/acre-foot).

The quantities of water used by each sector in 1980 with nominal agricultural demands indicate that as a consequence of the transfers, urban sectors are using more, and agricultural sectors less, than in Scenario 2 where transfers are not permitted. This pattern is repeated for 1995 and 2020. The quantity of water actually traded in 1995 declines as the impact of increasing energy costs outweighs the growth of demand attributable to population increases. For the period between 1995 and 2020, the quantities traded increase as the cost of energy stabilizes and demands for water continue to grow. By 2020, the magnitudes of water traded approach those traded in 1980.

With nominal demands for agricultural water, the quantities of water used statewide decline somewhat from the levels that would be experienced in Scenario 2. If the trading possibilities inherent in Scenario 3 are realized, total water use would be reduced by 833,000 acre-feet in 1980, 1.015 MAF in 1995, and 1.079 MAF in 2020. These quantities of water represent actual savings that could be realized by permitting trade between sectors. Viewed differently, failure to implement the institutional changes required to permit trade, would result in the use of additional quantities of water purely as a result of economically inefficient institutional arrangements.

The results for Scenario 3 under high agricultural water demands are presented in Table 4. The far right hand column shows the additional supplies that would be utilized by the northern and southern agricultural sectors in Scenario 3 if high demands replace nominal demands. The price of water to the agricultural sectors would be between $11.00 and $21.00 higher per acre-foot. One consequence of the higher demands (and prices) in the northern and southern agricultural sectors would be a reduction in the quantities of water exchanged between the northern agricultural and urban sectors. The absolute quantities of water used statewide under high demands would be 1.83 MAF greater in 1995 and 2.125 MAF greater in 2020 than under Scenario 3 with nominal demands.

A comparison of Scenarios 2 and 3 under high agricultural demands reveals patterns of prices and use quite similar to those that would prevail under nominal demands. The change in the prices of water in the southern agricultural, urban and Imperial Valley sectors remains the same since trade is unaffected. Prices in the northern agricultural and urban sectors increase somewhat more due to the reduced opportunities for profitable trade stemming from the increase in value of the agricultural water. With high demands, total water use under Scenario 3 is approximately 1.0 MAF less in both 1995 and 2020 than under Scenario 2. Again, this difference can be attributed to the inefficiencies inherent in existing water institutions.

The significance of the price increases should be clearly understood. In the Imperial Valley, for example, the impact of permitting trade is to increase water prices quite sharply. These price increases are accepted *voluntarily*, however, by users who find that the return they receive from selling the water is greater than the return from using it in irrigation. Users who elect to sell their water receive, in 1980, a price of $32.45 per acre-foot for water that costs them only $6.45. In 2020, they receive $49.81 per acre-foot for water that costs $27.69.

Table 4

Scenario 3: Water Prices and Quantities With
High Agricultural Demands

Region and Sector	Price (1980 Dollars)	Quantity (in MAF)	Change in Quantity (in MAF)
1995			
Northern agriculture	$ 52.97	13.68	+1.40
Southern agriculture	53.49	11.06	+0.43
Imperial Valley	37.78	1.74	-0-
Northern municipal and industrial	133.97	1.448	-0-
Southern municipal and industrial	206.79	2.95	-0-
Total		30.878	1.83
2020			
Northern agriculture	$ 66.93	14.36	+1.655
Southern agriculture	65.71	11.29	+0.470
Imperial Valley	49.81	1.423	-0-
Northern municipal and industrial	147.93	1.589	-0-
Southern municipal and industrial	218.81	3.44	-0-
Total		32.102	2.125

The benefits from transfer under nominal agricultural demands are summarized in Table 5 for 1980, 1995, and 2020. The right hand column of the table shows the annual benefits of trade to each trading region. The benefits of transfer under high agricultural demands are summarized in Table 6.

The magnitude of the estimates of total benefits reported here are subject to at least four qualifications. First, the demand functions for water have been cast in a linear form for ease of computation. The work of Howitt, Watson, and Adams suggests that the aggregate demand functions for agricultural water are curvilinear.[36] The use of curvilinear demand functions would likely reduce the estimates of benefits from transfer although probably not substantially. A second qualification stems from the assumption that real agricultural prices (adjusted for inflation) will remain relatively constant over the next 40 years. Should the price of agricultural commodities rise at rates higher than the general rate of inflation, as some experts have predicted, the willingness to pay for agricultural water would be increased, perhaps substantially.[37] This would serve to reduce the quantities of water that would be traded.

A third qualification attaches to the conservative nature of the assumption that the real price of electricity will rise only to $0.08/kwh. Chapter V of this volume suggests that this is the lowest likely increase and that the cost of electricity could rise to $0.15/kwh. Any increase in the price of electrical energy above what we have assumed in this paper will reduce the quantity of water that can be transferred economically. Indeed, since energy price increases affect the costs of both groundwater pumping and surface conveyance, sharply higher energy prices would tend to lock water into current sectoral patterns of consumption and would probably induce a reduction in the quantities of water used in all sectors with the possible exception of the Imperial Valley.

Table 5

**Benefits From Transfers With Nominal Agricultural Demands
(In 1980 Constant Dollars)**

Direction and Quantity of Transfer					Benefit
1980					
IMP	→ LA	1.1691 MAF	IMP	=	$15,198,300
SA	→ LA	0.652 MAF	SA	=	648,740
			LA	=	40,489,935
NA	→ SFB	0.7368 MAF	NA	=	718,380
			SFB	=	14,286,552
	Total				$71,341,907
1995					
IMP	→ LA	1.168 MAF	IMP	=	$13,099,120
			LA	=	28,107,920
NA	→ SFB	0.7196 MAF	NA	=	820,344
			SFB	=	23,973,474
	Total				$66,000,858
2020					
IMP	→ LA	1.4834 MAF	IMP	=	$16,458,323
			LA	=	36,469,389
NA	→ SFB	0.8108 MAF	NA	=	871,610
			SFB	=	29,346,906
	Total				$83,146,228

Key:

NA	=	Northern agriculture
SFB	=	Northern municipal and industrial
IMP	=	Imperial valley
SA	=	Southern agriculture
LA	=	Southern municipal and industrial

Finally, the results of this analysis are contingent, in part, on the assumption that marginal-cost pricing practices will be utilized in allocating water. Marginal-cost pricing normally ensures that water is priced according to its true scarcity value and, thereby, is devoted to its most valuable uses. The introduction of marginal-cost pricing would represent a significant departure from the average-cost or "melded" pricing practices currently employed by most water purveyors in California. Average-cost pricing ensures that costs are completely covered in the long run and prevents purveyors from accumulating profits. Without melded prices, a few water purveyors may have trouble covering costs, but under current circumstances such cases are likely to be exceptional and could be dealt with on an ad hoc basis. On the other hand, in the current California setting, most melded

Table 6

Benefits From Tranfers With High Agricultural Demands
(In 1980 Constant Dollars)

Direction and Quantity of Transfer					Benefit
1995					
IMP	→	LA	1.168 MAF	IMP =	$13,099,120
				LA =	28,107,920
NA	→	SFB	0.5432 MAF	NA =	315,056
				SFB =	13,658,764
		Total			$55,180,860
2020					
IMP	→	LA	1.4834 MAF	IMP =	$16,406,404
				LA =	36,469,389
NA	→	SFB	0.5792 MAF	NA =	220,096
				SFB =	14,975,216
		Total			$68,071,105

Key:

NA = Northern agriculture
SFB = Northern municipal and industrial
IMP = Imperial Valley
SA = Southern agriculture
LA = Southern municipal and industrial

prices are lower than marginal-cost prices. The consequence is that users are not confronted with the scarcity value (or opportunity cost) of water and there is, therefore, an inevitable tendency to use water excessively.

Although it is not always obvious, average-cost pricing compels those who use relatively low-cost supplies to subsidize the users of high-cost supplies. This occurs because average costs lead to prices which are higher than the marginal costs of cheap supplies and lower than the marginal costs of expensive supplies. Continued use of average-cost pricing in California would result in lower prices and greater use, compared to the marginal-cost pricing case in the three scenarios analyzed here. Additionally, for Scenarios 2 and 3, the use of melded prices would reduce the volumes of water traded and would undoubtedly justify the development of new supplies on a larger scale and at an earlier time than under marginal-cost pricing practices. Such outcomes would require the recipients of low-cost water to give up willingly some competitive advantage in the interests of those who would use high-cost supplies but are unable or unwilling to pay the full marginal costs of those supplies.

In contrast with these qualifications is the fact that gains from interregional trade probably represent a lower bound on the total benefits that could be realized from trade. This conclusion follows from the fact that trade is only permitted between regions and sectors. The third scenario does not encompass possibilities for trade between individual water users within the same region. Inasmuch as the intraregional transportation costs are likely to be significantly lower than the interregional costs, it is likely that the gains from intraregional trading would be substantially larger than the gains reported here.

In any event, the benefits from interregional trade are hardly negligible. An annual return comparable to the total benefits for 1980 would require an investment of nearly $900 million at a real interest rate of 8 percent. Additionally, it should be recognized that these benefits are, in effect, an opportunity cost that must be borne by water users if institutional arrangements remain substantially as envisioned in Scenarios 1 and 2. The limited market transfer opportunities envisioned in Scenario 3 not only ensure a modicum of efficiency in water use resulting in a savings of between one and two million acre-feet but also confer direct benefits upon trading parties. In short, the preservation of current institutions at a time of increasing water scarcity imposes real monetary costs in the form of inefficiencies upon the state of California.

V. CONCLUSIONS

In this chapter we have examined three scenarios of water use with the aid of an interregional trade model in an effort to illustrate some of the costs associated with preserving current institutional arrangements in the face of increasing competition for water supplies. If current institutions are maintained in substantially their present form for the next 40 years, water use will be sharply constrained in urban sectors. The price of all water will increase sharply as a result of increasing energy costs and increased competition for supplies. The increases will be especially sharp in urban areas.

The outlook for new water supplies that could alleviate the scarcity appears quite limited because of the costs. If water users do not defray these costs, the taxpayers will have to bear them. In the current political setting, we doubt that taxpayers will be willing to underwrite the costs of water projects to the same degree that has characterized the past. Fiscal limitations and increasing resistance to public funding of water projects suggests that perhaps 700,000 acre-feet of additional capacity would be provided over the next 40 years. This observation underscores the fact that California is indeed entering an era of relatively fixed supplies of water.

Scenario 3 is illustrative of one means of adjustment through a marketlike mechanism. An analysis of this scenario shows that urban water users will be considerably better off by virtue of cheaper supplies and somewhat more plentiful quantities. Agricultural water users will employ less water but they will do so voluntarily in response to prices offered for their water by urban sectors. This almost assuredly means that California agriculture will focus more intensively on the production of high valued crops. Low valued crops, especially those that are water-intensive, are likely to decline in importance. This response seems only reasonable for a state characterized by sparse rainfall and an increasingly dear supply of water.

Scenario 3 also demonstrates that marketlike institutional arrangements could confer real monetary benefits on water users. The costs of the institutional changes needed to reap these benefits are probably but a small fraction of the costs of capital facilities which would confer similar benefits. The institutions and policies of the past may permit us to cope with water scarcity, but they will do so only in a highly inefficient and costly way.

REFERENCES AND NOTES

1. This story is well told in Roderick Nash, *Wilderness and the American Mind* (Cambridge: Harvard University Press, 1967).
2. W. Douglas Morgan, "Allocating the Elixir of Life: Water," in *Economic Analysis of Pressing Social Problem,* Llad Phillips and Harold Votey, Jr., eds. (Chicago: Rand McNally, 1974), pp. 120-126; see also Jack Hirshleifer, James C. DeHaven and Jerome Milliman, *Water Supply: Economics, Technology and Policy* (Chicago: University of Chicago Press, 1960).
3. For a balanced and informed discussion, see *Water Policies for the Future,* Final Report to the President and to the Congress of the United States by the National Water Commission (Washington, D.C.: U.S. Government Printing Office, 1973), pp. 383-387.
4. Theodore J. Lowi, "Four Systems of Policy, Politics, and Choice," *Public Administration Review,* 32(1972):298-310; Dean E. Mann, "Relationship Between Distributive and Regulatory Politics," in *What Government Does,* Matthew Holden, Jr. and Dennis L. Dresang, eds. (Beverly Hills: Sage Publications, 1975).
5. David Seckler and L.M. Hartman, "On the Political Economy of Water Resource Evaluation," in *California Water,* ed. David Seckler (Berkeley: University of California Press, 1971), pp. 285-309.
6. See, for example, Richard E. Howitt, William Watson, and Richard Adams, "A Reevaluation of Price Elasticities for Irrigation Water," *Water Resources Research,* 16(August 1980):623-628; and Philip H. Carver, and John J. Boland, "Short- and Long-Run Effects of Price on Municipal Water Use," *Water Resources Research,* 16(August 1980):609-616.
7. California Department of Water Resources, Northern District, *Agricultural Water Purchase Plan,* July 1979.
8. Clifford T. Lee, *The Transfer of Water Rights in California: Background and Issues.* Governor's Commission to Review California Water Rights Law, Staff Paper No. 5, December 1977, pp. 57-70; Charles E. Phelps, Nancy Y. Moore, and Marlie H. Graubard, *Efficient Water Use in California: Water Rights, Water Districts and Water Transfers,* R-2386-CSA-RF (Santa Monica: Rand, November 1978.) (Also referred to as The Rand Study)
9. L.M. Hartman and Don Seastone, *Water Transfers: Economic Efficiency and Alternative Institutions.* (Baltimore and London: The Johns Hopkins Press, 1970).
10. Lee Brown, Brian McDonald, John Tyselling and Charles DuMars, "Market Reallocation, Market Proficiency, and Conflicting Social Values," in Gary D. Weatherford et al., *Western Water Institutions in a Changing Environment,* A Report to the National Science Foundation from the John Muir Institute, to be published by Westview Press, p. F. 91.
11. For a more thorough discussion of these legal arrangements see Bowden, Edmunds and Hundley, "Institutions: Customs, Laws and Organizations," this volume; for a more comprehensive treatment see Governor's Commission to Review California Water Rights Law, *Final Report* (Sacramento, California: 1978), and documents supporting the *Final Report.*
12. Hartman and Seastone, p. 25.
13. Lee, p. 13.
14. Ronald Robie, Statement of the California Department of Water Resources to the California Assembly Water Policy and Wildlife Committee at its special hearing on the *Rand Report,* May 14, 1980, pp. 3-4.
15. *Agricultural Water Purchase Plan,* p. 21.
16. Robie, p. 4.
17. Brown et al., p. F. 93.
18. Gary Weatherford et al., "Factors Underlying Irrigation Efficiency in the Tulare Basin of California," in *Western Water Institutions in a Changing Environment.*
19. Lee, pp. 31-36.
20. Phelps et al., op. cit., p. 33.
21. *Statutes of 1980,* ch. 933.
22. National Water Commission, pp. 209-260.

23. For a summary discussion of the problems of protecting in-stream uses, see State Water Resources Control Board, California Department of Water Resources, *Policies and Goals for California Water Management: The Next 20 Years*, Bulletin 4, June 1981, pp. 24-31.
24. Governor's Commission to Review California Rights Law, op. cit.
25. Phelps et al., op. cit., pp. 41-42.
26. Phelps et al., op. cit., p. 9.
27. Lee, pp. 51-52.
28. Phelps et al., op. cit., p. 29.
29. Robie, p. 5.
30. For various alternatives, see Sotories Angelides and Eugene Bardoch, *Water Banking: How to Stop Wasting Agricultural Water*, Institute for Contemporary Studies, San Francisco, 1978.
31. Brown et al., p. F. 92.
32. S. Enke, "Equilibrium Among Spatially Separated Markets: Solution by Electric Analogue," *Econometrica*, 19(1951):40-47, and P.A. Samuelson, "Spatial Price Equilibrium and Linear Programming," *American Economic Review*, 42(1952):283-303.
33. Space constraints prohibit full discussion of functions used in this model. A complete description is contained in the original version of this paper, available from the authors on request.
34. *The California State Water Project: 1977 Activities and Future Management Plans*, Bulletin 132-78, California Department of Water Resources, Sacramento, 1978. Calculations of interregional transfer prices for 1980, 1995, and 2020 are available from the authors on request.
35. T. Takayama and G.G. Judge, "Spatial Equilibrium and Quadratic Programming," *Journal of Farm Economics*, 46(February 1964):67-93.
36. Richard E. Howitt, William Watson and Richard Adams, op. cit., 1980.
37. See, for example, Harold F. Breimyer, "Outlook for Food Supply," *Challenge* 24(July/August 1981):55-59.

CHAPTER IX

INSTITUTIONS: CUSTOMS, LAWS AND ORGANIZATIONS

by

Gerald D. Bowden, Stahrl W. Edmunds, and Norris C. Hundley

ABSTRACT

California has entered an era in which the demand for water exceeds the currently developed supply; as long ago as 1974, according to the State Department of Water Resources, the water deficit already reached 2.4 million acre-feet annually. Confronted with this reality and the growing needs of an expanding population and economic base, Californians must reexamine their water-use institutions—the customs, laws, and organizations reflecting their values and governing their behavior. Of fundamental importance are customs, the unquestioned assumptions about appropriate behavior which constitute the heart of a culture. California custom has been to emphasize water as a commodity to be used and to deemphasize it as a common resource. The result has been a disorderly scramble for prior rights of water usage, massive water importation projects, and litigation in which California courts by the early twentieth century had issued more decisions on water disputes than on any other topic.

Out of these disputes emerged a complex and contradictory body of water law—the riparian right, appropriative right, groundwater right, pueblo water right, contractual right, and federal reserved right. The growth of this elaborate system accompanied the development of an equally complex water management system involving at least six major federal agencies, two major state organizations, and nearly a thousand public and private entities at the regional and local levels.

The major weaknesses today in California water law and management are primarily the result of this haphazard development of the allocation system. Among the most serious flaws are legal uncertainties over water rights which frustrate planning, investment, allocation, and efficient use of water. For example, about half of California's present annual water demand of 31 million acre-feet rests upon appropriative rights, but perhaps 25 percent of those are unrecorded pre-1914 appropriations. Another uncertainty is the indeterminate quantity of most riparian rights and the complex rules governing riparian status which seriously hamper transfers of rights or use of a market mechanism to allocate water to its highest demand. The groundwater situation is even more discouraging, and has resulted in the "tragedy of the commons"—the critical overdraft of basins.

Informed observers have recognized that the water-allocation system possesses a degree of intergovernmental and organizational heterogeneity that prevents effective coordination. The numerous local water management agencies are generally governed by boards of directors who represent large water users, who are more likely to be appointed than elected, and who, when elected, are put into office by a small number of voters. Socially and economically homogeneous, the directors are primarily concerned with expanding future water supplies from outside sources and avoiding interference from outsiders in their allocation decisions. The fragmented system, the popular view of water as a commodity, and the competition for privately owned water rights have fostered regional power politics dedicated to protecting water sources without sufficient regard to hydrological or environmental considerations. Lack of adequate cooperation between federal and state water agencies has further exacerbated the conflicts.

Such flaws in the system require new attitudes toward water and new approaches to law and water management. Among the alternatives for dealing with surface water rights are a measuring and recording of unquantified riparian rights, a quantification of the pre-1914 appropriative rights, a greater awareness of the social benefits that can be derived from transfers of water rights, and a clarification of federal reserved rights. Groundwater rights must be clarified and the overdraft of aquifers ended. Water agencies must be organized to meet future shortages and to promote wiser use of scarce supplies. The specific reforms outlined here will require determination and enlightened self-interest on the part of state and national leaders as well as all Californians.

CALIFORNIA INSTITUTIONS AND WATER USE

California institutional development and water use are closely intertwined. From the days of earliest settlement, the state's major institutions—the customs, laws, and organizations governing social behavior—have reflected the critical importance of water to a people attracted in ever greater numbers to those areas of the state least blessed with an abundant water supply. Success in establishing communities and a strong economic base required institutions that encouraged rapid development of water resources. That such success was achieved is readily apparent. In little more than a century following statehood, California has emerged as the most populous state in the Union and now ranks seventh among the nations of the world in annual production and income.[1] But while California's population and economic expectations continue to grow, its water supply—at least for the foreseeable future—is essentially fixed. Even a decision to develop a major new supply will produce no water for years because of the time required to construct the massive facilities necessary for such an undertaking. Implications for the present and future are profound, for California has already entered an era in which the demand for water exceeds the dependable supply—that is, the permanent supply available from groundwater pumping and current surface developments. According to the State Department of Water Resources, the water deficit in 1974 was already 2.4 million acre-feet.[2] Confronted with this harsh reality, Californians must reexamine their values and water practices. An analysis of the state's water institutions underscores the need for a wide range of changes if its citizens are to achieve wiser and more efficient use of water during the critical years ahead.

VARIABLES: CUSTOM, LAW, AND GOVERNMENT

California Water Customs

Of all society's institutions, customs are at once the most pervasive and the least subject to rapid change. Unlike more formal expressions of human action such as laws and public or private organizations, customs do not derive their identity from statute or private charter. Indeed, customs constitute the heart of a culture. They are the informal, long-established, and repeated practices that possess the character of tradition and social habit. As such, they reflect largely unquestioned assumptions about appropriate behavior and in turn shape the formal laws and regulations of society. Frequently, customary practices, while not law themselves, are stimulated or influenced by laws, administrative decisions, and the organizational structures devised by a society to regulate its activities. Thus the line separating custom from formal laws and political structure is often blurred. This is readily apparent in a glance at some of California's major water customs.

Traditionally Californians have overwhelmingly emphasized water as a commodity to be used and deemphasized it as a common resource belonging to all members of society. In so doing they have reversed the emphases of earlier civilizations. "By the law of nature," declared the Roman Corpus Juris Civilis nearly fifteen hundred years ago, "these things are common to mankind—the air, running water, the sea . . ."[3] The California legislature unequivocally reaffirmed the same principle in 1911 when it announced that "all water . . . within the State of California is the property of the people of the state."[4] But long before the legislature acted, Californians had already determined that water as a commodity for use in unlimited amounts took priority over water as a resource to be held in trust for all the people in the state. During the pioneer era and on into the twentieth century, the concern of Californians was with securing a water supply in order to survive and profit in a new land—not with worrying about its exhaustion or seeking to preserve its aesthetic or recreational values.

The emphasis on use so intensified as the population mushroomed that Californians very early began equating progress with the size of their water projects. Soon the new faith made commonplace massive projects to import water: the 233-mile Los Angeles Aqueduct completed in 1913 to the Owens Valley; the Hetch-Hetchy Aqueduct constructed in 1934 from the Sierra Nevada to San Francisco; the release of federal funds in 1935 for the ambitious Central Valley Project; the completion in 1941 of the Colorado River Aqueduct, a project that necessitated a series of huge dams, including Hoover Dam (at the time the world's largest), before water could be brought to the cities and farms on the southern California coastal plain; and the authorization by California voters in 1960 of the State Water Project which, when completed, will cost billions of dollars and consist of a network of power plants, dams, pumping stations, and a nearly 500-mile aqueduct from the humid north to the cities and farms of the Central Valley and southern California.[5] California pioneered in the construction of such engineering wonders and became the model emulated by other states and even nations.

As much a California tradition as the fascination with massive water importation schemes has been the preoccupation of the state's citizens with litigation and bureaucratic conflicts over water rights. The rush to use water combined with a lack of clear legal guidelines to produce a logjam in the courts. By the early twentieth century the California courts had issued more decisions on water disputes than on any other topic.[6] The conflicts at first centered in the state courts but soon broadened to include issues under federal law as California vied with other states for rivers they shared in common and clashed with the federal government over spheres of authority as well as over the water rights of federal lands, including Indian reservations. Complications emerged in the unfortunate California practice of virtually uncontrolled mining of groundwater in many areas, the refusal of users to recognize the relationship between surface and groundwater supplies, and the failure of courts and legislature adequately to clarify groundwater rights.[7]

The California tradition of legal conflict is of a piece with its laissez-faire attitude toward management of water resources. Californians have never been reluctant to ask the courts to settle private disputes, but they have customarily resisted legislative attempts to tell them how to use their water. Over the years federal, state, and local authorities have come to play an ever greater role as the cost of projects exceeded private means and as issues involving the public interest gained advocates. Even so, Californians have successfully avoided a mechanism for coordinating the activities of the hundreds of public and private water agencies or for developing a comprehensive management program.

California's water customs may have helped create the prosperous and populous state of today, but they are out of touch with today's realities. To continue unchanged the traditional emphasis on *using* water when that emphasis reduces the dependable supply, degrades the environment, and intensifies costly and time-consuming disputes over rights is patently self-defeating. Equally out of touch—at least for the present—is the custom of importing new water supplies. Enthusiasm for projects like those that dominated yesterday's thinking is waning because of the cost of such undertakings and because of stiff opposition from water-producing areas. Moreover, it seems apparent that Congress and the state legislature will be slow to endorse new projects unless patterns of water use are altered. Thus, there is a need to change those customs and attitudes that promote inefficient or unwise use of present water supplies. Such changes will be difficult to effect, but a beginning can be made by alerting the public to the consequences of their current behavior and by making careful alterations in those more easily changed formal extensions of custom—the law and the organizational structures for managing water resources. An understanding of the historical development of state water law and organizations can bring into sharper relief the specific changes that are necessary.

California Water Law: Historical Development

Present California water law is the product of more than a century of extensive conflict over water sources as well as over the meaning of constitutional provisions, court decisions, and statutes. That there would be conflict over water in a state where it is in short supply should come as no surprise, the more so because California entered the Union at a time when the western law of waters was in its infancy. Less clear, perhaps, are the ingredients that over the years have gone into producing California's special system of water rights.

Riparian Rights. A major element in the California system is the common law doctrine of riparian rights. When the first legislature in 1850 adopted the common law of England,[8] it automatically saddled the state with a water doctrine that had worked well in England and in the eastern United States but would prove ill-suited to California's drier climes. The riparian doctrine guaranteed to the owner of land abutting a river the full flow of the river, less only a reasonable amount taken by those upstream to satisfy so-called "natural uses"—domestic needs and the watering of domestic livestock. As for "artificial uses" for irrigation, commercial herds of stock, and industry, the California courts held that a riparian's right was reciprocal and correlative with the rights of all other riparians along a stream. Thus, owners' rights were equal and strictly usufructuary—that is, they had a right to use the water, but they did not own the stream itself and could not impair the rights of other riparians. Use was not necessary to create the right, nor did nonuse terminate it. Location alone was paramount and the right simply resided in the ownership of land bordering the stream and within the watershed.[9]

Appropriative Rights. Even before the legislature adopted the common law, many Californians recognized that it failed to meet their needs adequately. Especially of this mind were the thousands of gold seekers who poured into the area in the wake of John Marshall's discovery in 1848 and vigorously pursued their search for mineral wealth. This search soon relied heavily on the availability of water for working gold-bearing soil, especially the placer deposits which attracted most newcomers. Since the diggings were often located at great distances from streams, miners unhesitatingly responded in the only way that made sense to them: they diverted the water from rivers through flumes and ditches to the waiting sluice boxes, stamp mills, and other hydraulic machinery.[10]

Necessity, not the law, sanctioned such actions, but the law soon fell into line. At first the miners relied on their own self-imposed regulations. Acting on the assumption that natural resources like gold and water were free for the taking, they concluded that the person with the best right to them was the person who first appropriated them to his use. "Priority of discovery, location and appropriation" became the basis of all mining rights, and the principles were applied to water as well as to the mining claim to be worked. In 1855 in Irwin v. Phillips, these principles finally received the endorsement of the State Supreme Court and became popularly known as the doctrine of prior appropriation.[11]

As the doctrine emerged in California—and eventually in all other western states—it vested a water right in the first person taking water from a stream so long as he continued to use it beneficially. Others might appropriate water from the same stream, but priority of right went to the initial user. In times of shortage, latecomers were the first to lose water, and there was no pro-rata sharing of the reduced flow. The principle was a simple one—first in time, first in right—and it differed sharply from the riparian system. Unlike riparian law, the appropriation doctrine allowed a user to diminish the flow of a stream and even to change its course. It also severed water rights from the land, thus making them personal property, which could be sold without selling the land.[12]

The California Doctrine. Within just a few years of statehood California had acquired two different systems of water law. Conflict was inevitable, and in 1886 the two principles finally clashed head-on in the State Supreme Court. In the landmark case of Lux v. Haggin, the court in a feat of legal legerdemain upheld both riparian law and the appropriation system, but it did so in a way that would trouble Californians for generations. In announcing what became popularly known as the "California doctrine," the court reaffirmed that the riparian principle had been adopted by the first legislature, but it also recognized the legitimacy of appropriation. The appropriator possessed the superior right if he began using water before a riparian land owner had acquired his property. If the appropriator began using water later, then his right was junior. Put another way, riparian rights inhered in all public lands when those lands passed into private hands, but they were also subject to appropriations made before the transfer of title.[13]

So long as the relationship between population pressures and water supply remained relatively balanced, no major alterations occurred in the legal system, though its hybrid nature kept the courts busy. Especially troubling by the turn of the century was the lack of a mechanism for systematically recording rights or the quantities of water held under those rights. An individual acquired a right simply by diverting water and putting it to beneficial use until challenged. Such a system not only encouraged costly lawsuits, but also inhibited planning and investment.

In 1914 voters responded to the growing confusion by approving a referendum that established a state permit system and required the recording and quantification of appropriative rights.[14] Today this authority resides in the State Water Resources Control Board.

Another major development in the legal system occurred a decade and a half later in the wake of renewed conflict between riparians and appropriators. Riparians had to abide by a "reasonable use" standard in their relations among themselves, but they did not think they were subject to such a restriction in disputes with appropriators. Appropriators disagreed, but in 1926 in Herminghaus v. Southern California Edison, the State Supreme Court sided with riparians.[15] The practical effect of the decision was to permit riparians to use water in ways that were often flagrantly wasteful. The public reacted with a howl and in 1928 amended the state constitution to prohibit any unreasonable use of water. The legal test of a right—riparian or appropriative—became "reasonable and beneficial use," a principle that remains "the central theme of modern California water rights law."[16]

Groundwater Rights. California law governing rights to groundwater developed more slowly than surface water law. This reflected the greater initial interest in more easily acquired surface supplies. Soon, however, the demand for water prompted the sinking of wells, and the availability of electricity made possible extensive pumping operations. By the turn of the century the competition for groundwater, especially in rapidly growing southern California, had reached the point where legal guidelines became a necessity. The State Supreme Court responded in 1903 with the "correlative" rights doctrine. In Katz v. Walkinshaw, the court held that the paramount right to subterranean water belonged to the owner of the overlying land.[17] If there was more than one landowner, then they each possessed a right to a reasonable share of the water. No one possessed a prior right, but rather a "correlative right" in common with the others. Surplus water not needed by the overlying landowners could be appropriated by others on a first-in-time, first-in-right basis. Thus groundwater was subject to both correlative and appropriative rights. It could also become subject to a "prescriptive" right. Anyone who took more than his correlative share or who pumped nonsurplus water for his appropriative right might succeed in establishing a prescriptive right to the additional water. This possibility encouraged widespread pumping of groundwater until the overdraft on some supplies forced competitors into the courts to clarify their conflicting claims. In 1949 in Pasadena v. Alhambra, the State Supreme Court attempted to resolve the uncertainty by creating the doctrine of "mutual prescription." Through this device prescriptive rights were awarded to every user, and the court determined the formula to be followed in establishing the quantity of each user's right.[18] That formula was based on each user's highest five years of pumping. Once determined, the uses of each party were then reduced proportionately until the total extraction did not exceed the safe yield of the basin.

Rather than resolving the problem, the 1949 decision sent people scurrying to the pumphouse in an effort to establish their uses at as high an average as possible. The legislature responded in 1951 by permitting southern Californians to use alternate supplies of water without losing or impairing their unused groundwater rights. Two years later lawmakers authorized the State Water Rights Board to seek injunctions against pumping that threatened to destroy basins through ocean water intrusion. None of the legislation modified groundwater rights and both measures applied only to areas of southern California. More far-reaching was the 1975 decision of the State Supreme Court in Los Angeles v. San Fernando. The court held that private users could not obtain a prescriptive right against a public agency.[19] The decision enhanced the position of public entities in the scramble for water and made it highly unlikely that private parties would invoke mutual prescription to resolve disputes in basins where there were private and public appropriators.

Pueblo Water Rights. Still another principle successfully litigated by two California cities—Los Angeles and San Diego—is the pueblo right. As early as 1881 in Feliz v. Los Angeles, the State Supreme Court held that a former Spanish or Mexican pueblo—in this instance, Los Angeles—had "succeeded to all the rights of the . . . pueblo," and among them was the right to all the water of any river running through or adjacent to the community. Subsequent cases extended the right to the subterranean flow of the river.[20] The large number of California's former pueblos (Los Angeles, San Jose), presidial pueblos (San Diego, Monterey, San Francisco, Santa Barbara), and mission pueblos (San Luis Obispo, San Juan Capistrano, San Juan Bautista, Sonoma) suggests the possible significance of this right for future generations.

Contractual Rights. During the last half century the federal and state governments have played an increasingly dominant role in the area of water rights. This has been largely the result of the lands (and water rights) that they possess and the massive water transportation schemes that they have underwritten. The federal government, as a result of the Boulder Canyon Act of 1928 and the release of funds for the Central Valley Project in 1935, built facilities capturing flood runoff and negotiated contracts allocating the water to users. The state government followed the same pattern with its State Water project which, when fully operational, will supply approximately ten percent of California's water needs. In these instances when new water has been made available, the project operators possess appropriative rights to the water which they allow others to use under contracts that vary from project to project, but which invariably supply water to agricultural users at prices considerably below those of urban customers.[21]

Federal Reserved Rights. The federal government has also profoundly influenced water distribution, especially during the twentieth century, in its capacity as owner of national parks, monuments, and other public lands. According to the U.S. Supreme Court, the federal government possesses rights to sufficient water to fulfill the purposes for which it has set aside these lands, including Indian reservations—of which California has many, especially in the southern and drier part of the state. In 1963 in Arizona v. California, the U.S. Supreme Court determined the rights of several federal reservations to the waters of the lower Colorado River,[22] but the extent of those rights elsewhere in the state is far from clear.

California Water Governance

The growth of California's elaborate system of water law accompanied the development of an equally complex water management system. Authority is presently shared by hundreds of private and public agencies at the federal, state, regional, and local levels. At least six major federal agencies, two major state organizations, and nearly a thousand public and private entities at the regional and local levels possess water management responsibilities.[23] These responsibilities at all levels developed piecemeal and, as in the case of the state permit system, in response to a particular problem rather than as a result of systematic planning or efforts to coordinate activities. Most numerous are the so-called "special districts"—more than eight hundred of them—created as a result of general or special acts of the state legislature and responsible for a wide range of services, including irrigation, recreation, generation of hydroelectricity, sewage treatment, flood control, and much else.

FLAWS IN CALIFORNIA WATER LAW AND GOVERNANCE:
IMPLICATIONS FOR THE FUTURE

The major weaknesses today in California water law and management are primarily the result of the haphazard development of the allocation system. That patchwork process did not prevent California from becoming the most populous state in the Union and one of the most prosperous places in the world—but the present flaws, when combined with the overdraft on the presently developed water supply, threaten to undermine the economy and to damage the environment permanently. A review of these flaws suggests alternatives which may be viewed as options.

Legal Uncertainties

Among the most serious weaknesses are legal uncertainties. Court decisions, statutes, and constitutional amendments have clarified many of the ambiguities that troubled earlier generations, but serious legal uncertainties remain which continue to frustrate planning, investment, and wise and efficient use of water. Especially serious is the unclear scope of many pre-1914 appropriative rights. The referendum of 1914 required all new appropriators to secure a state permit for a specific quantity of water, but it placed no such requirement on earlier appropriators. A 1965 law to correct this oversight was ineffective because no penalty was attached to noncompliance. Recent estimates indicate that about half of California's present annual water demand of 31 million acre-feet rests on appropriative rights, and perhaps twenty-five percent of those uses are unrecorded pre-1914 appropriations.[24]

Several additional uncertainties stem from the uneasy nexus between the riparian doctrine and the need to obtain optimum social benefit from the state's scarce supply of surface water. A major difficulty derives from the indeterminate quantity of most riparian rights. Except for the few streams where there has been a quantification of riparian rights, the riparian owner's claim has not been fixed at a specific volume of water. Instead a riparian is limited to an amount that does not interfere with the reasonable requirements of other riparians.[25] Such a flexible entitlement obviously poses a serious obstacle to rational planning. In 1980 the state legislature took a major step forward by making it possible to transfer riparian rights which have been statutorily adjudicated and quantified, but the social benefits of this legislation will not be realized until many more such rights have been quantified.[26]

Three major rules have evolved which act as constraints on the unquantified riparian right. First, some part of the benefited land must touch the stream or lake; second, the land must lie within the watershed of the stream or lake to which it is riparian; and third, if title to some riparian land not directly touching a stream or lake is sold (without reservation of water rights) then the severed parcel may never reacquire its former riparian status.[27] The effect of these interrelated rules is nearly to preclude the private transfers of water rights held by riparians or the employment of market mechanisms to allocate water where demand is the greatest.

Another major difficulty with the riparian right is the rule protecting the right from loss by nonuse. In 1913 the legislature attempted to circumvent this rule by stipulating that a riparian right would be lost after ten years of nonuse, but this statute was declared unconstitutional in 1935. In 1979 the state legislature declared that failure to use an adjudicated right for five years (earlier it was three years) would result in its loss. Even if this statute applies to adjudicated riparian rights (and that is not altogether clear) the immediate impact would be slight since few riparian rights have been adjudicated and quantified. Also, in 1979 the State Supreme Court held that the unexercised riparian right could be assigned a priority lower than all rights (including appropriative) being exercised along a stream, but the court refused to allow the right to be extinguished.[28] The result has been the virtual indestructibility of the riparian right and reinforcement of the principle that rigidly confines the right to land along streams and lakes instead of allowing it to be reassigned—when such reassignment would not be environmentally harmful—to other areas where demand may be greater. The burdens of riparian principles are growing heavier by the decade in California where, according to recent estimates, as much as ten percent of the annual water demand may be claimed by riparians.[29]

The California constitutional amendment of 1928 checked the wasteful abuses of many riparians with its "reasonable use" requirement, but it also generated considerable debate—and litigation—over the meaning of "reasonable." In recent years that debate has broadened to include the legality of retaining water within streams for aesthetic or fishery purposes. The state's Wild and Scenic Rivers Act of 1972 stated that such purposes constituted a use under the law, but the California Supreme Court has not yet addressed the issue and the lower courts have challenged the legislature's position. In 1979 the State Court of Appeal held that in-stream uses could not be secured by a water right since there was no physical control exercised over the water as required by law.[30] Here looms again the persistence of the California tradition of diverting and *using* a stream. As noted in 1978 by the Governor's Commission to Review California Water Rights Law, "the impairment and loss of instream values continue to grow."[31]

Still another reason for anxiety among many Californians is the uncertainty of federal reserved rights, especially Indian water rights. As long ago as 1908 the U.S. Supreme Court, in Winters v. United States, held that an Indian reservation possessed a special water right not lost by nonuse.[32] In 1963 in Arizona v. California, the court reaffirmed the earlier decision and announced that the quantity of the Indian right was determined by the extent of the "practicably irrigable" acreage on the reservation.[33] The implications of that decision for California water users, both Indian and non-Indian, are as yet unclear in spite of the costly and time-consuming litigation that it has generated.

Debate also continues on the "counties of origin" provisions in the state legislation authorizing water projects. Doubt remains about the enforceability of such provisions, which allow California's northern counties to retain water now going (or proposed to be sent) south if they should need it in the future.

The legal situation of groundwater is even more discouraging than that of surface water. The State Supreme Court has held that unexercised groundwater rights are not lost by prior and inconsistent use of water by neighboring landowners.[34] On the other hand, the court has also held that those rights can be lost through prescription to a prior user who consistently utilizes the water in an overdrafted basin. The result of such rulings has been the "tragedy of the commons": overlying landowners, seeking to maximize their uses and to avoid loss of rights by prescription, have overdrawn the resource to the detriment of all users and have made the implementation of water plans virtually impossible in California's many overdrafted basins.[35] Still another doctrinal impediment to water planning is the rule that groundwater may be "appropriated" for off-site uses only if the needs of overlying users have been met first.[36] This rule frustrates the goal of allocating water on the basis of need, rather than on the basis of fortuitous location.

Correlative, appropriative, and prescriptive rights have obviously been less than successful as a means of effective regulation of groundwater. Overdraft of supplies averages more than two million acre-feet annually. "California's groundwater," sadly notes the Governor's Commission to Review California Water Rights Law, "is usually available to any pumper, public or private, who wants to extract it, regardless of the impact of extraction on neighboring groundwater pumpers or on the general community."[37] The impact of such extraction includes costly litigation, threatened exhaustion of aquifers, seawater intrusion, and land subsidence. Compounding the problem is inadequate recognition of the interrelationship of groundwater and surface water supplies. Though significant progress in the management of groundwater has occurred in some large urban areas of southern California, the problem remains serious throughout the state and has reached crisis proportions in the San Joaquin Valley.

Weaknesses in Water Governance

Of a piece with the legal uncertainties is the patchwork administration of California's water resources. There is no overall coordinating agency or comprehensive management program. Jurisdictional disputes among the federal, state, regional, and local agencies are legendary. So, too, is the need for reform. Several scholars recently put it best:

> . . . [The] water allocation system in California is characterized by a degree of intergovernmental and organizational heterogeneity that sometimes defies the imagination...[and by] the lack of efficient and effective coordinating mechanisms. This lack of coordination contributes to uncertainty over ground rules, and leads to a confusion of ends and means, and to needless conflict that does nothing but distract attention away from the fundamental problem of allocating scarce water resources.[38]

The most numerous of the water management agencies are the more than eight hundred special districts providing a variety of water services on the local level. These decentralized water districts generally have narrowly defined management objectives: to develop plentiful supplies of cheap water for their local constituencies; to provide water at the lowest average cost; to maximize local use and development within district boundaries without regard for water needs elsewhere; to protect their rights to local water sources; to seek new water supplies from external sources, often subsidized with public funds in order to minimize local costs; to maintain local control over district water; to consume their entire allotment when necessary to prevent loss of their right (or any part of it) because of nonuse; and to foster the legal and political means needed to maintain their entitlements.[39] The product of these goals has been a water management system that is highly fragmented, self-interested, and often wasteful.

Other unfortunate by-products of the present decentralized water management system emerge on analysis. The directors of local districts tend to represent the large water users in the area; directors are more likely to be appointed than elected; when elections are held, they are infrequent and voter turnout is low. Several scholars recently came to the following conclusions about water district directors: directors are socially and economically homogeneous; most directors are primarily concerned about future water needs and expanding supplies; conservation and environmental issues are not of primary importance in district management; directors are anxious to avoid interference from outsiders and seek to preserve maximum independence; the desire to serve as district director appears related to protecting or improving personal and group financial interests; and directors show a high degree of uniformity in their decisions with little disagreement among themselves.[40]

The management and staff of water districts share the directors' goals and attitudes. Most managers are former engineers whose principal goal is to maximize supply at the lowest possible cost.[41] Given the supply orientation of management and the insularity of its personnel, little attention has been given to analyzing the price for additional increments of demand and supply, or competitive rates for the cost of capital. Thus the normal tests of economic efficiency have not been applied with the social or economic welfare of all California citizens in mind.

The state legislature recently took major steps toward correcting this situation. In 1979 it sought to combat waste of water by modifying the "use it or lose it" principle. An appropriator would not lose the right to any water unused because of conservation efforts—that is, using less water to accomplish the same purpose or using less water because of the need to rotate crops or allow land to lie fallow. In 1980 the legislature permitted an appropriator to retain an unused right for five years—instead of the earlier three—before forfeiting it. Lawmakers also authorized both temporary and long-term transfers of rights where no substantial harm would be done to other users. In addition, they gave a boost to water-conservation efforts by vesting exclusive right to reclaimed wastewater in the person who salvaged the water.[42] Only time will reveal the impact of such measures, but a significant move forward seems to have been made.

POSSIBLE FUTURE SCENARIOS
FOR CALIFORNIA'S WATER INSTITUTIONS

Three scenarios for California's water institutions are here examined: (a) maintenance of the status quo; (b) development of new water sources; and (c) reallocation of present water supply. While these scenarios are discussed separately for illustrative purposes, they are by no means mutually exclusive. Indeed the most likely course of events is that many aspects of the status quo will remain dominant for the next decade, especially the nature of water law and water district management; but gradually, in the face of impending shortages, a limited amount of new water development will take place among the lower cost projects, followed by later measures to reallocate existing supply.

Scenario One: Maintenance of the Status Quo

Issues and Impacts. Most of what has already been said about California's water institutions constitutes a compelling argument for change and against maintenance of the status quo. Moreover, common sense suggests that a policy based on preserving the status quo would collapse under public pressure during a water crisis. The resulting intervention would be hurried and too late to prevent or lessen the effects of the more complex and severe social dislocations. More to the point, there is evidence that some changes are already underway, and others can be anticipated. For example, farm irrigation practices are beginning to reflect a realization of water scarcity, demonstrated in the increasing use of drip irrigation, sprinkling rather than flooding, and laser land-leveling technology. Political pressure to alter the present water management system can be expected to intensify significantly as powerful interest groups, such as urban residents, come increasingly to recognize that other groups, such as farmers, pay considerably less for water than most users. The State Department of Water Resources will doubtless come under greater pressure to separate its role as guardian of the state's water resources from its role as operator of the state's development and delivery system. As conflicts among water users intensify, environmental groups can be expected to focus on the state's dual roles as a conflict of interest and to insist on their separation.

Scenario Analysis. The maintenance of the status quo is facilitated and embedded in present customs, laws, and organizations and will tend to prevail given no water shortages. On the other hand, drought, population growth, and increasing overdrafts will change the status quo and, when severe, cause a water crisis.

The interventions to be expected in severe water shortages will be (a) limitations on water uses, (b) regulation of new subdivision connections, (c) transfers among large water districts (as occurred in 1976-77), (d) surcharges to pay emergency transfer costs, and (e) rationing of water supplies. Competition for water will increase sharply in the areas of extreme shortage and will result in heavy public pressure to obtain water supplies by transfers from elsewhere. Minimum human needs for water in urban areas will take priority over other uses, probably followed in priority by essential industrial and agricultural uses. The impact of water rationing is likely to be felt most heavily upon residential landscape-users of water, and the residual impact shared by pro-rata reductions in supplies for agriculture and industry.

Scenario Two: Development of New Water Sources

Issues and Impacts. A scenario that calls for the development of new water sources as the solution to increased competition for the available supply might or might not result in major institutional change. If such changes are not exacted by government in exchange for more dams and aqueducts, then the key questions will be those of capital cost, who pays, whether environmental consequences would be acceptable, whether energy gains would exceed energy demands of a new project, and similar issues that are analyzed elsewhere in this volume. On the other hand, if the federal and/or state governments insist upon institutional changes as a prerequisite for funding new water projects, then those changes will be the result of the give-and-take of a future political process as well as the social and economic conditions prevalent at the time—none of which can now be predicted.

Scenario Analysis. The development of new water sources is most likely to occur under conditions of: (a) national and international food shortages or (b) an affluent economy with state budgetary surpluses available for investment in new productive facilities. Current budgetary stringencies of state and federal governments make this scenario improbable for the present.

New supplies which are likely to be economically feasible under a market transfer system (as proposed in Chapter VIII) include the Peripheral Canal at $72 per acre-foot, New Melones at $124 per acre-foot, and Glenn Reservoir at $148 per acre-foot. Other potential sources of new supply, such as Cottonwood Reservoir, Auburn Dam, Los Vaqueros Reservoir, and High Shasta, are estimated to deliver water (without transfer or pumping costs) at about $259 per acre-foot and upward—prices which would be feasible only with large public subsidies.

The development of large new water supplies would reduce competition for water and shift to the fiscal and political arenas the conflict over the distribution of the water subsidy burden. Assuming subsidy burdens are distributed as in the past, the main beneficiaries would be farmers, and the main burden would fall upon middle-income taxpayers, who currently are resisting additional tax burdens.

Scenario Three: Reallocation of Present Water Supply

Issues and Impacts. The central institutional issue here is whether government, the private market place, or some combination of the two should determine the reallocation of the present water supply. There can be no doubt that decisions made in the market will not always correspond to those of public agencies. In short, shifting power to government or the market will have the effect of diminishing the influence of one of them. Whether this is perceived as good or bad depends in part on one's political philosophy and the faith one has in economic choice to determine public policy. Associated with this issue is the question of how existing public agencies will react. All bureaucracies resist change, especially when that change reduces their power. Another issue is how environmental groups would respond to a shift in favor of the market. Since the market tends to discount or ignore environmental amenities, environmental groups might be expected to resist such devices. Still another issue is whether monopolistic tendencies of a market or quasi-market approach could be controlled. The history of California water, as we have noted, has demonstrated a tendency for large users to dominate the water market. If market transactions become more widely used, even larger segments of the water market may be captured by high-volume users.

Scenario Analysis. The conditions most likely to bring a revision in the present water allocation system would be water shortages coupled with taxpayer resistance to new water development. Taxpayer resistance is probable under conditions of low economic growth rates, inflation, unemployment, high interest rates, high tax burdens, and tight state budgets. Under such stringent circumstances, citizens might be influenced by the recent gasoline shortage to conclude that there is no absolute shortage of water but only shortages of water at existing prices (which are as low as $3.50 per acre-foot and range as high as $250). That is, public attitudes may assume that extremely low-value water is going into low-value uses, which might be curtailed without great social loss (otherwise the low-value uses would command higher prices). Intervention in this case would be toward the creation of a state-regulated market for water. The creation of a market-like mechanism for water has been discussed in other chapters in this volume.

The net result of a market mechanism for water would be to optimize the allocation of water to its higher-value uses. Conflict over water would be reduced in that shortages would be mitigated and the existing supply would be allocated among users by competitive pricing. Those activities that currently would gain by market prices for water would be those which can economically afford such water—for example, all moderate- to high-value agricultural crops, as well as industrial, residential, municipal, and tourist users. Those activities which might lose by a market reallocation would be the marginal and low-value agricultural crops, including possibly some acreage in hay, pasture and rice. Even here, however, yields might not decrease significantly; for example, in the 1976-77 drought, the rice acreage decreased by 40 percent as marginal lands were removed from cultivation but rice yields declined only 10 percent.

Impacts of a market system on other water uses are uncertain; environmental and recreational effects, for example, would depend upon how well external social costs are incorporated into market prices. On the whole, the beneficiaries of a market allocation system would include the overwhelming majority of California's agriculturalists and residents.

RECOMMENDED COURSE OF ACTION
FOR INSTITUTIONAL CHANGE

Our assessment of California's water institutions leads us to conclude that the public interest is most broadly served by the third scenario—a reallocation of the present water supply. Such a reallocation, we believe, should rest on two major areas of institutional change. First, customary attitudes and perceptions regarding water and its proper use must be altered. Second, water management agencies and laws affecting the distribution of supplies must be restructured.

Customs. As already noted, the attitudes and values of a society are often most accurately revealed in its customs. Implicit in California's historical experience are a number of traditional attitudes toward water which must be reassessed if the public is to avoid severe social conflict in the coming era of increased competition for water.

Ownership. Californians have traditionally viewed water as a commodity to be reduced to private ownership as rapidly as possible and have largely forgotten that water in its natural state belongs to all the people. Case law, however, unequivocally quashed the popular notion of many landowners that their uses of surface and groundwater are somehow beyond the regulatory power of the state.[43] Developing a water policy based on the wise use and distribution of water would be substantially less disruptive if the facts of water ownership were more generally understood. A related problem derives from the regional self-interest that has historically characterized California water politics.

Regionalism. Water policy in California has traditionally turned on regional power struggles. A plethora of regional alliances and interregional feuds has eclipsed the legal point that water falling on one part of the state belongs to the people of the state as a whole, not just to those who reside where it fell to earth. Californians have paid a high price for indulging their regional chauvinism. Political leaders in the north have sometimes succumbed to this popular vice because they are unaccountable to voters in the south (except when they infrequently run in statewide elections); politicians in the south have callously disregarded the environmental consequences of building thirsty cities in deserts watered from great distance at great price. Too often leaders throughout the state have treated water supply and demand as regional political issues rather than as hydrologic problems ultimately involving the entire state and often much of the West, including Canada and Mexico.[44] Desperately needed among state and federal leaders is a broader vision—a water statesmanship—that is sensitive both to the ecology of each watershed and to the legitimate needs of people regardless of where they live.

Ground versus Surface Water. The traditional proprietary attitude toward water is held with particular passion in the case of groundwater. The Blackstonian notion that land ownership consists of absolute dominion over a wedge extending from the earth's core upward into the cosmos continues to dominate popular perceptions of groundwater rights. This literalist view of ownership permits a shared entitlement to water flowing across several parcels of land, but it does not easily admit a similar caveat in the case of groundwater. If Californians are to fully address the problems raised in planning for the future, this popular attitude must change. They must cease thinking of groundwater as ground and start thinking of it as water. Put another way, they must recognize that all water is part of the same hydrologic cycle. The realization that groundwater is a shared resource akin to air must be substituted for the destructive misconception that it is more like oil or coal.

Water Use and Agriculture. Another popular attitude impeding wise water management is the belief that water use is of secondary importance to land use. Farmers are especially strong proponents of this view. Since agriculture is a vital industry, they reason, sufficient water must be found to support it. The fact is that California agriculture is already heavily overdrawn at the water bank. Farmers are mining water at a higher rate than it is being replaced. In some areas, the use and reuse of both ground and surface supplies have led to the dangerous build-up of salts and other minerals which have drastically reduced—and threaten to destroy—the productivity of once fertile lands. Thus, the attitude that allows water to be abused in the name of land-use interests can result in the despoliation of the land as well. Moreover, the privileged position accorded to agriculture in the pricing of water encourages waste and frustrates attempts to distribute scarce supplies where they are most needed. The subsidization of agriculture (and, indirectly, the consumers of California agricultural products) through cut-rate prices for water may have made sense during the early years of the twentieth century when the government sought to get people onto the land, but it is out of step in today's world of agribusiness and water scarcity.

In-Stream Uses. Another popular attitude out-of-step with the present is the traditional assumption that every drop of water reaching the sea is a drop wasted. In reflective moments some Californians acknowledge the need for enough water in streams to provide habitat for aquatic birds and spawning fish, but state water policies have been overwhelmingly driven by developmental values. These values have all but excluded the requirements of natural plant and animal communities, and have also tended to exclude many aesthetic and recreational amenities associated with unaltered streams. Achieving balance between the economically productive uses of water and the demands imposed by natural ecological communities will require changing the public attitude toward the beneficial use of water. Californians must abandon the notion that water is wasted unless it is put to some human use with direct economic value. Otherwise they will be unable to address many pressing issues raised by water-policy planning.

Still another reason for attention to in-stream requirements is that a major hydrologic function of a stream is to transport sediment. Reduced rates of water flow mean lower levels of sediment transport, higher levels of stream deposition, erosion of beaches, and destruction of natural habitats. These disruptions in sediment transport and deposition argue powerfully for a new attitude toward the wisdom of extracting every possible drop of water from the state's surface streams.

The Law and Water Management

Because of the enormous political controversy surrounding water policy, proposals for major reform in laws and organizational structure tend to be seen as naive and unrealistic. Common sense nevertheless demands that major changes be made before the end of this century. Common sense, as well as an understanding of California's complex water development record, also suggests what some of these changes should be.

Surface Water. Several modifications in the legal entitlements of surface-water users seem desirable. First, unquantified riparian rights must be quantified in order to reduce uncertainty and to permit socially beneficial transfers of water. Second, greater clarity regarding pre-1914 appropriative rights is needed. Third, the scope of federal reserved rights must be clarified. Finally, in-stream flow standards must be established to ensure the protection of natural plant and animal communities as well as recreational uses of surface water. This may require public acquisition of water rights or more vigorous regulatory procedures. Much needed clarification could be achieved by fuller use of statutory adjudication procedures as recommended in 1978 by the Governor's Commission to Review California Water Rights Law.[45]

Groundwater. Ameliorating the disabling consequences of present groundwater rights law will be especially difficult. One reason is that the law distinguishes groundwater from surface water. Another is that many powerful water districts depend on groundwater for their supply. Changing either of these situations will require public education and political fortitude. So, too, will several additional reforms that must be made.

First, prescriptive rights to groundwater must not be expanded and new claims based on prescription should not be recognized. Second, all extraction of groundwater must be regulated by permit or subjected to basin adjudication to ensure that basins are not damaged through overdrafts. Third, the requirement that only "surplus" groundwater may be transferred beyond a water basin must be altered to permit more efficient use of aquifers as storage receptacles. Altering groundwater law in this way would help lessen the need for additional costly surface reservoirs. Groundwater reservoirs are cheaper, more efficient, and more consonant with natural hydrologic processes than relying on large, expensive, and short-lived surface water impoundments. The "Groundwater Management" approach proposed by the Governor's Commission to Review California Water Rights Law is a promising approach to dealing with this problem.[46]

Water Management. An obstacle to developing a rational water plan for California is that, in the words of the present State Department of Water Resources Director, "it is easier to move water from Sacramento to Los Angeles than it is to move it from Concord to Walnut Creek or from Pasadena to Alhambra."[47] The state system, in other words, is more adaptable than local systems because the state system is interlinked and local systems are not. It is patently obvious that the administrative apparatus spawned in the nineteenth century is ill-equipped to serve California's needs in the twenty-first century. Californians cannot reasonably expect the atomized policies of eight hundred or more agencies pursuing their individual self-interests to yield water policy for the state as a whole. Planning to meet future water needs is also severely hampered by the absence of a distribution system (pipelines, canals, and other hardware) capable of effecting efficient transfers of water. Such a system will be enormously expensive and for that reason particularly difficult to achieve.

What should be done, then, is fairly clear. The difficulty has been how to do it politically, in view of the strength of the self-interest groups that seek to retain their own water entitlements unimpaired. One managerial approach to this classic conflict problem is to promote participation among the conflicting parties and to provide incentives for compliance. Fortunately, the state of California has ample legislative power to do both; it also has a number of precedents to serve as examples of how to do it.

The first precedent may be found in state planning requirements imposed upon local governments. The state requires city and county governments to develop general plans for dealing with such issues as land use, housing, conservation, open space, and seismic safety, among others.[48] The legislature could adopt a similar approach to water allocation questions. Water districts could be required to develop plans in which they classified water usages, assigned priorities to water needs, and established means for responding to a water shortage through transfers, water rationing, queuing, and pricing changes that would promote conservation of water and allocation of it to those most in need. If each water district had a water-shortage plan, the state could design strategies for meeting water shortages in various areas. Responsibility at the state level could be vested in a coordinating agency, which could seek to harmonize the interests of the numerous special districts and provide a point of contact between them and other state agencies.

Given an adequate information system, the state coordinating agency would then need the means to supply water to the areas of shortage. In the event of a critical shortage like that experienced in 1976-77 or worse, costs would be incurred in making water available to regions of deficiency. Such costs would be for facilities for interbasin transfers or to bring in supplies from a new source. The state could meet these costs by creating a Water Shortage Fund to which all water users of California would contribute on the grounds that all are ultimately the beneficiaries of such a system. The state has an appropriate method for assessment in the beneficial use tax, which might take the form of a surcharge designed to cover the cost of delivering the needed supplies to areas of shortage. The surcharge could be levied upon water districts, which, in turn, could transfer it to water users and consumers.

Incentives could be developed to induce voluntary efficient water use. For example, the water shortage surcharge could be waived for those water districts which on their own initiative consolidated and undertook to supply water to needy areas. Another incentive might be to waive the surcharge for users willing to sell their water entitlements. Those agricultural or municipal users, for example, who have excess water entitlements that they might otherwise use inefficiently in order to preserve their rights, could sell the water at marginal cost—i.e., the cost of supplying an equivalent volume of new water. By avoiding the surcharge, the seller would be assured of a windfall profit. The profit would be especially handsome in those areas where the average historical cost of water has been very low and the marginal cost of new water very high. (One might ask why the individual seller of water should be entitled to a large windfall profit. The frank answer is political expediency—to induce sellers to change behavior that would otherwise be difficult, if not impossible, to change within the existing pattern of water rights. If water rights are not shifted voluntarily or by inducement, the only recourse is compulsion under the police power of the state, a move that would surely encounter intractable opposition).

The goal under this option is the creation of a quasi market which will move water at the margin to shortage areas while leaving undisturbed the main body of water entitlements under the present tangle of legal doctrine. Even so, the creation of such a quasi market could only be accomplished by removing several current legal obstacles. One such obstacle is that water allocations and entitlements usually reside in the water district rather than the individual; the individual as a resident has only a claim to water service. Legislation would have to be enacted to recognize that individuals possess transferable interests to contractual water rights that are independent of the district's entitlement. Similarly, legislation would have to recognize the transferability of groundwater rights, divorcing these rights from the land and making them marketable so long as such transfers are not environmentally destructive.

Some may object that these options are an elaborate and costly way to transfer water in the event of shortages—but California already possesses a much more complex, costly, and wasteful water management system. Short of the wholesale dismantling of present water law and the creation of a centralized state management that overrides present water rights and district management—neither of which appears to be politically feasible—there seem to be few alternatives available to meet water shortages. We believe our suggestions are more likely to induce compliance and to be politically attainable.

Federal Role. No discussion of water management can ignore the important role played by the federal government. There can be little doubt that until the state and federal systems are brought under a common administrative structure, the practices of these two systems will continue to be mutually disruptive. Moreover, a state-coordinated quasi-market system, based upon taxes and price incentives, cannot be made to work if a large portion of the water supply remains outside of its jurisdiction. There appear to be three possible approaches to this problem: merge the federal system into the state system; merge the state system into the federal system; or maintain separate management systems but impose a common set of rules, procedures, and pricing methods on both systems.

State acquisition of the federal system would surely be resisted by the consumers of cheap federal water. It may, however, be attractive to a president and congress anxious to rid the federal government of a major drain on the national treasury. Federal acquisition of the state system to form a western equivalent of the Tennessee Valley Authority is likely to generate widespread opposition from state agencies as well as from those who fear that Washington will be insensitive to local environmental and fiscal concerns. The most promising alternative to the present dual system appears to be the imposition of a common set of required practices to be followed by both state and federal water agencies. The precise nature of those practices should be determined jointly by the congress, the president, and state leaders who clearly acknowledge the negative consequences of the bifurcated state-federal water system. Only with such an acknowledgment are these leaders likely to take steps necessary to ameliorate the existing condition. In view of the radical disparity between the prices charged to consumers of federal and state water, any move to establish a common set of guidelines will obviously meet with stiff political opposition. But the day is not distant when strong political opposition to the current system can also be expected.

*   *   *

California's water institutions are a complex and closely interconnected mosaic of customs, attitudes, laws, myths, and organizational structures. They are a product of the state's historical experience as well as that of the nation. To tamper with any of them is to tamper with all of them. Common sense demands that state and national leaders bring these institutions into harmony with the overriding necessities of today and tomorrow. To persist in the outmoded practices of an earlier era is to wreak havoc on the future.

REFERENCES AND NOTES

1. Walton Bean, *California: An Interpretive History* 3rd ed., (New York: 1978), p. xvii.
2. California Department of Water Resources, *The California Water Plan: Outlook in 1974,* Bulletin No. 160-74 (Sacramento: November 1974), p. 2.
3. Thomas C. Sandars, ed., *The Institutes of Justinian* (London: Longmans, Green, and Co., 1941), p. 90.
4. *Calif. Stats.* (April 8, 1911), p. 821.
5. For a good brief description of each of these projects, see William L. Kahrl, ed., *The California Water Atlas* (Sacramento: State of California, 1979), passim.
6. Lucien Shaw, "The Development of the Law of Waters in the West," *California Law Review,* X (1922): 444.
7. Kahrl, ed. *California Water Atlas,* pp. 103-104.
8. *Calif. Stats.* (April 13, 1850), p. 219.
9. Wells A. Hutchins, *The California Law of Water Rights* (Sacramento: Office of the California State Engineer, 1956), pp. 220-221.
10. For the use of water in the diggings, see John W. Caughey, *Gold Is the Cornerstone* (Berkeley: University of California Press, 1948) and Rodman Paul, *California Gold: The Beginning of Mining in the Far West* (Cambridge, Mass., Harvard University press, 1947).
11. *Irwin v. Phillips,* 5 Cal. 140 (1855).
12. The classic studies on the emergence of the appropriation doctrine are Clesson S. Kinney, *A Treatise on the Law of Irrigation and Water Rights,* 2nd ed., 4 vols., (San Francisco: 1912) and Samuel C. Wiel, *Water Rights in the Western States,* 3rd ed., 2 vols., (San Francisco: 1911). For a brief summary, see Norris Hundley, Jr., *Water and the West* (Berkeley and Los Angeles: University of California Press, 1975), pp. 64-73.
13. *Lux v. Haggin,* 69 Cal. 225 (1886).
14. Gordon R. Miller, "Shaping California Water Law, 1781 to 1928," *Southern California Quarterly* LV (1973), p. 28.
15. *Herminghaus v. Southern California Edison,* 200 Cal. 81 (1926).
16. *Calif. Constitution,* Article XIV, Section 3 (Nov. 6, 1928); Governor's Commission to Review California Water Rights Law, *Final Report.* (Sacramento: December 1978), p. 9.
17. *Katz v. Walkinshaw,* 141 Cal. 116 (1903).
18. *Pasadena v. Alhambra,* 33 Cal. 2d 905 (1949).
19. *Calif. Stats.* (1951), Chap. 1361; (1953), Chap. 1690; (1955), Chap. 1887; *Los Angeles v. San Fernando,* 14 Cal. 3d 199 (1975).
20. *Feliz v. Los Angeles,* 58 Cal. 73, 79 (1881); *Los Angeles v. Pomeroy,* 124 Cal. 597 (1899); *Los Angeles v. Hunter,* 156 Cal. 603 (1909); *San Diego v. Cuyamaca Water Co.,* 209 Cal. 105 (1930); *San Diego v. Cuyamaca Water Co.,* 209 Cal. 152 (1930).
21. Kahrl, ed., *California Water Atlas* passim; Donald E. Owen, Chief, Division of Planning, California Dept. of Water Resources, personal communication, July 1, 1981.

22. *Arizona v. California,* 373 U.S. 546 (1963).
23. James Jamieson, Sidney Sonenblum, Werner Z. Hirsch, Merrill R. Goodall, and Harold Jaffee, *Some Political and Economic Aspects of Managing California Water Districts* (Los Angeles: UCLA Institute of Government and Public Affairs, 1974), pp. 9-25; Merrill R. Goodall, John D. Sullivan, and Timothy De Young, *California Water: A New Political Economy* (Montclair: Allanheld, Osmun, 1978), pp. 4-16; Charles E. Phelps, Nancy Y. More, Morlie H. Graubard, *Efficient Water Use in California: Water Rights, Water Districts, and Water Transfers* (Santa Monica: Rand, 1978).
24. Governor's Commission to Review California Water Rights Law, *Final Report,* pp. 11, 18.
25. Kahrl, ed., *California Water Atlas,* p. 65; D. Anderson, *Riparian Water Rights in California* (Sacramento: Governor's Commission to Review California Water Rights Law, background paper, 1977), p. 2; *Prather v. Hoberg,* 24 Cal. 2d 549, 150 P.2d 405 (1944).
26. *Calif. Stats.* (1980) Chap. 933.
27. Kahrl, ed., *California Water Atlas,* p. 65; *Hudson v. West,* 47 Cal. 2d 823, 306, P.2d 807 (1957).
28. *Calif. Stats.* (1913), p. 1012; *Tulare Irrigation District v. Linday-Strathmore Irrigation District,* 3 Cal. 2d 489, 45 P.2d 972 (1935); *In re Waters of Long Valley Creek Stream System,* 25 Cal. 3d 339 (1979); *Calif. Stats.* (1979) Chap. 1112.
29. Governor's Commission to Review California Water Rights Law, *Final Report,* p. 11.
30. *California Trout v. State Water Resources Control Board,* 90 Cal. App. 3d 816 (1979); *Fullerton v. State Water Resources Control Board,* 90 Cal. App. 3d 590 (1979).
31. Governor's Commission to Review California Water Rights Law, *Final Report,* p. 112.
32. *Winters v. United States,* 207 U.S. 564 (1908).
33. *Arizona v. California,* 373 U.S. 546, 596-601 (1963).
34. *Hudson v. Dailey,* 156 Cal. 617, 105 P. 748 (1909); *Burr v. Maclay Ranch Water Co.,* 106 Cal. 268, 116 P. 715 (1911).
35. Governor's Commission to Review California Water Rights Law, *Final Report,* pp. 143-144; *Los Angeles v. San Fernando,* 14 Cal. 3d 199, 537 P.2d 1250; 123 Cal. Rptr. 1 (1975); *Tehachapi-Cummings County Water District v. Armstrong,* 49 Cal. App. 3d 992, 122 Cal. Rptr. 918 (1975); Calif. Dept. of Water Resources, *Ground Water Basins in California,* Bulletin 118-80 (Sacramento: Calif. Dept. of Water Resources, 1980), passim.
36. See *Katz v. Walkinshaw,* 141 Cal. 116, 135 (1903); *Lodi v. East Bay Municipal Utilities District,* 7 Cal. 2d 316, 341, 60 P.2d 439, 450 (1936).
37. Governor's Commission to Review California Water Rights Law, *Final Report,* p. 136.
38. Donald Erlenkotter, Michael Hanemann, Richard E. Howitt, and Henry J. Vaux, Jr., "The Economics of Water Development and Use in California," in Ernest A. Engelbert, ed., *California Water Planning and Policy: Selected Issues* (University of California, Davis: Water Resources Center, June, 1979), p. 177.
39. Jamieson et al., *Some Political and Economic Aspects of Managing California Water Districts,* pp. 49-96. See also U.S. National Water Commission, *Water Policies For the Future: Final Report to the President and Congress* (Washington D.C.: U.S. Government Printing Office, 1973), pp. 227-293.
40. Jamieson et al., *Some Political and Economic Aspects of Managing California Water Districts,* pp. 97-121.
41. Ibid., pp. 121-140.
42. *Calif. Stats.* (1979) Chap. 1112; (1980) Chaps. 933 and 1100.
43. U.S. National Water Commission, *Water Policies for the Future,* Recommendations 7-21, 7-22.
44. See, for example, Hundley, *Water and the West,* passim; Hundley, *Dividing the Waters: A Century of Controversy Between the United States and Mexico* (Berkeley and Los Angeles: University of California Press, 1966), passim; Kahrl, ed., *California Water Atlas,* passim.
45. Governor's Commission to Review California Water Rights Law, *Final Report,* pp. 113-114. On the possibilities of invoking the public trust principle to protect in-stream uses, see Harrison C. Dunning, "The Significance of California's Public Trust Easement for California Water Rights Law," *U.C. Davis Law Review* XIV (1980), and U.S. Department of the Interior, Fish and Wildlife Service, *The Public Trust Doctrine, Instream Flows and Resources,* by Felix E. Smith (Sacramento: March 1980).
46. Ibid., pp. 165-169.
47. Ronald Robie, Director, California Dept. of Water Resources, personal communication, February 13, 1981.
48. *Calif. Code,* Sections 65040.2, 65100, 65101, 65300, 65302, 65303.

CHAPTER X

POLITICAL DYNAMICS AND DECISION MAKING

by

Eugene C. Lee and Harrison C. Dunning*

ABSTRACT

The physical and human environment within which California politics takes place is both distinct and diverse. Its elements include the state's geography, patterns of urban settlement, economic development, agricultural production, and complex ethnic and racial groupings.

Water policy is also affected by a politics which is highly personalistic and particularistic, and in which neither the two political parties nor their leaders have played an effective role. The role of interest groups is dominant, and scores of such groups are active in water politics at all levels of government. Bureaucrats, government water specialists and the courts constitute additional categories of political actors. All of these operate in a context of "direct democracy," in which measures can be placed directly on the ballot by the initiative or referendum.

Within this general framework, a strong consensus over water policy in California can be reached only on issues of minimal controversy. In general terms, water reclamation and reuse and conservation command overwhelming support among a large number of interest groups. The consensus collapses with respect to issues of the allocation, pricing, and regulation of water use, concerning which development-oriented groups oppose and environmental groups support stronger governmental action. The split continues concerning development of additional water projects, although the positions of most groups are reversed.

The difficulty of reaching a consensus is seen in the record of the Governor's Commission to Review California Water Rights Law, whose report in 1978 recommended a state/local regulatory program designed to reduce groundwater overdraft, to preserve in-stream flows, and to facilitate the transfer of water and water rights. The failure of the legislature to act on these recommendations can be attributed to many factors, including a narrow mandate which prevented the building of a consensus involving both development and regulation viewpoints. In contrast, the ability of Arizona to provide for state management of groundwater and mandatory conservation indicates that compromises and consensus can be achieved in the process of bargaining among key interest groups and with strong leadership on the part of the governor.

For California, serious reform may be achievable only when major projects appear untenable to the water industry, on either legal or economic grounds; when some interest-group alignment takes place; when direct interest-group bargaining occurs; and when additional political leadership or external forces press for change.

*The authors acknowledge the contributions of Laura Lake, University of California, Los Angeles, in the formulative stages of this paper.

THE SIGNIFICANCE OF POLITICS
FOR CALIFORNIA'S WATER POLICY AND PROGRAMS

Water and politics? The words fit together like "hand and glove." Indeed, the issues surrounding water in California, as the papers in this volume illustrate, are manifestly political, involving such fundamental questions as the distribution of wealth, the use of land, the location of industry, the character of labor, urban settlement patterns, the price of food and energy, and thus inflation and the overall economy.

The dominance of politics arises from the fact that, more than anywhere else in the nation—and perhaps the world—Californians have chosen not to adapt to the environment, but rather to adapt the environment to their own perceived needs. This development is not, of course, unique to California, but parallels the American experience generally. But the degree of human intervention— technological, social, economic—involved in this, the world's preeminent "hydraulic society," has thrust government, and thus politics, to center stage.

Water, as much or more than any other basic societal need—food, housing, energy—involves public decisions. The housing crisis of the 1980s will, for example, be shaped primarily by decisions of the private marketplace, although government and politics will play a decisive role. To a far greater degree, in contrast, critical issues of water in California will be resolved by public agencies, cities and water districts, the legislature and the governor, the congress and president, and by the political structure and processes which involve all of these.

In California, water politics involves not only classical legal and institutional questions of water rights and regulation, but massive public works—dams, aqueducts, power plants—which become political issues in their own right. The financial implications of control and development are enormous. To a degree unsurpassed in any other phase of the economy—with the possible exception of defense spending—government decisions impact upon the water economy. In an earlier day, the control of surface water rights shaped the creation of the first California fortunes. Today, the issue of groundwater regulation involves immense personal stakes. In parallel fashion, the development of water projects and the distribution of the "new" water created can be responsible for impressive capital gains, while the exportation of that water from its place of origin or normal flow may involve potential losses.

In addition, the competition for water in the 1980s has brought new problems and new political interests related to the soaring costs of energy. On the one hand, large quantities of cooling water are needed for the generation of electricity, water which can be obtained most readily by buying the water rights of current agricultural users. On the other hand, the costs of pumping that water over the Tehachapi Mountains will soar, as contracts with power companies expire in the mid-80s and are renegotiated at many times their current rate. For the individual farmer and consumer, an expert on water use has predicted that:

> Certain food prices may double and some of California's fresh produce may disappear because of water and electricity price hikes in the 1980s. . . Cheap water will become a thing of the past. After 1985, water may double or triple in price . . . Some farming operations will go out of business.[1]

In circular fashion, therefore, decisions concerning water in California will affect every citizen, interest group, and political figure. But at the same time, each of these will have an impact upon these decisions.

Political Variables That Will Be Important in Determining Water Policy

Politics reflects the society of which it is a part. In California, this environment is distinct from that of any other state. It remains true, as Carey McWilliams wrote in 1949, that California is "the great exception."[2] The elements of this diversity each have their own political impacts and, to one extent or another, add to the complexity of water politics.

The geography of the state provides the first example. The size of California is matched by its variety of terrains, soils, climates, natural resources—not distributed evenly throughout the state, but highly specific in their regional impact. Nowhere, of course, is this more evident than in the differential rainfall from north to south, and in the extraordinary vulnerability of the state to the Sierra snowpack, the amount of which is neither regular nor reliable.

This vulnerability is not just a result of nature's vagaries, of course, but also of society's attempts to overcome nature in patterns of urban settlement and agricultural production. There is no sign as yet that Californians are ready to concede. Net immigration into the state in 1980 approached 300,000, and the 400,000 births (as contrasted to the birthrate) were at an all-time high. As preceding chapters have indicated, the urban/industrial share of water is expected to increase from 15 percent of total usage to 20-25 percent by the year 2020, though it is far from clear how agriculture will accommodate to this shift.

Competition for water will take place in the world's largest advanced industrial society, a society in which the service sector is dominant, in which social and economic interdependence is high, and in which California's ties to the national and international economy are increasingly close. This is especially the case for water-intensive agribusiness, which plays an important role in international trade and which brings into play a host of additional political factors and participants, both at the state and national level.

In addition to geographical diversity, demographic growth, and economic complexity, the state is characterized by an ethnic and racial variety matched only by Hawaii. While legal immigrants from Asia, undocumented migrants from Mexico, and a fast-growing Latino population may not have a specific impact on the demand for water, they are increasingly important elements in the state's political culture.

A central element in this political culture is the fact that California is the most heavily urbanized state in the nation. While 85 percent of the state's water may be used in agriculture, over 90 percent of the users are city-dwellers. Insofar as a specific issue involves voting, either for representatives in Sacramento or Washington or on initiatives and referendums, it will be urban voters who settle the fate of agricultural users. The issues will be resolved in the midst of an increasingly crowded political agenda which, in the 1980s, will include such controversial and complex questions as a criminal justice system that does not seem to work, educational institutions that do not seem able to teach, ever more costly medical care, a cracking freeway system, and a border highly permeable by hundreds of thousands, if not millions, of migrants from an expanding and volatile Mexico.

Equally important and of direct relevance to water politics is the ongoing tax revolt, spawned in California as Proposition 13, whose ramifications are only now becoming fully apparent. Indeed, the well-recognized groundwater overdraft has been matched in the last three years by the overdraft of state revenues, with a resulting draw-down on the surplus (i.e., year-end balances) to the vanishing point. There is little indication the electorate is willing to change direction.

Against this general backdrop, water policy will be affected by a number of specific political institutions, each of which interacts with the others in ways which complicate generalization.

Importantly, California is a state where there is very little intermediate linkage between voters and interest groups, and elected officials—state legislators, governor, congressmen. It is a state in which politics is highly personalistic and particularistic. Political parties are far from meaningless as labels differentiating large numbers of voters and politicians, but they are relatively unimportant as programmatic, organizational bodies.

With respect to water, one cannot look to the political parties to develop coherent policy, or necessarily address the issue at all. This is particularly the case when the current titular leaders of the two parties—the governor and lieutenant governor, respectively—fail to exercise a leadership role.

In the legislature itself, the politics of water transcends party lines. The main divisions are less partisan than regional and economic. The split within Democratic ranks was nowhere more evident than in the contrasting positions of Assemblymen Leo McCarthy and Howard Berman in their contest for the speakership in 1980. Various promises of support for or against major water legislation in Sacramento were used by the two men in their attempt to persuade undecided legislators to support their particular cause.

In this context of ineffective party, gubernatorial and legislative leadership, the role of interest groups is greatly enhanced. Scores of these are involved in water politics: agricultural, business, labor and environmental organizations; federal and state agencies; local governments and water districts. This involvement can be seen daily in the halls of the Capitol, where lobbyists and legislators interact. It is less visible but equally manifest in legislators' concern over the next election.

This concern is increasingly evidenced by a drive for campaign funds. Although California law governing the disclosure of campaign contributions is strict and apparently complied with, the sums involved are large and unlimited. Individual congressional campaigns have involved in excess of $1 million, and state offices only proportionately less. Such funds are often used by incumbents to finance other candidates' races, thus building personal—as opposed to party— ties and organizations. The end result is greatly to increase the role of money in politics and the role of groups which have the resources to participate in this critical aspect of political life.

A recent Common Cause report describes the impact of the "top twenty" contributors to state legislative campaigns—organizations which gave a combined total of $10.6 million over the past five years. Their ranks include several groups with a vital interest in water politics: labor (Teamsters and the State Labor Federations); finance (the California Bankers Association); utilities (Southern California Edison). One need not necessarily agree with Common Cause's advocacy of public financing for political campaigns to agree that these groups, and others like them, participate in a system where "the vast majority of legislators will remain heavily dependent on special-interest dollars, and those dollars will continue to command undue influence. . ."[3]

A third category of political actors involves the bureaucrats and staff of the various executive agencies and legislative committees. Typically with more experience, and often with more expertise, than their principals, government water specialists do much to shape the agenda and the alternatives presented to the policy makers and to the people. The extent to which an agency is dominated by an "engineering mentality" with a bent toward capital construction, for example, or a committee by a staff committed to an environmentalist ethic, will do much to influence the character of the policy outcome.

In a different context, a fourth arena of water politics includes the courts. As is clear from the preceding chapter, a great deal of water law and policy has emerged via the judiciary. The selection of cases, the role of litigants and their attorneys, the skill and knowledge of the judges and the quality of their opinions are all vital to an understanding of the origins and implementation of much water policy.

The politics of legislator, lobbyist, bureaucrat and judge takes place in a context of "direct democracy"—the initiative and referendum—which means the ability of the voters to place both statutes and constitutional amendments directly on the ballot, on the one hand, and to suspend the implementation of a statute, on the other. Although there have been only 45 successful initiatives in the state's history (and until 1981 the referendum had not been employed at all since 1952), the existence of this institution has become a key factor in state politics. While little employed in recent water policy development—with the exception of the ill-fated wild and scenic rivers protection act in 1974—the threat of an initiative may force legislative action, or, on the contrary, preempt legislative consideration altogether.

Like candidate campaigns, the politics of direct democracy is highly particularistic, permitting direct contact between interest groups and the voter, often with only the 60-second TV commercial as an intermediary. Such contact is costly, and initiative campaigns can involve the expenditure of millions of dollars. Unlike most candidate elections, the expenditure of such huge sums does not ensure the success of a measure, although it will generally suffice to defeat one. However, grassroots organizations can play a vital role in this arena, as evidenced by the successful coastal conservation and political reform issues of the 1970s.

Also, regardless of initiative petitions, constitutional amendments and bond issues must be approved by the voters. These elections can be both controversial and closely contested. The history of the State Water Project itself illuminates the shifting positions of political actors and interest groups. Although opposed by the Metropolitan Water District of Southern California, which favored a constitutional amendment guaranteeing water delivery, a bond act passed the legislature in 1959, subject to voter ratification. While the act attempted to strike a balance between competing regional interests, as described in *The California Water Atlas,* "The campaign for authorization of the bonds in 1960 nevertheless became one of the most fiercely contested elections in the history of the state."[4] Only four days before the election, the MWD board reversed its earlier opposition, adding its support to what became a narrow victory. A shift of less than 90,000 votes out of a total of 5.8 million ballots would have caused the defeat of the Project.

In short, water policy makers must take into account either the need to obtain popular approval or the ability of interest groups to put measures directly on the ballot regardless of legislative views and intentions, a practice which is in marked contrast to most other industrial states, as well as to the congressional arena.

With respect to that arena, California has by far the largest congressional delegation, and it will rise to 45 members in 1982. The very size of this delegation, however, as well as the diverse society that it represents, has prevented a unity of viewpoint or action. In 1981, the delegation is almost evenly divided between the two parties, and includes the widest range of political views. This diversity is clearly revealed in water politics, both between the parties and between members of the same party. The same divisions which affect the state—urban/rural, public/private, conservationist/developer, north/south—prevent the delegation from presenting a "California position" to the national administration or to the federal bureaucracy.

In this Washington environment, the position of California members on key committees is crucial, especially if the member is in the majority party. A well-placed subcommittee chairman may be more important than the governor with respect to a national water policy decision, even one dealing exclusively with California. It is no surprise that California interest groups are as active in Washington as in Sacramento, and that their role in congressional electoral politics is no less pronounced. No less than in Sacramento, too, the politics of competing federal bureaucracies—most visibly the Corps of Engineers and the Bureau of Reclamation—shape the national water agenda.

These complex state and national political ties reflect the fact that, to a degree unmatched anywhere else in the nation, two immense and complicated water systems, one national and one state, exist side by side; both are inextricably intertwined with equally complex regional systems. Thus virtually every problem of water competition involves power relationships—legal, administrative, fiscal and political—among at least three levels of government. Now, as in the past, different interests take their case to whichever level of government is most favorable at the moment, and this can vary with changes of administration in both Sacramento and Washington.

The local delivery structure for water is even more complicated and even less understood. The politics which determines the role and decisions of the more than 1,000 water districts of various sorts is generally out of the mainstream and public view, and thus beyond accountability, despite its importance. Nowhere is this more evident than with respect to the Metropolitan Water District of Southern California, frequently termed the second most important legislative body in the state. With responsibility for the water needs of half the state's population, its policies have been described recently as "[underwriting] Southern California land booms for the past 40 years . . . a *carte blanche* for development and agricultural interests . . . [through its] wonderfully generous pricing policies.   Governed by a nonelected board, where votes are weighted by the relative assessed valuation of the member units, the MWD is virtually invisible to and untouchable by normal political institutions.

In such a political environment, what of the public? In recent Field polls, the following were some of the most striking findings:[6]

• By a 40 to 30 percent margin, Californians think current state water laws are unfair to regional interests, including 54 percent of Northern Californians and 31 percent of Southern Californians.

• Most Californians believe that new water facilities are needed to meet future demand, but there is equal agreement that conservation is very important.

• Most Californians have a total misperception of the distribution of water usage in the state, greatly overestimating the extent of urban use and underestimating agricultural demands.

• Californians are polarized by region, as on no other issue in recent history, over the Peripheral Canal. In May 1981, 53 percent of Southern Californians favored the project, as contrasted to only 21 percent of those polled in the North. Importantly, 26 percent of Californians had no opinion on the project—32 percent in the South and 16 percent in the North.

The political variables which will shape California's water policy in the coming decades are, as described above, interrelated and often ambiguous. They derive from a society which is wondrously complex and undergoing continuous change. But certain predictions may be offered:

• The basic structure of governmental institutions will remain much the same as it has been over the past 50 years.

• The political process will continue to be particularistic and personalistic, despite efforts to revitalize the political parties.

• The overall role of interest groups in the political process will grow, although specific interests will wax or wane in influence.

• While the tax revolt as such will abate, there will be little sentiment for a return to pre-Proposition 13 or pre-Reagan levels. The public sector—defense spending excluded—will continue at present levels. Competition for limited tax resources and related pressures for water projects to show their cost-effectiveness will intensify.

• In such a political environment, consensus will be more difficult to achieve, and few governors or legislators will find it in their interest to attempt or within their ability to achieve more than modest, incremental changes from the status quo in almost any policy area, water included. In the absence of elected leadership, bureaucratic politics will become more important.

• The use of the initiative to enact legislation will continue to flourish, providing opportunities for both special-interest groups with well-financed campaigns and grassroots organizations with volunteer workers to seek direct influence over public policy. Depending upon the outcome of the Peripheral Canal vote, interest groups may seek more frequently to overturn legislation through the referendum.

• The federal government will continue to be a critical force in shaping state water policy, with respect to capital projects, conservation, water quality, and a host of other issues. In planning, constructing, operating, pricing, and regulating, parallel political tracks will have to be followed in both Sacramento and Washington for almost any major policy.

• Litigation and ensuing judicial opinions will continue to be a significant source of water policy, both at the state and national levels.

What of water? Will its storage, distribution, pricing, conservation and alternative uses—now barely in the public consciousness even after the drought experience—join energy as a more highly visible political issue? If so, will public attitudes assume a larger role in decision making, and public understanding of the facts become more central to decision makers? What would be the political impact of such public knowledge? Will water policy makers—grassroots environmentalists or development-oriented water districts—turn to the initiative process to work their will, when representative institutions fail to deliver in the desired manner?

The answers to such questions are unclear for 1984, much less for 2020. Their dimensions may be measured, however, by an attempt to analyze the political implications of "alternative water futures."

THE POLITICS OF ALTERNATIVE WATER FUTURES

Three scenarios illustrate possible futures of water policy in California. The first assumes no basic shift in policy or practice, although short-run adjustments might follow a drought or other natural phenomenon. Improvements in reclamation and conservation would continue to take place, but only modest incremental changes in the overall pattern of water allocation would occur. A second scenario projects only minimal change in the supply of water in the state, but assumes major changes in the institutional mechanisms for allocating and distributing that water. A final scenario provides for significant increases in the supply of water through the construction of new storage and transfer facilities, unimpeded by the referendum on SB200.

Clearly these three alternatives are not mutually exclusive. All could take place simultaneously—increased conservation, shifts in allocation practices, and capital development. Indeed, it may take action on more than one front to permit any movement at all. As indicated throughout this discussion, the forces favoring and opposing different courses of action are in close balance, at least as reflected by legislative voting. Compromises between advocates of development and conservation may be necessary, if either side is to advance its cause.

Despite this interrelatedness, the political dynamics of the three scenarios are distinguishable. It is useful to attempt to analyze them as pure types, recognizing their distance from the real world of political trade-offs and negotiated legislative settlements.

In an analysis of alternative futures, the views of contending interests are, of course, a crucial variable. Fortunately, a recent survey of 31 organizations and governmental units on nine critical issues of water policy has been conducted.[7] Part of a much larger study of water-policy formulation, the results of the survey presented in Table 1 provide a lens through which the three scenarios may be more closely examined.

These 31 organizations are grouped in the table according to broad categories. The nine issues follow the order of the three scenarios, from minimal change, through reallocation and regulatory adjustments, to increases in supply resulting from major capital projects. The resulting matrix offers few surprises but is illuminating in its consistency.

Table 1

Policy Positions of California Interest Groups
on Nine Selected Issues of Water Policy

KEY:
SS = Support Study
S = Support
QS = Qualified Support
NP = No Position
QO = Qualified Opposition
O = Opposition

ORGANIZATIONS (By Category)	Scenario #1: Conservation & Reclamation			Scenario #2: Reallocation & Regulation			Scenario #3: Construction & Development		
	Water Reclamation and Reuse	Water Conservation Alternatives	Employment of Water Pricing Practices	Revision of Water Rights to Improve Efficiency	Revision of Water Rights to Modify Instream Uses	State Policy for Local Groundwater Management	Construction of the Peripheral Canal	Enlargement of Shasta Dam	Development of North Coast Rivers
Agriculture and Forestry									
Agric. Council of Calif.	NP	QS	NP	O	O	O	S	SS	NP
Calif. Farm Bureau	QS	QS	O	QS	O	O	S	SS	S
Calif. Forest Prot. Assoc.	QS	NP	NP	QO	QO	O	NP	QS	O
Calif. State Grange	S	NP	O	QO	O	SS	QS	SS	O
Water Organizations									
Assoc. of Cal. Water Agencies	QS	QS	O	S	O	O	S	QS	S
California Mutual Water Cos.	S	S	S	O	O	O	S	SS	S
Calif. Water Resources Assoc.	S	QS	QO	O	O	O	S	SS	S
Business & Labor									
Calif. Chamber of Commerce	QS	QS	O	O	O	O	S	SS	S
Calif. Manufacturers Assoc.	S	S	QS	S	QS	QS	NP	NP	S
State Bldg. & Trades Council	S	S	NP	NP	O	NP	S	SS	S
Civic									
California State Bar	NP	NP	NP	NP	NP	NP	NP	NP	NP
Calif. Taxpayers Assoc.	NP	NP	NP	NP	NP	NP	NP	NP	NP
League of Women Voters	S	S	S	S	S	S	NP	O	O
Environmental									
Calif. Env'l Defense Fund	S	S	S	S	S	S	O	NP	O
California Trout	S	S	QS	S	S	NP	O	SS	O
Planning & Conserv. League	S	S	S	S	S	S	O	O	O
Sierra Club	S	S	S	S	S	S	O	NP	O
Federal Government									
Army Corps of Engineers	S	S	QS	QS	NP	NP	NP	NP	NP
Env. Protection Agency	S	S	S	S	S	S	QS	SS	NP
Fish & Wildlife Service	S	S	NP	S	S	S	QS	SS	O
Bureau of Reclamation	S	S	O	QS	NP	S	QS	SS	NP
State Government									
Dept. of Fish and Game	S	S	NP	S	S	S	S	SS	O
Dept. of Water Resources	S	S	QS	S	S	S	S	SS	O
Public Utilities Commission	S	S	S	NP	NP	NP	NP	NP	NP
Water Resources Control Bd.	S	S	S	S	S	S	S	SS	O
Local Government									
Calif. Special Districts Assoc.	S	S	S	QO	NP	QO	NP	NP	QS
County Supervisors' Assoc.	S	QS	NP	NP	NP	NP	NP	NP	NP
League of California Cities	NP	QS	NP	NP	NP	NP	NP	NP	NP
Urban									
City of Fresno	S	QS	NP	QS	NP	NP	NP	NP	NP
East Bay MUD	S	S	S	NP	NP	NP	NP	NP	NP
Metropolitan Water District	QS	QS	NP	O	O	O	S	SS	O

Source: Adapted from Ernest Engelbert and John F. Munro, "California Water Policy Decision Survey", July 10, 1979 (unpublished).

The Alternative Future of Limited Change: Scenario #1

The politics of the status quo in water policy has, in effect, been described in the two preceding sections of this paper. It is, as suggested, a highly pluralistic, particularistic politics, with a weak institutional base for producing a political settlement on issues which severely divide the interested parties. Few political figures find it in their own interest to be water policy leaders, as was Governor Edmund G. "Pat" Brown in his successful drive to pass the State Water Project in 1960. Instead, in such a politics, agreement can be reached only on issues of minimal controversy, unless an external event—a drought or federal intervention, for example—force initiative or action.

Table 1 is suggestive of the kind of change which is possible, absent such external pressure. Virtually every interest group listed is supportive of better water reclamation and reuse, and of pursuing conservation alternatives. To be sure, a consensus might disappear with respect to a specific feature of such a program, but as a general policy area this would appear to be a promising field for far more aggressive action, both public and private. And indeed, there is ample evidence in preceding chapters that reclamation and conservation are taking place in both the urban and agricultural sectors.

The Alternative Future of Reallocation and Regulation: Scenario #2

The consensus immediately collapses, however, with respect to changes in present practices of the allocation, pricing, and regulation of water use. Previous chapters have described various alternatives to current economic and institutional arrangements. It is clear that most if not all of the proposals are opposed by an impressive list of interest groups, including the California Farm Bureau Federation, the California Chamber of Commerce, and, significantly, the Metropolitan Water District of Southern California. (The California Manufacturers Association is a noteworthy exception.)

In contrast, state and federal agencies, environmental organizations, and the League of Women Voters are united in their support of change. It is important of course, to note that the survey was completed during the tenure of the Carter Administration. It remains to be seen what policies and directions in the areas of water rights and regulation will emerge under the leadership of Secretary Watt. Regardless, the sharp division of opinion between the supporters and opponents of change illustrates the level of difficulty confronting a governor or legislator in attempting to lead in this policy area.

Nor does it seem likely that issues like water rights or pricing will find their way to the ballot via the initiative process. "Save the Groundwater" is not a slogan designed to move an urban electorate, regardless of the fundamental importance of the issue and the grassroots-organizing abilities of environmental activists.

Instead, absent political leadership and popular appeal, controversies over regulation and reallocation will take place more in the courtroom than in the Capitol. Unless other factors intervene, litigants rather than legislators or voters will shape this alternative future, as currently evidenced by the Inyo County suit against Los Angeles to halt the city's pumping in the Owens Valley.

This scenario could be markedly affected, of course, by federal policy and practice, not only over the allocation of water per se, but in connection with such matters as water quality—e.g., in the Delta, or in groundwater threatened by toxic substances.

The Alternative Future of Development: Scenario #3

The actors remain much the same with respect to the politics of increasing California's water supply through the development of additional water projects. However, the roles of many are reversed. Now it is the Farm Bureau and state Chamber of Commerce which favor and the environmental groups which tend to oppose these programs.

But several important groups shift position from the sharp dichotomy of the preceding scenario, and there are also important exceptions as to position. Expansion of the Shasta Dam, for instance, is seen by a variety of groups as suitable for further study, evoking little opposition even among environmentalists. But support begins to fall off for the Peripheral Canal, while development of the North Coast rivers polarizes attitudes as did the reallocation and regulation issues discussed in Scenario #2.

Unlike Scenario #2, however, the politics of development must deal with the possibility of large-scale expenditures at both the state and federal levels. While perhaps no more important in its overall impact on water utilization than are the strategies of reallocation and regulation, the development of new water is much more visible to the public. This is especially true when general revenues or subsidies are involved, which directly pit water against other programs in the battle for already limited tax resources.

This visibility and public awareness increase the political stakes for the urban representatives who dominate the legislature, and also make more likely attempts to reach voters directly through the initiative and the referendum, as evidenced by the battle over the Peripheral Canal.

In this more visible and overtly political arena, the overall demographic trends noted above will increase the relative interest and role of urban interest groups in water policy. Their voice will be heard not only in the metropolitan regions of the state, but in the once rural, now exurban foothills of the Sierra. California's fastest growing communities are the small towns on the rim of the Central Valley. They will have their own needs and press their own demands for domestic water, at times in competition with agriculture, which now shares its once-dominant economic position in these areas with light industry and second-home and retirement communities.

The Alternative Future of Compromise: Scenario #4

As suggested above, the three scenarios are abstractions for analysis, not projections of reality. What *is* real in politics is negotiation, compromise, a balancing of the positions of private interests and governmental organizations and public attitudes until a majority position can be obtained. This majority need not be a consensus, as the extraordinarily narrow vote in 1960 in favor of the State Water Project clearly demonstrates.

In the 1980s, however, a bare majority should no longer be acceptable. Decisions that will bind future generations to a course of action they might not have chosen themselves should, if at all possible, involve something more than "politics as usual." Water policy is this sort of decision. Here, above all, the political system should attempt to produce judgments and reach decisions which go beyond the narrow self-interest of individuals, economic groups, bureaucrats and elected officials—that is, attempt a consensus.

Certainly, with regard to water policy, the choice need not be conservation *or* development, cost-effective systems of allocation *or* increased supply, environmental protection *or* a prosperous agricultural and urban society.

All can be obtained, but—as the above discussion has indicated—consensus may be even more difficult to achieve in the political environment of the 1980s and beyond. There exists as yet no political scenario to promote this alternative future.

TOWARD A POLITICAL CONSENSUS

Water Policy Reform in California: A Political Stalemate

The experience of the Governor's Commission to Review California Water Rights Law, and that of a parallel effort in Arizona, illustrate both the difficulty of creating a future that could command the support of Californians and the ways in which those difficulties could be overcome. The commission, established by executive order during the severe drought of 1976-77, was instructed to review existing California water rights law, to evaluate proposals for modifications in this law, and to recommend appropriate legislation in a report to the governor.[8]

Some of the commission's minor recommendations have been enacted into law.[9] But the commission's principal recommendations—that a state policy and a state/local program aimed at the eventual elimination of most groundwater overdraft be adopted, that the regulatory mechanisms for preservation of instream flows be strengthened, and that transfers of water and water rights be facilitated—have never come close to legislative approval.[10] Four general reasons explain the failure to achieve a political consensus in favor of the commission's proposals.

First, the general political climate was—and remains—inhospitable to the kinds of changes proposed. At a time when the popular mood favors less government and lower taxes—as represented in Washington by limited deregulation and in California by Proposition 13—the commission recommended *more* government, particularly in proposing groundwater regulation for those overdrafted basins (notably in the southern part of the San Joaquin Valley) not now subject to effective district control or to court decrees. At a time when the environmental movement has been put on the defensive, the commission recommended *more* environmental protection, particularly in proposing strengthened instream flow preservation. And at a time with a crowded political agenda and popular fatigue with many recurring issues, the commission recommended changes which command little grassroots understanding or committed support, but which generate intense opposition from directly affected interest groups such as farmers.

Second, the commission's membership and mandate were organized in a way that made political consensus very difficult. The sponsor of the commission, who chaired the State Water Resources Control Board, initially conceived of the commission as a nonpartisan, independent and expert group which would make recommendations of a "technical" nature—something like those provided by the California Law Revision Commission. Consequently, no legislators were appointed to the commission, members were asked to serve as individuals rather than as representatives of interest groups, and lawyers with interested parties as clients—initially excluded from consideration for fear of bias—were included only as a result of outside pressure. A distinguished and competent group of commission members was ultimately assembled, but the assumption that the key decisions could be treated as technical ones by impartial experts—rather than highly political ones requiring interest-group compromises—proved untenable. The decisions—such as whether to have increased groundwater management and the respective roles of state and local governments in such management—were political, but the political wheels had not been greased. The commission itself lacked political power, the various interest groups were not directly involved in the bargaining process, and the commission had no powerful political patron. It was gubernatorial in name only. Aside from one press conference given upon receipt of the final report, the governor did virtually nothing to advance the commission's proposals. And the commission lacked effective political ties to the legislature, in marked contrast to the situation a decade earlier when substantial revisions in California's water quality law had been made.

Furthermore, the commission's mandate was probably stated too narrowly to allow for political consensus. Directed to study California water rights law, staff and members of the commission believed it was beyond the scope of their charge to examine either the law or current state policy concerning water development projects. Yet, as noted above, many interest groups believe that more such projects are needed and—of critical importance—regard any effort to improve the management of existing water supplies as implicitly suggesting that additional supplies should not be developed. Thus, groups such as the Association of California Water Agencies, the California Farm Bureau Federation, and the California Chamber of Commerce, which favor further water construction projects, took strong positions against the recommendations for improved management.

In contrast, environmental groups such as the Planning and Conservation League and public interest groups such as the League of Women Voters generally supported the recommendations. However, the commission believed it lacked a mandate which would allow examination of a comprehensive approach involving a mixture of management changes and development projects. Nor did the Brown Administration see fit to link in any way the commission's management recommendations, which it nominally supported, with the development proposals it supported with great vigor.

A third reason for the commission's lack of political success was its inability to generate broad public support. There was no crisis—such as the Santa Barbara oil spill, which a decade earlier sparked federal concern over oil pollution of water. The drought, which had led to the commission's creation, ended before doing serious harm to either the economic well-being or the lifestyle of most Californians. (It is by no means clear whether more years of drought would have provoked public support for management reforms rather than for dam construction.) The commission had among its members no well-known figure who could draw attention to its work, as Pardee, the popular ex-governor, had done with respect to the work of a similar commission he chaired many decades ago.[11] Other than the anadromous fishery losses which were (arguably, at least) associated with water development projects, it was difficult to build a dramatic and convincing factual case that business-as-usual would cause any significant harm to the general public. The threat of federal action suggested by the early work of the Carter Administration on a new national water policy soon lost credibility. And the commission itself was unable to achieve unanimity, which may have had an adverse political effect.

A final reason for the political defeat, at least initially, of the commission's proposals was the misfortune of having its key proponents within the executive and legislative branches either removed or seriously weakened at critical junctures. The chair of the State Water Resources Control Board—who sponsored the commission, was a highly articulate spokesman for its views, and was the executive branch official most thoroughly committed to pursuit of the recommended changes—was appointed to another state position, out of the mainstream of water politics, just before the commission's proposals came before the legislature. And the speaker of the assembly, who repeatedly had spoken publicly and forcefully in favor of the commission's general approach to water policy, was embroiled in a devastating leadership battle just as the commission's proposals were being considered in committee.

A Brief Contrast: The Achievement of Political Consensus in Arizona

Lack of approval for the commission's recommendations does not necessarily mean that political consensus will never emerge; recent events in Arizona attest to that. This state radically revised its original law in 1980, to provide for state management of groundwater aimed at pumping limited to "safe yield" in the three overdrawn areas projected to contain major urban populations by the year 2025.[12] Pump taxes, the permanent retirement of irrigated land, prohibitions on the development of subdivided land without a water supply assured for at least 100 years, and mandatory conservation measures—including continued reductions in per capita use—are all provided for in new legislation which passed the Arizona legislature by an overwhelming margin.[13]

These dramatic changes in Arizona are but the latest steps in a controversy over groundwater overdrafting in that state which goes back at least to 1938.[14] Several commissions have addressed the problem, and, in fact, reform legislation which eventually proved ineffective was passed in 1948. As recently as 1979 the commission then appointed to study the problem seemed stalemated. Within a few short months, however, political consensus was achieved.

Several factors appear to have contributed to the ability of this neighboring state to accomplish that which has proved so elusive in California. First, it was evidently clear to all that with the construction of the Central Arizona Project (CAP), no significant water development projects remain to be built; there is no longer a realistic prospect of water development projects in the Pacific Northwest for the benefit of the lower Colorado basin. Thus, interest groups such as mining firms and cities were forced to look at reallocation of existing supplies to get more water. Second, a court decision in 1976 threw into question the validity of even intrabasin transfers of water,[15] much less interbasin transfers. Third, when the public process of debate within the special blue-ribbon commission on groundwater appeared ineffective, a private process of bargaining among representatives of three key interest groups—mining, cities and agriculture—began. Fourth, Arizona's governor personally spent hundreds of hours involved in these private negotiations, underscoring the enormous importance of a solution for the future of the state. Fifth, at crucial junctures the United States Secretary of the Interior threatened dire consequences—such as a construction slowdown on the Central Arizona Project or allocations of CAP water in a way unfavorable to non-Indian interests—if an adequate groundwater management law was not forthcoming. The governor was able to make effective use of these threats to force the negotiating interests to reach a compromise solution.

It is impossible to know whether the Arizona groundwater management statute will be held valid by the courts, will be preserved in its present form by the legislature, or will prove to be effective in practice. The statute is now being tested in litigation challenging its constitutionality,[16] and recently the construction and financing industries—not, it should be noted, groups which had participated in the private negotiating process described above—succeeded in having some modifications in the legislation enacted.[17] Nonetheless, the mere fact that the Arizona groundwater management statute was adopted is impressive proof that a political consensus among deeply antagonistic forces can achieve major changes in the management of water.

Some Possible Implications for California

Despite obvious differences between the two states, several lessons may be drawn from the Arizona experience for California. First, consensus for serious management reforms may be achievable only when further major water development projects appear untenable to the water industry. In the context of California, this may occur only when the North Coast rivers appear as beyond reach as did the Pacific Northwest rivers to Arizona—either because the costs of development make it unthinkable, or because political limits appear effectively to have placed these rivers indefinitely out of bounds. Second, political consensus may be possible only with some interest-group realignment, so that groups with long-standing stakes in the state's water resources decide to shift their position to support management reform. The most likely candidate for such a decision appears to be urban interests. If, for example, the Metropolitan Water District of Southern California were greatly to increase its emphasis on improved management and reallocation of developed water supplies, which might permit a moderation of its development policies, the political ramifications could be profound. The Arizona experience suggests that direct interest-group bargaining may be more efficacious than the usual commission study/legislative debate route. Finally, fortuitous factors, such as sustained federal pressure, inspired gubernatorial leadership, or a new initiative campaign, could play an important part in bringing about significant change based upon a durable political consensus.

The divisiveness created by the recommendations of the Governor's Commission to Review California Water Rights Law, the debate and referendum over the Peripheral Canal, the disagreement over the protection to be given the North Coast rivers, and the continuing impact of water diversion from the Owens Valley and Mono Lake, all dramatize the difficulties confronting the people of California and their political leaders. That these difficulties can be overcome is also clear. The next generation of Californians deserves no less.

REFERENCES AND NOTES

1. "Water Specialist Predicts an Increase in the Costs for Food and Water," *University Bulletin* (University of California), May 11, 1981, p. 2.
2. Carey McWilliams, *California: The Great Exception* (New York: Current Books, Inc., 1949).
3. Walter A. Zelman, in *Twenty Who Gave $10 Million: A Study of Money and Politics in California* (Los Angeles: California Common Cause, 1981), p. 1.
4. William Kahrl, ed., *The California Water Atlas* (Sacramento: Office of Planning and Research, 1979), p. 51.

5. Bob Gottlieb and Peter Wiley, "Water District's Policies Encourage Land Boom in South State," *Sacramento Bee,* July 21, 1981 (reporting on a recent study conducted by the Urban Planning Department, UCLA).

6. The Field Institute, "The Peripheral Canal and Related Water Issues," *California Opinion Index,* August 1980; "The California Poll," May 6, 1981.

7. Ernest Engelbert and John C. Munro, "California Water Policy Decision-Making Survey," July 10, 1979 (unpublished).

8. State of California Executive Department, Executive Order B-26-11 (May 11, 1977), as reported in Governor's Commission to Review California Water Rights Law, *Final Report* (1978), p. 2.

9. These statutes are codified as California Water Code Sections 100.5, 109, 1011 (see also 1010), 1210-1212, 1241, 1243, 1345-1348, 1704.1-1704.4, 1725-1730, 1735-1740, 1745, 1825, 1831-1836, 1840, 1845, and 1850-1851 (Deering Supp. 1981).

10. Although in 1980 the legislature adopted a new section 109 of the Water Code which expresses a policy of encouragement for "the voluntary transfer of water and water rights where consistent with the public welfare of the place of export and the place of import," the various changes proposed by the commission to implement this policy were not approved. A similar but more promising "first step" toward the elimination of groundwater overdraft was taken by the legislature in 1978 when Water Code Section 12924 was adopted, directing the Department of Water Resources to identify groundwater basins "subject to critical conditions of overdraft." DWR Bulletin 118-80, published in January 1980, identifies eleven such basins.

    No legislative response whatsoever has been forthcoming to the commission's recommendations on the preservation of in-stream flows. In an apparent response to these recommendations, however, the State Water Resources Control Board has by regulation promulgated procedures for protecting in-stream beneficial uses. 23 California Administrative Code §§ 1050-1060.

11. Report of the Conservation Commission to the State of California (1912).

12. James W. Johnson, "The 1980 Arizona Groundwater Management Act and Trends in Western States Groundwater Administration and Management: A Minerals Industry Perspective," 26 *Rocky Mountain Mineral Law Institute* (1980), pp. 1031-1103; Philip R. Higdon and Terence W. Thompson, "The 1980 Arizona Groundwater Management Code," 1980 *Arizona State Law Journal,* pp. 621-671.

13. The bill in unamended form was approved by more than a two-thirds vote in each house of the Arizona legislature. Higdon and Thompson supra note 10 at p. 621.

14. See generally Dean E. Mann, *The Politics of Water in Arizona* (Tucson: The University of Arizona Press, 1963).

15. *Farmers Investment Company v. Bettwy,* 113 Arizona 520, 558 P.2d 14 (1976).

16. *Town of Chino Valley v. City of Prescott* (No. C-28568) and *City of Chandler v. Kyrene Water Company* (No. C-397751). Interestingly, the statute reverses the usual practice by including a *non*-severability clause—if *any* part of the statute is found unconstitutional by the courts, the entire statute will fail. By this device the Arizona legislature "tried to ensure that the courts will not consider any detriment to any particular water user without also looking at the corresponding benefits to that user and the corresponding detriments to other water users." Johnson, supra note 10 at p. 1063.

17. Act of April 22, 1981, Ch. 192 §17 and Ch. 203.

CHAPTER XI

AN OVERVIEW: THE CONFLICTS AND THE QUESTIONS

by

L.T. Wallace, Charles V. Moore, and Raymond H. Coppock

An overview of the preceding chapters, and of California water problems and opportunities in general, grew out of three days of intensive discussion at the Asilomar Conference of September 30 through October 2, 1981. This chapter is based largely on comments and suggestions of those who took part in that conference. It contains no policy recommendations because participants were not expected to reach consensus on substantive issues. The only prevailing agreement was that in water policy decision making there must be more accommodation by contending interests, to assure resolution of California's water problems in the future.

An important assumption of the conference, and of this volume, is that California will have continuing water policy problems. In the future, voters of this state will have to decide again and again on questions of water development, allocation, or use. Immediate water policy decisions obviously will have their impact; but the discussion in this chapter focuses on the longer-run issues and choices.

BACKGROUND

Areas of Uncertainty

Despite almost 40 years of planning and developing a State Water Plan, and an even longer history of local, regional and federal or state water development, uncertainty persists about the future of California's water resources and water supply. This uncertainty results from geographical and demographic factors, from institutional arrangements, and from public attitudes.

The geographical and demographic factors include desertlike conditions in the southern half of the state, abundant water in the north, and the immense system of reservoirs, canals and pumps that transports water from north to south. The nine southern counties constitute 60 percent of the state's population and are expected to add another 6.7 million people by 2020. Most agricultural irrigation, from both surface and groundwater sources, is in the San Joaquin Valley where considerable overdraft of groundwater already exists. Prices for delivered irrigation water in California range from less than $2 to more than $200 per acre-foot. These cost differences—as well as climate, soil, management and other factors—result in vastly different cropping patterns and farming profitability throughout the state.

Uncertainty also results from institutional and legal factors. Water rights law, water district formation and financing, public water development policy, and water quality control are some of the areas requiring legal and institutional "rules of the road."

The third reason for uncertainty is attitudinal. For example, many farmers fear that urban interests have the votes and the money to take water away from them; many city people perceive agriculture as having a virtual monopoly of the state's water, often at "subsidized" prices; and environmentalists view water as a resource in desperate need of protection. Such differences of perspective create various interpretations and analyses of California's water "problems."

Before considering the specific agreements and disagreements generated by the Asilomar Conference, let us look at two factors that affect the entire spectrum of water policy issues in California—increasing costs, and the central role of agriculture.

Increasing Costs

Various types of cost influence water use and water policy. Two of the most important are the cost of new development and the cost of pumping water.

Economic trends have created a different and more difficult situation than ever before for water planning and development. For one thing, California now faces a physically limited supply of developable water, particularly as long as the North Coast streams are classified as wild and scenic rivers. In addition, the state may be approaching the limits of economically feasible water development. Figure 1 indicates that future projects, as presently planned, will cost substantially more per acre-foot of yield than past projects did—even in uninflated (1980) dollars.

Underscoring the fact that the era of cheap water has ended is the trend in real costs of electric power for pumping. Figure 2 shows that those costs were almost constant between the mid-1960s and 1973—and, in fact, actually dropped in comparison to the Consumer Price Index. For several years thereafter, pumping costs fluctuated due to the oil embargo, the 1976-77 drought, and the ending of the drought. (The drought reduced hydroelectric power, forcing a temporary shift to more expensive fossil fuels.) In 1979, however, a sharp upward trend began. Since then, the rate of inflation in electric energy costs for irrigation pumping has increased twice as fast as the Consumer Price Index—significantly affecting the economic outlook for use of groundwater as a resource.

The Role of Agriculture

In addition to escalating costs, another factor that shapes all aspects of water policy in California is agriculture's dominance of water use. The fact that irrigated farming accounts for all but about 15 percent of water put to use in the state means, among other things, that:

  • Agriculture is considered a potential "source" of water by other users of the developed supply, many of whom are able to pay more for it than most farmers.

  • Of all users of developed water, agriculture has the most to gain or lose as a result of water policy decisions.

A realistic view of the state's agricultural industry and its future water use is needed. Farm spokesmen insist that an important, and often underrated, reason for water development is simply to ensure economic health and growth for California's agriculture—to maintain farm output, to feed the state's expected

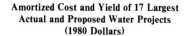

Figure 1

Amortized Cost and Yield of 17 Largest
Actual and Proposed Water Projects
(1980 Dollars)

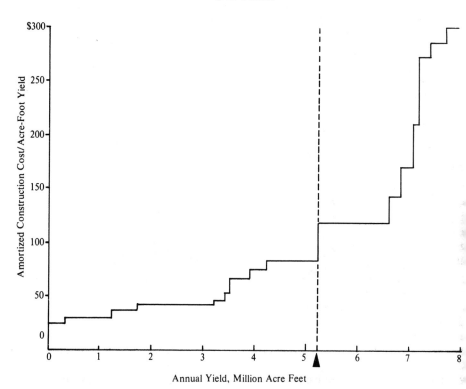

Source: Meral, Gerald H., Managing California's Limited Water: Prospect for Future Supplies,
Speech, January, 1981

population increase, to help feed the nation and the world, and to help maintain the nation's balance of payments. Yet there are differing views. How important is the historic competitive advantage of the state's agriculture, especially its unique specialty crops, to California? To the U.S.? To the world?

It is evident that California farmers play a crucial role in the state's economy and control much of the land-based wealth. Still, nonfarm employment accounts for about 3 out of every 4 jobs in the state and provides almost 84 percent of the state's gross income. Agriculture, while of immense importance to California, simply is no longer the dominant economic force.

Another consideration is that California's agriculture is not geared to feed the world's hungry. Our state does not export large amounts of staples such as food grains that the less developed nations need for calories and protein—except for rice and, in recent years some wheat. California's chief overseas exports are

Figure 2

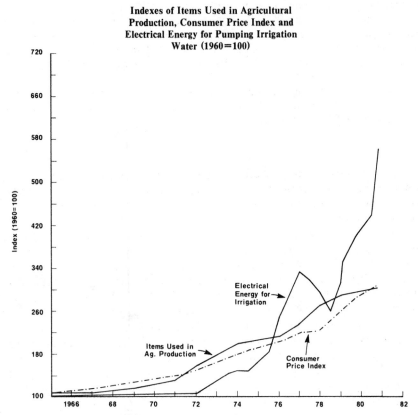

Indexes of Items Used in Agricultural
Production, Consumer Price Index and
Electrical Energy for Pumping Irrigation
Water (1960=100)

specialty crops, which have an important role in the diets of more affluent populations. In the future, California's agricultural role will continue to be oriented primarily to the developed economies of the world, those with money to pay for the high-cost, high-value crops produced here.

Sales to developed nations are the ones that contribute most to the national balance of payments, so this state's farm exports are important in that regard. One potential problem, however, is that as farmers grow more dependent on food demand overseas, they also become vulnerable to economic or political instability abroad, including trade barriers.

A related question is more specific. Is the economic heath and impact of the state's agriculture important enough to Californians to justify public financial support of new irrigation water supplies? Some argue that since most benefits of California crops go to consumers elsewhere and since overseas export of those crops doesn't significantly relieve world hunger, the state's taxpayers have little to gain by subsidizing water to farmers. To this, agricultural spokesmen reply that the in-state economic impact of food and fiber production, processing and marketing is itself ample reason for public concern and at least some degree of public support. Some farm spokesmen at the conference said they do not ask for subsidized water; they are willing to pay their share of the cost of new development projects as long as other beneficiaries pay theirs.

We need to know more about possible future impacts on agriculture of more costly and/or scarce irrigation water. Some important information is available—for example, it is possible to estimate the economic value of water on a specific crop growing in a specific area. Yet more facts are needed, particularly since most answers are site-specific. Farmers and policy makers alike remain confused on such questions as: How much could farmers afford to pay for water and still largely retain their existing crops? What shifts in cropping patterns would result from even higher prices for water, and what would be the secondary impacts? At what price level might agriculture become clearly and permanently unprofitable, resulting in losses not only to farmers but to farm workers, financial institutions and local communities and governments?

POLICY THEMES

Like breaking a logjam, the resolution of certain key water policy issues in California may well clear the way for a surge of decisions and—it can be hoped—progress toward solution of the state's water difficulties. The question is, which are those key issues?

Only time can give an exact answer. However, certain issues involving questions of both fact and value surfaced repeatedly during the Asilomar Conference. Some of them run as a continuous strand of concern through the foregoing chapters. They are briefly described here, and the arguments summarized. The purpose of this section is not to argue for any particular policy approach, but to examine the debate in the context of:

• The expertise, and prejudices, of the academic authors of the previous chapters, who in many cases recommend water policy action although they do not always agree among themselves.

• The expertise, and prejudices, of the nonacademic participants in the conference, many of whom also expressed strong, and sometimes conflicting, policy preferences.

The broad issue behind almost all others at the conference was that of development versus belt-tightening—that is, building new water projects or reallocating the existing water supply, including conservation. Most participants did not see this as an either/or question; also, there was recognition that as a policy issue it is unmanageably broad and complex. Still, this ever-present issue should be stated, if only because those who emphasize development of new water insist that a broad viewpoint is needed. They say that it is necessary first to inventory the state's overall needs (or desires) for additional water, considering, for example, population growth trends, overdraft in the San Joaquin Valley, and the state's contracts to deliver more water to the south. In light of those factors, the need for new development would be clearer.

The opposing arguments point (1) to possibilities for using the existing supply of water more efficiently, and (2) to the looming and unavoidable constraints on new development. These constraints are of two kinds:

(1) Economic, primarily the problem of escalating energy and construction costs. This leads to the issue of cost-sharing for new projects, and particularly to the question of public support or subsidy.

(2) Environmental, primarily the problem of in-stream requirements for water. This leads to the question of less tangible but important values of environmental resources.

To succeed in California, a new water project would have to overcome both economic and environmental constraints. Political feasibility, also essential, depends on that process of accommodation.

Within this framework, it is clear that a first step would be agreement on certain specific issues. These involve questions of both fact and value. To the extent that facts can help resolve them, information is needed so that policy decisions will not be swayed solely by subjective values.

Conservation

Residential users can cut their demand for water substantially without extreme sacrifice, as demonstrated during the 1976-77 drought. Still, since irrigated farming will continue to account for most of the water put to use in California, the concept of water "saving" as a strategy in state water policy points inexorably at agriculture. What is not known is how much of its present or hoped-for future supply agriculture could give up, at what cost. We also need to know who would pay that cost; and who would benefit, and by what means.

Those who say agriculture should use less water argue that: (1) out of such a vast supply, even relatively small overall savings would be significant for nonfarm use, and (2) in many farm areas, more water appears to be applied than the crops really need. Farm spokesmen and water scientists reply that this viewpoint results to some extent from wrong assumptions or misinformation. Where water is scarce or higher-priced, farmers already reduce waste voluntarily, for economic reasons; and where more water is allowed to run off, it usually supplies important down-stream or water basin uses.

Possible impacts—good and bad—of using less water for agriculture are a central point of dispute. The question is not only how much water would be "saved," but where the "savings" would exist within the water system. For example, reducing return flows through conservation may dry out wetlands, or reduce in-stream water quality.

In order to seriously consider agricultural water conservation as a part of state water policy strategy, we must determine whether it would reallocate the existing supply to recharge, to other farmers, or to municipalities—and what would be the methods of transfer. Or should conservation simply substitute for proposed new water projects?

In the debate over water policy, some confusion grows out of the difference between physical efficiency of water use and economic efficiency. With good engineering, and by paying the cost in dollars and environmental impact, it is possible to reduce excess use of irrigation water almost to nothing. This is physical efficiency. Economists, however, argue that an additional criterion should be whether the water is being put to the use that generates most income. This raises the question of how to evaluate in-stream values.

Water Market Proposals

The idea of an institutional/regulatory shift in the direction of permitting water rights holders to sell water to the highest bidder created shock waves at Asilomar, as it has throughout the state since the report of the Governor's Commission to Review California Water Rights Law. The proposal, discussed in detail in Chapter VIII, generated some outspoken opposition from participants at the conference, and even more reservations based on unanswered questions.

The reasons for doubt are complex. Some of those voiced were:

• The "willing seller" question. Under some limited circumstances, water rights holders already are free to sell their water; but, apparently, most do not want to. There may be fear of losing water rights, or other reasons; this needs to be determined. Those arguing for more market freedom say that once the system is openly established, some of those with low-cost supplies will see more profits to be made in water sales than farming, and will offer to sell at last part of their supply.

• The "Owens Valley syndrome." Some spokesmen for agriculture and water districts, and others, fear that market pricing would increase water prices for all farmers so much that many growers would go out of business. Proponents of marketing respond that, in reality, only relatively small quantities would be bought from agriculture for nonfarm uses. There is, after all, a limit to how much additional water would be useful to urban areas.

• The need for a broker. Concern was expressed for protection of third parties in any water transfer, especially the environment and those who depend on return flows. Can the broker who brings the potential buyer and potential seller together and helps negotiate a price also act to protect the seller's title and be the guardian of third party interests? No agreement was reached on whether these functions should be undertaken by a public, quasi-public or private entity.

An alternative mentioned by some participants was that water prices could be reset by administrative action to more accurately reflect true market value.

Development Cost Strategies

Basic questions of public policy grow out of the cost increases for new water projects. An important question of fact is how much nonfarm California taxpayers benefit from new water projects. In any case, what is the cost limit that the nonfarm public will tolerate for developing agricultural water? Can private interests tackle large water development projects, or is public financing—state or state-federal—a necessity?

Proponents of development argued that public support is essential, and that the public can and will help finance water projects. They conceded that water from such developments will be much higher priced.

Generally, environmentalists and other nonfarm spokesmen at the conference opposed agriculture's receiving the benefits of vast development projects without paying the full cost of their water. As reported before, at least some farm spokesmen said they were willing to pay their fair share if beneficiaries from such activities as salinity control in the Delta, white-water recreation, and fishery protection also pay theirs. Farmers also pointed to other trade-offs, including agriculture's provision of open space.

Environmental Protection

Several aspects of the controversy over environmental impacts of new water development surfaced at the Conference:

• The "wild rivers" debate. Opponents of development say a decision to keep a river in its natural state can be changed, if necessary, in the future; but a decision to build a dam is irreversible. Proponents point out that more than half of California's streamflow is still undiverted.

• Protection of in-stream flow. Environmentalists insist that early planning for a new project must include consideration of the needs of fish, wildlife and the environment (as well as municipal and agricultural use) and the project designed accordingly. Evaluation of less tangible environmental values is a primary problem here.

• As always, water quality in the Delta is a prime concern.

Federal-State Coordination

The question of future joint federal-state water projects, as well as even closer coordination of existing projects, is one of the key on-going public policy decisions faced by California. How much state control over the water resource should or can be maintained? In addition, dissatisfaction with the sheer volume of governmental regulations was expressed. Still, it was pointed out, some form of regulation aimed at protection of the various interests seems inevitable in return for government help with water development.

CRITICAL PERSPECTIVES

Participants at the conference not only debated California water policy in general but reacted to policy analyses and approaches contained in the preceding chapters of this volume. This section summarizes some of those reactions.

The Role of Economic Values

A number of participants objected to what they viewed as a too-narrow economic approach to policy evaluation. Few water policy decisions, they argued, are or should be made strictly on economic grounds.

The criticism was aimed particularly at the repeated recommendations for economic efficiency in the form of a free water market. Such an arrangement, the critics fear, might not take into account the secondary impacts of unfettered water transfers. For example, sale of agricultural water to nonfarm uses, or to distant farming areas, could change cropping patterns. In the process, the role of certain lower-value crops such as alfalfa—a mainstay of the dairy industry and an important rotation crop—might be underrated.

Academia vs. the "Real World"

Water policy proposals, no matter how carefully researched and argued, are only a first step. Policies also must be tested against the realities of political dynamics and water institutions, public and private. Some at Asilomar criticized what they called the university authors' "ivory tower" proposals, unfitted for the pressures and constraints of the real policy-making arena.

For example, it was charged, the preceding chapters largely ignore the pressure for water development growing out of already existing commitments to increase the water supply—specifically, contracts held by the DWR to eventually deliver 4.43 million acre-feet of water yearly. This amount cannot possibly be furnished with existing facilities. Whether that fact justifies building of new facilities is a crucial issue.

The Need for Reliable Data

Despite criticism of proposals in authors' papers, most of the discussion groups at the conference reported that applicable research on water policy by the University is needed. A consensus prevailed that this research should span all aspects of water resources—physical, technical, social and economic—if California's water problems are to be solved. The participants all agreed that the University could play an objective role in a continuing program of public education concerning complex water policy issues. In their evaluations of the Asilomar Conference a number of the participants stated that the discussions had provided them new insights and that the University should be encouraged to continue to foster dialogue and forums for the state's citizenry.

OUTLOOK

If there was consensus on any point during the conference it was that a workable state water policy outcome must include a combination of different approaches including conservation and management, institutional change, and water development. In small discussions and in plenary sessions, many participants said they would be willing to accept some form of balanced solution.

There was seeming agreement that:

● Efficient use and conservation are important, but cannot alone satisfy the total demand for water.

● Even with these measures, some form of institutional change will be required to allow effective redistribution of "saved" water to deficit areas.

● In addition, areas with current high efficiency in water use and continuing deficits (the San Joaquin Valley) will require newly-developed supplemental supplies to avoid significant economic damage in the long run.

The Question of Leadership

What may be missing is a clear constituency in support of a negotiated solution. Wild rivers have their political action groups, agriculture has its defenders, cities have their spokesmen; but there seems to be no attempt to build a broader-based political constituency that cuts across segmentalized water interests. Any strong position on water policy by a major political figure, or even a strong attempt to negotiate or compromise, appears to be politically dangerous.

It may be that only a severe crisis such as drought could build a significant degree of consensus on California water policy. If so, this implies that long-range water planning and dependable policy implementation are obsolete under ordinary circumstances in today's world of highly specialized and contending interest groups.

This is not to say that long-range planning is absent. For example, state resource agencies have recently proposed specific water policies and projects, linking water development with tighter water management and conservation during the next two decades.* Nevertheless, building a broad political constituency is

---

*"Policies and Goals for California Water Management: The Next 20 Years," a joint report of the State Water Resources Control Board and the Department of Water Resources (June 1981, 53 pp).

another matter. Could agriculture, which uses 85 percent of the developed water and clearly has most to gain or lose, take a leadership role?

In any case, political leadership willing to stake its success on a coalition approach to water problems seems absent. Like a rudderless ship on a sea with currents, counter-currents and changeable winds, California water policy has followed a shifting course in the past and may well do the same in the future. Until now, the shifts have been largely due to the relative political power of local and regional interests, both urban and agricultural. In the future, political forces, possibly realigned, will continue to exert strong influence, but a new consideration may become paramount—the fact that huge new water projects would put a multibillion dollar burden on state and regional fiscal resources.

Despite the difficulties in developing agreement, financial realities may engender some changes in the way water is planned for and allocated in California. A conference agreement seemed to be that increasing costs and increasingly diverse forces representing both consumptive and nonconsumptive water uses will bring about a mix of water-policy approaches—some new development, conservation and protection of in-stream flows, groundwater management, and some institutional changes. There was no consensus as to what that mix might be.

AUTHORS AND CONTRIBUTORS

Gunther Barth, Professor of History, University of California, Berkeley

Gerald D. Bowden, Associate Professor of Environmental Law, University of California, Santa Cruz

Ted K. Bradshaw, Research Sociologist, Institute of Governmental Studies, University of California, Berkeley

William H. Bruvold, Professor of Behavioral Sciences, University of California, Berkeley

Mark N. Christensen, Professor of Energy and Resources, University of California, Berkeley

Roger W. Clark, Assistant Professor of Forestry and Resources Management, University of California, Berkeley

Raymond H. Coppock, Communications Specialist, Cooperative Extension, University of California, Davis

John Cummins, Director, California Policy Seminar, Institute of Governmental Studies, University of California, Berkeley

Noreen Dowling, Director, Public Service Research and Dissemination Program, University of California, Davis

Harrison C. Dunning, Professor of Law, University of California, Davis

Stahrl W. Edmunds, Professor of Administration, Director of Dry Lands Research Institute, University of California, Riverside

Ernest A. Engelbert, Professor of Public Administration, University of California, Los Angeles

Don C. Erman, Professor of Forestry and Resource Management, University of California, Berkeley

B. Delworth Gardner, Professor of Agricultural Economics, Director, Giannini Foundation of Agricultural Economics, University of California, Davis

Robert M. Hagan, Professor of Water Science and Extension Water Specialist, University of California, Davis

Glenn W. Harrison, Staff Research Associate, Graduate School of Management, University of California, Los Angeles

Richard E. Howitt, Associate Professor of Agricultural Economics, University of California, Davis

Norris C. Hundley, Professor of History, University of California, Los Angeles

Larry J. Kimbell, Associate Professor of Business Economics, University of California, Los Angeles

Eugene C. Lee, Professor of Political Science, Director, Institute of Governmental Studies, University of California, Berkeley

Robert S. Loomis, Professor of Agronomy and Range Science, University of California, Davis

Curtis D. Lynn, County Director, Cooperative Extension, Tulare County, University of California

Dean E. Mann, Professor of Political Science, University of California, Santa Barbara

Frank G. Mittelbach, Professor of Management and Planning, University of California, Los Angeles

Charles V. Moore, Agricultural Economist, University of California, Davis

Richard L. Perrine, Professor of Engineering and Applied Science, University of California, Los Angeles

D. William Rains, Professor of Agronomy and Range Science, Director, Plant Growth Laboratory, University of California, Davis

Ann Foley Scheuring, Editor, University of California, Davis

J. Herbert Snyder, Professor of Agricultural Economics, Director, Water Resources Center, University of California, Davis

Michael B. Teitz, Professor of City and Regional Planning, University of California, Berkeley

H. J. Vaux, Jr., Associate Professor of Resource Economics, University of California, Riverside

Edward Vine, Staff Scientist, Energy and Environment Division, Lawrence Berkeley Laboratory

Richard A. Walker, Assistant Professor of Geography, University of California, Berkeley

L. T. Wallace, Economist, Cooperative Extension, University of California, Berkeley

Christian Werner, Professor of Geography, University of California, Irvine

William W. Wood, Jr., Economist, Cooperative Extension, University of California, Riverside

REVIEWERS

Raymond F. Dasmann, Environmental Studies, University of California, Santa Cruz

William I. DuBois, California Farm Bureau Federation

William G. Dunn, Consulting Civil Engineer

Arthur C. Gooch, California Department of Water Resources

D. W. Kelley, D. W. Kelley & Associates

C. B. McGuire, Energy & Resources Group and Graduate School of Public Policy, University of California, Berkeley

Gerald H. Meral, California Department of Water Resources

Charles V. Moore, U.S. Department of Agriculture—Economic Research Service at University of California, Davis

W. Douglas Morgan, Department of Economics, University of California, Santa Barbara

Peter B. Moyle, Division of Wildlife and Fisheries Biology, University of California, Davis

Donald E. Owen, California Department of Water Resources

Hal Salwasser, U.S. Department of Agriculture, Forest Service

Anne J. Schneider, Downey, Brand, Seymour & Rohwer

Seymour I. Schwartz, Division of Environmental Studies, University of California, Davis

Harry Walker, Department of Land, Air and Water Resources, University of California, Davis

Geoffrey A. Wandesforde-Smith, Division of Environmental Studies, University of California, Davis

William E. Warne, Water Resources Consultant

Clarence L. Young, California Department of Health Services

DISCUSSION LEADERS AND RECORDERS

David Allee, Department of Agricultural Economics, Cornell University

Gilbert Axt, Security Pacific Bank, Fresno

John A. Dracup, Engineering Systems, University of California, Los Angeles

George E. Goodall, Cooperative Extension, Santa Barbara County

Alvin J. Greenberg, Water Committee, Sierra Club

Julie Harkins, Bank of America, San Francisco

Jeanne Harvey, Water Committee, League of Women Voters of California

Otto J. Helweg, Water Resources Center, University of California, Davis

James Rote, Assembly Office of Research, State of California

Anne Sands, California Reclamation Board

James Schaaf, George S. Nolte Associates

Rita Schmidt Sudman, Western Water Education Foundation

Mary K. Shallenberger, Governor's Office of Planning and Research, State of California

Frank G. Tiesen, attorney (Vista Irrigation District)

Arliss L. Ungar, Delta Environmental Advisory Committee

Gary D. Weatherford, Center for Natural Resource Studies, John Muir Institute